"This is a moving story p
when war dislocates fai
extraordinary stresses battering
*Taylor and his fiancée Nettie are played out against the background of the
Siege of Malta. Difficult communications allow anxiety, jealousy and
suspicion to encroach on the rational, so that living for the moment becomes
the norm.*

*This is the first narrative I have come across from a medic in 30
Company RAMC serving in Malta during the Second World War. Any
soldier reading George's tale, who has ever served in conflict, will have no
problems relating his experience to those challenges faced by George and
Nettie."*

Colonel (retired)Walter Bonnici, RAMC,
creator and administrator of the RAMC Malta website
maltaramc.com

*"This is a love story. True, the diary kept secretly by George Taylor
between 1940 and 1943, when he served in the Royal Army Medical Corps
on the island of Malta, reports on the siege when the island faced daily raids
and attacks from Axis forces. But the real theme of the diary is his anxiety
for the survival of his relationship with Nettie.*

*The diary was kept secret because it had to be. Taylor knew he would be
in trouble if it were found. There is no censor in the diary."*
Scottish Association of the Teachers of History

"This is a most unusual military history book. *There are few
military non-combatant accounts of life in the Second World War, fewer still
from an Other Rank. Based on words and feelings recorded at the time, it is
probably unique.*

*It is an interesting and informative account of the Siege of Malta, with its
devastation of the islanders' jobs, properties, health and social communities,
and of the sacrifices made by sailors and airmen to maintain the island and
drive off the aggressors.*

*Obviously a high-minded young man, his eager adoption of the Masons'
codes and customs is to his credit and must make very interesting reading for
those who are of the Brotherhood."*
Don Marshall, Military History Enthusiast

Faithful Through Hard Times

Jean Gill

Jean Gill's previous publications
Novels
The Troubadours Quartet
Book 4 *Song Hereafter* (The 13th Sign) *2017*
Book 3 *Plaint for Provence* (The 13th Sign) *2015*
Book 2 *Bladesong* (The 13th Sign) *2015*
Book 1 *Song at Dawn* (The 13th Sign) *2015*

Someone to Look Up To: a dog's search for love and understanding (The 13th Sign) *2016*

Love Heals
Book 2 *More Than One Kind* (The 13th Sign) *2016*
Book 1 *No Bed of Roses* (The 13th Sign) *2016*

Looking for Normal *(teen fiction/fact)*
Book 2 *Fortune Kookie* (The 13th Sign) *2017*
Book 1 *Left Out* (The 13th Sign) *2017*

Non-fiction/Memoir/Travel
How Blue is my Valley (The 13th Sign) *2016*
A Small Cheese in Provence (The 13th Sign) *2016*
Faithful through Hard Times (The 13th Sign) *2018*
4.5 Years – David Taylor (The 13th Sign) *2017*

Short Stories and Poetry
One Sixth of a Gill (The 13th Sign) *2014*
From Bed-time On (National Poetry Foundation) *1996*
With Double Blade (National Poetry Foundation) *1988*

MAP OF WW2 MALTA

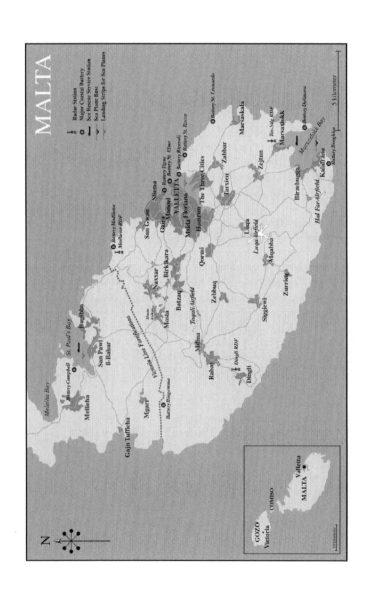

MALTA

Radar Station
Major Coastal Battery
Sea Rescue Service Station
Sea Plane Base
Landing Strips for Sea Planes

5 kilometer

Battery St. Leonardo
Marsakala
Battery Delimara
Ta's-Silg RDF
Marsaxlokk
Battery Benghisa
Marsaxlokk Bay
Zejtun
Zabbar
Kalafrana
Battery Rinella
Battery St. Rocco
Hal Far Airfield
Birzebuga
Battery St. Elmo
Tarxien
The Three Cities
Battery Fiene
VALLETTA
Msida
Floriana
Manoel
Hamrun
Gzira
Luqa
Luqa Airfield
Sliema
San Gwan
Mqabba
Qormi
Battery Madliena
Madliena RDF
Naxar
Birkirkara
Zurrieq
Battery St. Roque
Batzaq
Zebbug
Siggiewi
Mosta
Mosta Lines
Ta'qali Airfield
Mellieha Bay
Bugibba
St. Paul's Bay
San Pawl
B-Bahar
Mtha
Dingli RDF
Dingli
Battery Campbell
Victoria Line Fortifications
Rabat
Mellieha
Mgarr
Battery Binġemma
Gajn Tuffieha

N

GOZO
Victoria
COMISO
Valletta
MALTA

MAP OF WW2 VALLETTA

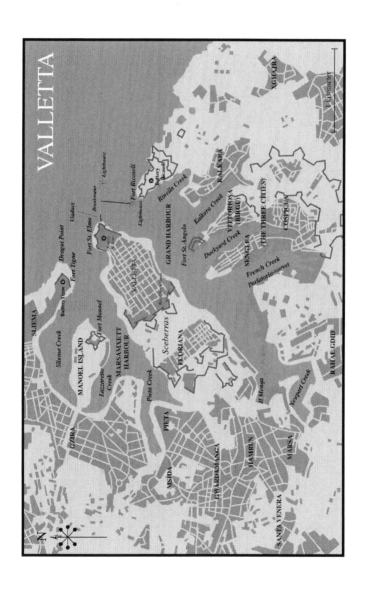

For George and Nettie

Remembrance:
love's last gift.

Glossary

Military Ranks and abbreviations

CO – Commanding Officer

NCO – Non-Commissioned Officer

RSM – Regimental Sergeant Major

WO – Warrant Officer

Staff Sergeant

Sgt – Sergeant

Cpl - Corporal

L/Cpl – Lance Corporal

Private – the lowest rank

Padre – a Christian minister attached to an army unit

OCTU – Officer Cadet Training Unit, through which a NCO could gain a commission and become an officer.

Slang

Civvies – civilians or civilian clothing (non-uniform)

Blighty - England

Bully beef – tinned minced beef, common in rations, also known as corned beef

Bumped – demoted

Dear John letter – a letter from a girl back home ending the relationship

Eyeties – Italians (derogatory)

Jerry – A German or the Germans (derogatory)

Johnny – a British pilot (familiar and friendly term)

Gofer – an assistant to 'go for' anything required

The pictures – the cinema / the movies

Rugger – the game of rugby

Scramble – the order to pilots to take to the air immediately

Smokey Joe – a minesweeper, a navy boat used to detect and blow up mines

U.S. – useless, an abbreviation of 'unserviceable'

Army Uniform and Life

Elephant shelters – bomb shelters of a type used in WW1, that could be erected in cellars.

Fire picket – a duty as a fireman, giving the alert for fires and putting them out. The relentless bombing frequently started fires. (Called 'fire piquet' by George)

Flak – anti-aircraft

MDS – Main Dressing Station

M. E. – Middle East

M.E.F. – Middle East Forces

NAAFI – Navy, Army and Air Force Institute, a forces General Store, in which George bought his writing pad.

Ordnance – military stores

Parashots – seeking enemy parachutists who'd bailed out of damaged planes or who'd deliberately landed on the island. They were supposed to be captured, not shot.

Pips – the metal buttons on a uniform shoulder to show officer rank

Puttees – bandages worn to protect the lower leg

Stripes – cloth stripes on the uniform sleeve to show NCO rank

V.C. – Victoria Cross

VIP – Very Important Person

Diseases

Malta Dog – dysentery

Malta fever – brucellosis, also known as undulant fever

Poliomyelitis – polio (also called 'Poly' by George)

T.B. – tuberculosis

Forces

RAF – Royal Air Force

RAMC – Royal Army Medical Corps

RIF – Royal Inniskilling Fusiliers

The Manchester Regiment – (called 'the Manchesters' by George)

Currency, sterling
Pounds, abbreviated as £
Shillings, abbreviated as /-
Pence, abbreviated as d

Malta Life

Mtarfa (called Imtarfa by George, British-style) – the site of what was the only military hospital in 1940
Gharry – horse-drawn carriage used as a taxi service
Auberges – the 'Houses' or Lodges of the Knights of St John
Langues – the Order of St John was divided into 'Langues' or tongues/ Languages

AXIS – Germany, Italy and other powers who fought against the ALLIES in WW2

Luftwaffe – German Air Force
Fliegekorps – a German Air Regiment
German planes - Junkers 88 and Stukas (bomber), Messerschmitt 109 (fighter)
Regia Aeronautica – Italian Royal Air Force
Italian planes – Macchi (fighter), Savoia-Marchetti (bomber)
Decima Flottiglia Mas – Italian 10th Light Flotilla

BRITISH planes and weapons

Fighter planes – Spitfire, Fulmars, Hurricanes, Gladiators
Bomber – Swordfish,
Bofors guns – anti-aircraft guns
3.7 positions – the QA 3.7-inch AA was a heavy anti-aircraft gun

Chapter 1.

Every road towards a better state of society is blocked, sooner or later, by war, by threats of war, by preparations for war... war, which is mass murder organized in cold blood.
Ends and Means

Young men died in wars and old men lied about what they had done in them; George had no intention of falling into either category. He was going to keep his head (when all around were losing theirs), do a good job for a short while and return as soon as possible to Nettie.

He smiled ruefully. Why the silly girl had joined up herself, he would never know. It had quite spoilt their secret engagement ceremony, him knowing that she was off to play at soldiers. Perhaps he should not have told her so.

There had been one of those stormy moments when she tossed her black curls and wondered that he thought so little of her. He hadn't pressed the point; time would do that for him. Time when she was wearing the scratchy, unbecoming fabric of army uniform, time following the orders of some other girl, who could also be better occupied.

Follow orders? Nettie? When, one day not too far away, she promised in church to obey him, she would probably cross her fingers. How could he protect her if she tossed her head and went her own way? Nettie was supposed to be at home, safe, waiting for his return, not charging off round the countryside. She could have no idea what real soldiers like him would be doing on a daily basis.

Truth to tell, he had little idea himself yet, but it had been made clear during the six months training that he must keep his kit in impeccable order and run long distances carrying heavy weights. Whatever its military purpose, (his being not to reason why), he was on his first visit across the border from Scotland, his first trip abroad, and, for all his wide reading, he was open-mouthed as a child at the foreign sights.

For centuries, the British upper classes had sent their children on a Tour of Europe at their coming of age; for young men of all classes, the Second World War enforced such a Tour on a scale never seen before. For twenty-two-year old Private George Swan Taylor, his Tour started with a lump in the throat.

Goodbye to his parents had not stirred by a hairsbreadth from the Victorian restraint which ruled all their relations. The emotional temperature had risen just enough for his father to say, 'Of course, I no longer expect you to repay your university fees, not with this...' and his slight hand gesture indicated the station platform, crowded with men in khaki, their sobbing women and small children taking what might be a last look.

'It will just take longer,' George replied, earning a nod of approval.

Perhaps George had imagined a flicker of envy in his father's eyes, his Headmaster father who was recalled from his regiment in 1914 because his country needed its teachers. The photograph of his father in his Black Watch kilt stood proudly on the dresser but the uniform had never left for France with its regiment.

Or perhaps George was wrong, and it had been fear for his elder son, controlled through habit. His mother's, 'You will write, dear,' struck him more as a command than a plea, and it had been, as always, Nettie's hazel eyes which showered him with love and pride. Even if she said nothing, her heart was always in her eyes, sparkling as she smiled for him.

'Do I look all right?' she asked him, and he regarded her forehead, clear and shining under its halo of fashionably rolled back curls, her red wool coat with a black velvet collar – a present from her sister Jean, who enjoyed spoiling the baby of the family – and he had said, 'You look fine.'

That was not enough and she pressed, 'I want you to remember me.' For two pins he would have run away with her there and then, let the army go hang, let Hitler win the war, but the same eyes would not have let him (she would not have loved him so much, loved he not honour more).

He understood that about his girl only too well. She was in love with romance itself as much as he was in love with her. All he could say was, 'I'll remember you,' and he had looked away from her disappointment. One day he would find the words she wanted.

The glitter in her eyes spilled onto her cheek. She waved, and he watched her through the bobbing heads and shoulders beside him, crowding the train doorway. He screwed up his eyes to sharpen his last glimpse. It was going to be a long... year? Yes, surely a year would do it, earn him time at home, and then back to it, beating the Hun.

How his younger brother David had looked at him when he came home for the weekend and said he'd signed up for the full seven, not just for the duration of the war.

'Why?' David asked.

George told him, 'Makes no difference; it will last that long anyway.' *But why had he signed up at all? Too many reasons to explain to his younger brother.* Britain and France had declared war on Germany on 3rd September 1939 and George had signed up straight away. He had read the papers, understood some of what didn't get reported, and made his choice. Hitler's invasion plans for Western Europe were as vast as they were increasingly likely to happen. If nobody stopped Hitler, everyone and everything George loved was under threat, and he could not stand by while others stepped up to the mark. It was his duty to protect his country and his family, and he could not live with himself if he did not.

David himself had missed conscription by a narrow squeak, using Uncle Willie's connections to join the Signals and avoid the Infantry, just before George announced his news.

And then there was a train, and men, and endless physical drill, turning left on command, right on command, eating to command, *yes sir no sir three bags full sir* until you even breathed in unison. Basic bodily functions were an act of anarchism, surprising you with the reminder that anything, other than your rank, could be private, that anything could be beyond army control.

When he signed up with the Royal Army Medical Corps in September 1939, George left a Chemistry degree course at the University of Dundee for a different sort of higher education. If he were honest, he had been restless, not convinced that he was cut out to be Mr Taylor, the Pharmacist, for the rest of his life, even with Nettie beside him.

Instead, he was becoming Taylor, regressing to the relationship with officers which he'd had with his high school teachers, remembering how to disappear into safe insignificance, doing what he was told. Too many Scots for him to become 'Jock' or 'Haggis' but he supposed those too might become an option. George was ceasing to exist.

Despite the confusion of a heavy snowfall, marching orders, a lorry and another train took the men to Southampton docks, where they boarded *the Amsterdam* within an hour, claimed their fifty cigarettes and a pack of what passed for food, which everyone called an 'iron ration'. Then they bunked down, three to a cabin. They were delayed at Spithead from 3pm till midnight, waiting for an accompanying convoy, but their boat safely reached

Cherbourg at 7.30 am on the 15th February 1940.

George managed a wash and shave in the water trough on the station platform and then forced down some 'stew' for lunch, a slop of meaty mess which made him nostalgic for his mother's cooking. He took up the offer of a visit to see the town with an anticipation which quickly turned to anti-climax. His accompanying officers and sergeant seemed equally unimpressed by the shabby grey buildings and the slovenly air about the town, as sour-faced locals reluctantly opened shutters to poorly stocked shops. If this was the Continent, he had no idea why the rich would holiday here.

Perhaps David would have made more of it, speaking French as he did, but even he would have had to work hard to charm a welcome. At least George had time to stretch his legs before cramming with seven others of the party into a second-class carriage at the end of the train, knowing he was lucky to have that much room, as the men had been split into three groups, each looking after a train.

After a surprisingly good night's sleep, George visited the train cookhouse and was revitalised by two slices of ham and bread, and tea. He passed the time when off-duty playing cards or reading his copy of *Ends and Means*, a work he found very much to his own way of thinking. Huxley would have been amused to hear his philosophical work being passed off as 'ways of improving at cards' when George suffered a few pointed queries on his choice of material. It was easier to get on with other chaps if you didn't flaunt your brains too much, very like schooldays.

The French countryside flashed reflections across the pages of George's book, whitening the shadows as the snow thickened, softening trees and fields to rounded silhouettes, icing bridges over broad, shivering rivers.

Standards dropped at lunchtime when George faced more stew but the bar of chocolate at teatime saved the day. There was no drinking water available, so the men had to rely on their water bottles and an occasional tea. Before he signed up, George had never really considered what he ate and drank, nor when, but it quickly became the timetable, highlight – or disappointment – and conversation topic of his day.

Duty consisted of an hour with four patients in the Medical Room, at 9pm and 3am, allowing George two spells asleep, which terminated at 9am in a mild, rainy Marseilles. Despite the all-too familiar weather, this was more like it, with the sort of bungalows and scenery that might attract a chap to explore further. No such luck this time and the train took them relentlessly right to the docks and the waiting *Duchess of Atholl*, twenty thousand tons of the best of British shipbuilding, from the Clyde, no doubt. This was definitely more like it; hammocks, four course dinners and waiter service – everything the third-class passengers would have had – and paid for. Marvellous!

Bolstered by the good food, a fortnight's pay and a ten-shilling sub, a welcome advance payment, George found his sea-legs and his way to the dining-room, with only a few wrong turnings. Even they rewarded him with dazzling blue, beyond his experience of Leven and Largo, his Scottish coastal home; a blue to tempt him out on deck in shirt and pants, sunbathing, in February.

Even when the seas grew wilder and ropes were put in place to enable safe movement from door to door, the only grey was the accompanying destroyer. Some of the party were detailed as sentries and submarine look-outs but George was free to sway with the roughening sea, rocking to surprisingly sound sleep in his hammock.

Morning brought the usual army routine of inspection, followed by an hour's gym but the rumour that they would reach Malta at four o'clock lifted the men through early tea, into full marching orders and standby, keeping them buoyant for the two hours until they finally docked.

George later recorded his first impressions in black ink, in his flowing, looped hand with a hint of angularity to digits and each letter 'r', contradicted by extravagance in the tall initial stroke of a 'p' or the additional curling loops on a capital 'W' or 'T'. His makeshift diary was a Stores Writing Tablet of thin lined paper, with a grey card cover.

Darling,
It is due to the fact that one is not allowed to write much that has made my mind up to chronicle to a certain extent the details of my now somewhat varied existence.

Monday 19.2.40
The first sight of Malta from the harbour is wonderful – maybe you have seen it in the pictures? The houses tiered on the hills all round with arches and semi-tropical trees. Then it began to get dusk and the moon started shining. All the lights around began to twinkle, and it added more charm to the scene.

About 6.45pm we started to disembark – I can't describe it – all I can say is 'marvellous and wonderful'. All the lights on the hills round about, the moon, the ships' lights for disembarking and the little gondolas sailing around – each with its fairy lamp.

We got to the shore at 7.15pm and were met on the landing at Valletta. We were taken to buses and driven about seven miles across the island to what is known as Imtarfa. On arriving we were given supper and then – after talking, went to bed – and I didn't need to be rocked.

Tuesday 20.2.40
Up at 6am – washed, shaved, cleaned and on parade at 7.15am. Given another Medical Inspection.

Breakfast at 8.15am. Wrote a letter to you about 9am and at 10am we were chased out to permit inspection of room. Went across to the NAAFI (Navy, Army and Air Force Institute) which is only a minute away and I had a nice cup of tea and two cakes. Came back and laid kit for inspection.

At two o'clock, the barber walked in and asked if I wanted a haircut – so I did. It's fine when the barber comes to you!

Then we had inspection until 3.30pm and I think I made a good impression. After that we had tea and four of us went for a walk. (Here we do not wear respirators as it is still a peace time station but we must wear belts, with holsters and arms, for protection)

I saw anemones in full bloom – tropical trees and do you remember that cactus my Mother had about 2 feet high – Well! I saw one the same – only it was fifteen feet high! On our walk we were pestered all the time – boys selling things and begging halfpennies.

One man collared us and said he would show us the Catacombs – after about twenty yards, I said I wasn't going and turned back. I had only gone a few yards when another joined me as he didn't want to go either. About half an hour later we saw the other two again and they hadn't gone. He had asked them into a 'pub' first and they had managed to get out of it and leave him. The 'natives' will run a mile if you take off your belt but sticking a knife in you in the Catacombs would be a pleasure. Anyway, we got back quite safely at 5.30pm.

Then I went to the NAAFI and bought this writing pad – then beat a fellow nicely at table tennis and then went to the pictures in the NAAFI at 6.30pm. It was a very good picture and I got back at 8.30pm when I started writing this.

It seems ridiculous, I know, but my face is red as a beetroot with the sun! I wasn't sick on the boat but since I came off it, the ground still insists on rocking! We have a wireless in every barrack room; although the time here is one hour ahead of that in Britain.

I think I have done very well for tonight so I will reserve the rest for a later date.
Goodnight Darling.

Goats on Floriana in the days when goats were taken round the houses and milked on people's doorsteps – when there were still goats on the island.

Fruit and vegetable sellers

Lady wearing traditional Maltese faldetta

Chapter 2.

The ideal man is the non-attached man. Non-attached to his bodily sensations and lusts. Non-attached to his craving for power and possessions. Non-attached to the objects of these various desires. Non-attached to his anger and hatred; non-attached to his exclusive loves. Non-attached to wealth, fame, social position… Non-attachment to the self and to what are called 'the things of this world' has always been associated in the teachings of the philosophers and the founders of religions with attachment to an ultimate reality greater and more significant than the self.

Ends and Means

'What the hell are you doing here?'

George turned from his organisation of rows of labelled bottles to face a belligerent fellow-soldier, framed in the dispensary doorway.

The Maltese washer-up muttered, 'I told him there wasn't enough work for me, never mind another dispenser, but the Sarge said he,' a head-flick at George, 'knows what he's doing.'

'We'll see what the CO has to say about that!' The doorway emptied as fast as it had filled, leaving George full of righteous indignation. Still sweating from the march to the military hospital at Mtarfa from Valletta, he had been singled out to work in the dispensary, while the others went to wards, the cookhouse, clerical jobs and the island's mental asylum. He had been soothing himself with the familiar names, tincture of iodine, camphor B.P., benzocaine, when he was interrupted.

'Who was that?' he asked the Maltese, whose inexpressive back remained firmly turned towards him.

'Ward dispenser.'

It would be annoying if the fellow kicked up a shindy and George was blowed if he'd lose such a pleasant post without a fight – even if the man never talked to him again. George completed a third concoction then gratefully accepted a half-day.

Wednesday 21.2.40

The average height of the Maltese man seems to be under five feet so it makes me seem bigger than ever! Some of the women go around with peculiar hoods around their head – something like a small cab hood. I don't know why yet but maybe I'll find out later.

As I am writing (now two o'clock) in the barrack room there is a cool breeze blowing through the wide-open windows, and the sun is brilliant outside. Today it is equivalent to one of our finest summer days – I just remarked a few minutes ago that it is ideal for a bathe. I am beginning to think that it will become somewhat hot when summer does arrive – in four months' time!

Our barrack room is one in a huge building which looks marvellous when seen from the next hill. All the buildings here are of solid stone – no 'bricks' at all, which gives everything a solid appearance. There is also wonderful architecture, with arches, pillars, etc. which makes the place very picturesque. For beauty of scenery, this has got Hawaii and all the other places beat to a frazzle. Neither wonder the millionaires live here! – (some of their daughters are nurses!)

Our barrack room is about 40ft broad and 80ft long (15 feet high) with eight pillars spaced in the centre. The floor is brown stone and the wall is yellow till half-way up, then a 2ft black band and white all above that. Outside, a solid stone veranda runs the length of the building with arches all the way along. You see the island is solid rock and all the earth has been imported as duty. Thus, there is an unlimited supply of water. Labour is also very cheap and so everything is very ornate. The veranda outside is the same colours as inside.

Here, you see, the weather is so fine and everything is so clean that the white stays pure white. Everything seems to be so pale here – even our Service Dress goes pale with the bleaching of the sun. It is lovely and clean, and, having cleaned my boots, it looks as if I have only to flick them until the rain next winter! No mud, no dust.

As John Brown once said to me, 'England's a cold place' – well! I certainly agree – and dirty too! To tell you the truth, at the present minute I am thinking that after this it would almost be impossible to stay in Scotland again.

Our beds consist of mattress, canvas sheet, 2 sheets, 4 blankets, pillow and slip. We have also each a blue carpet 6ft × 3ft so that we don't stand on the cold floor! Nice work – eh?

Did I tell you that on my arrival I saw a chap, who came here on the last draft, that I knew at Crookham – a dispenser too. He told me he was on a ward as orderly.

Well! all the other lads on half-day today are away playing football or hockey. Personally, I thought it a little too warm for such strenuous games and I wanted to do a bit of writing anyway. Well! I've done it now and that is everything up to date.

Later:

I popped into the dance for an hour just to see what like it was. It was quite good to see that there were too many 'stripes' and 'pips' there so I just had the <u>one</u> and left and was in bed about 9.30. The crowd came back about 12.15 roaring and singing and then they stuck a mop in my face to wake me up! They are going to be blooming sorry for it yet!

There had been nothing to an Army Dispensary anyway and he would learn more about another highly interesting and very technical subject, George told himself as he reported to the X-ray Department. Where there were medical cases, there was always a need for X-rays.

When dismissing him from the dispensary, The Regimental Sergeant-Major had merely told him that one dispenser was enough so it was not clear whether there had been a complaint or merely a reorganisation; either way, it had done George a favour and everybody was quite jealous.

To judge by the pips and stripes at the dance, promotion prospects on the island looked good, and George was sure he had made a good first impression on the Radiologist, a Major. It was galling to know that others had started off with stripes, a present in war-time, but he would earn his. He tied his white overall at the back and investigated the system for storing plates.

Daily routine was already cast in solid Maltese stone and started with a six o'clock wake-up call; then, make the bed, dress, sweep the floor; six-thirty parade for roll call; wash, shave, clean buttons and boots, breakfast; seven-thirty be on parade across at the Military Hospital for inspection and roll-call; after all this, dismissed for duties. Added to this were the weekly excitements of Pay Parade – so far, he was two weeks in advance, so not complaining – and Thursday's debugging. This weekly duty was one he took very seriously, as his sensitive skin reacted strongly to the insects which otherwise infested his bed.

On a Thursday morning he would take his bed to pieces, laying it and the bed-clothes on the veranda in the sun, where the display from all the barracks was spread out like an Arab souk. At teatime, the process was completed with a blowlamp, applied to the metal bed. Boy, did the bugs sizzle, but the worst was the smell. They would be back within days and you became so sensitive, you would react to the movement against your skin and kill the little blighters – you knew you'd got one because of that smell.

Making the bed was no picnic either. George had sewn the required five slips onto his blankets and knew to ensure that the labels showed, or he would fail the 7.15pm stand-to-your-beds inspection, carried out regularly by the Commanding Officer.

Bedding laid out correctly

Before a CO's inspection, George would contribute to the big clean-up after work. They polished the smooth stone floor to a skating-rink; cleaned out their lockers and replaced contents in the approved manner; ensured respirators were to hand, ready to place on top of the blankets, which had to be in a row with labels exact, and all equipment had to be in the correct fashion on pegs.

Other regular variations in drill included fire practice and a visit to the Gas Chamber to test masks; there seemed to be a general conviction higher up the chain of command that an offensive against the island would probably start with gas attacks on a wide scale.

Parades could sometimes lead to drill; the men would meet on the football field and then there would be an hour doubling the square, in full service dress and wearing respirators, as the Officers did not consider it to have reached summer temperatures yet. That would have been quite amusing in frosty England but when the sweat was running down the inside of his tunic, George didn't see the joke.

Then, still sweating, it was back to the X-ray room, to find that yesterday's Corporal was today's Sergeant.

'Do I have to create a minor disturbance to find out whether I'm permanent here or not?' George demanded.

'I tried this morning but the CO was busy – he'll see me tomorrow,' was the new sergeant's response.

'Well I'm not a fat lot of use so far.'

'Couldn't manage without you – it's just rubber-stamping and the job's yours.'

George had been in the army exactly six months, one fourteenth of his chosen sentence, long enough to mistrust rubber-stamping, but he was slightly reassured at the promise of radiography training. He would have been more optimistic if he hadn't heard the rumours of orders – confirmed by the Sergeant – that no radiographers or masseurs were to be trained abroad during the war. What an army.

As if that wasn't enough to make a man cynical, health advice from HQ Fortress Malta was enough to make any RAMC man tear his hair out. To prevent heat sickness, *Frequent drinking of sea water when bathing in the open sea is easy in Malta and should be encouraged.'* Neither wonder, soldiers went sick!

Another equally hilarious health notice advised staying in bed in the morning: *'After a restless night a refreshing sleep is often obtained in the morning hours, so that a very early reveille is not to be recommended.'* Well! You could only laugh, or you'd cry.

George played the tourist when he could and took photos of local events and landmarks. This is the Feast of St Dominic, Valletta.

The Palace Armoury, Valletta

The Roman Villa, Rabat

Hagar Qim Neolithic Temple

Castle and key of Gibraltar, Milorda Gardens, Floriana, dating from 1889: a monument to the Pompadours Anglian Regiment

Before the war really affected Malta, the swans sailed peacefully on the pond in the grounds of San (Saint) Anton Palace

Another way of passing the time was sport. The men are playing football on a makeshift pitch, 'probably the only one in existence that was solid stone' according to George, who broke his leg in three places during one match.

Chapter 3.

Of the significant and pleasurable experiences of life only the simplest are open indiscriminately to all. The rest cannot be had except by those who have undergone a suitable training.
Ends and Means

Thursday 22.2.40

I finished about 6.15 and then went up to the Recreation Room upstairs – two rooms – one billiard room and the other with easy chairs, tables, writing paper, ink, wireless and everything. I played for an hour and a half – free too! You can see how everything is so handy here. In one minute you can have food, tea, pictures, dance, tennis, billiards, draughts, ping pong and it's a couple of minutes to the football pitch and the <u>other</u> NAAFI. There is a terrific difference here too in that there is never a crush as was always the case at Boyce. I think the company is about 90 strong at present but some are leaving at the end of the week. There are always some on duty which keeps things quiet too!

Tonight, walking back from the recreation room in the full moonlight it was really like daylight – although I bet no-one ever thought of reading in it!! Walking along in the moonlight, jacket and shirt neck open, in the delightfully cool air, has a peculiar effect on me – soothing certainly – and surprise at such magnificent beauty. There is but one way to convince you of the truth in my ravings and that is for you to see everything yourself *and then I'll defy you to express in words how you feel. Off to bed now! Goodnight Darling.*

No-one wakened them the next morning and George scrambled to the 7.30am parade conscious of his stubble, not jet black like his brylcreemed hair, nor oddly ginger like his tentative moustache, but dark enough to be an embarrassment. He knew his buttons would pass muster as they could easily go two days, but he was lucky to get away without shaving.

Mid-morning, George would break for tea, cake and a smoke at the NAAFI and that was where he found that his suspicions about the wake-up, or rather lack of it, were shared.

'Something fishy about this morning business.'

'Some sod thinks it funny to see us hopping around with our pants down.'

'Nothing for it – Spoof's keen. Put him in charge. Least we'll wake up, then.'

George had become Spoofer, then Spoof, after a Spoofer Taylor in a boys' magazine. There was hardly a pause for George to accept his new responsibility before all eyes were on their hopes for a perk.

'Now then, Scouse, what can you do for your mates?'

Scouse, whose real name George didn't even know, had been placed in the cookhouse. He grinned. 'Fancy tea in bed, boys? Or at least in your bedroom.'

'Best offer we've had all week.'

'Dress up for us an all?'

'No chance. Time you paid a visit to Straight Street, you randy sod.'

'Oooh, choosy!'

Scouse turned serious. 'Make sure it stays on the QT boys, it's–'

'–More than my job's worth,' they chipped in.

'I'll slip a pail up to you, mornings, half five, and evenings, eight o'clock, best I can do – all right?'

'Wonderful. Football, anyone? Three this afternoon.'

The football pitch was probably the only one in existence that was solid stone. Despite seeing cases all week being X-rayed for injuries caused by 'organised games', George couldn't resist joining in, not even when he was reminded to wear his identity tags in case the medics on duty had to sweep him up. As it turned out, a three-all draw, with only minor injuries all round, offered a pleasant way to pass the time. And time was passing too slowly.

Saturday 24.2.40

I was told today that I am to be trained as a radiographer so I must be doing all right and be quite suitable.

It is now 6.15pm and I haven't anything thought of for tonight yet. All the other lads are out so I'll pop off somewhere I expect. I am just wondering where you are and what you are doing at this minute. Have you got the initials on the ring? Have you got the photograph? – And how I curse the fact that the Censor makes it impossible to write what I think instead of having to fall back on the bad habit of thinking what to write.
Love, George

He had proposed to her in the bluebell wood, where they courted in the springtime with another couple, their friends, Joan and Jack. She chose sapphires 'like your eyes' for her engagement ring, which should be uniting their initials at this very moment on the third finger of her left hand.

Bluebells. She said his eyes deepened bluer when his heart beat faster. She asked for a photograph to carry next to her heart at all times, and she frowned at his comment that it would become rather crumpled and bathing would be difficult, but he promised to send one all the same. Her image was on its way to him; but then, her image had never left him. At the sudden recollection of her face, he felt an ache, which he was too much a man of science to diagnose.

Sunday 25.2.40

Somehow or other I've missed you more than usual, Darling. I suppose it's just that I'm paying less attention to my surroundings and so think of you more.

Everybody else is out – away to Valletta, which is one shilling for a return by bus. You take a horse cab (if you want) for a three-mile roundabout road to the bus stop for the large sum of 3ᵈ each. I haven't been in Valletta since the night we came here. To tell you the truth, I am spending quite enough without galivanting away 'to town'.

I think my average is about one shilling and 3ᵈ a day – roughly 2½ᵈ for cigs, 3ᵈ for tea and cake in the forenoon and the rest for supper. Then I was at the pictures once – 6ᵈ – and I see 'Idiots Delight' is on tonight so I think I will go 'and chase the shadows away!'

Anyway, you will see that the present rate of expenditure leaves very little over at the end of the week, so it will have to be cut down somehow in order to save a bit. I could do with a pair of light boots – which one is permitted to wear on duty – only they cost 18 shillings made to measure, so that is out of the question at present.

Today, about thirty men left for home and what surprised me was that they seemed to be going just because they had to and not because they wanted to. This certainly was the case with a few I spoke to, who were absolutely disgusted.

After dinner, I went up to the Billiard Room and played all afternoon. And now I am going to write you a short note for posting, in which will be written as little as possible. I do hope that you do not misunderstand my short, dry letters but I just can't help it.

Love, George

P.S. I was wrong about the price of cigs – it's 2½ᵈ for ten but I only smoke ten a day anyway.

It was too bad that every word he wrote in letters was not only read but censored; if he so much as mentioned the price of cigarettes, the sentence was likely to be ripped out as a threat to national security, and he could do without the ensuing reprimand, too.

He studied the photo he was sending. He looked as bald as a baby with his hair hidden under his cap but he'd seen worse mug-shots. He looked extra spick, with cap-badge and buttons gleaming, but the jacket looked so bare; he hoped it would not be too long before he could add some stripes. Still, his mother and his girl needed a picture of him now and he would not disappoint them.

He thought of Nettie at odd moments during the day, predicting what she would be doing, wondering if he was right, and wondering how she was coping with their enforced separation. Was she coping *too* well? He was not allowed to tell her he missed her or anything at all that might give the enemy the impression that British army spirits were vulnerable to any human emotion.

He was probably allowed to tell her that he had seen a snake about 18 inches long and ¾ inch thick but didn't know if it was poisonous; he could also tell her that he had seen clouds for the first time in a blue Maltese sky.

What would she think of him, talking about the weather? He flung his pen across the bed and went to the NAAFI to play draughts.

His spirits lifted the next day when he heard that there was a letter for him – only to drop further when he found it was for a different Taylor, forwarded from Crookham on 9ᵗʰ January so goodness only knew when the other chap would get it.

Strange to think of some other man's fragile contact with home contained in this plain envelope. Was his alter ego even now looking at Nettie's handwriting?

Then, when he went to wash some hankies after tea, some man washing himself accosted him with, 'Blimey, just the guy I wanted to see – I could twist your neck.'

'Me?'

George recognized the Sergeant in charge of X-ray. 'You're the idiot who posted the Major General's X-ray to him, then?'

'No idea what you're talking about. I dropped in a special report to the hospital office if that's what you mean.'

'Well, the report's missing and the wires have been red-hot all afternoon. There will be some stripes missing in this district if that report reaches the patient, I can tell you, so you'd better hope it's not been sent where the Sergeant in charge thinks!'

George knew better than to point out that he'd just followed orders in passing on the report. He had a fair idea why both sergeants were nominating him as villain of the piece. 'Perhaps it will turn up with the body that went missing out the mortuary,' he said. Caused a fair stink, that had and upset the post mortem mightily. George continued washing his hankies.

Outpatients seemed determined to refer all their clients for X-rays the next morning, including a Maltese lady whose case-notes queried 'Twins?' in the Medical Orderly's scrawl.

George took the chance to try out the local phrases he'd been learning, earning shy smiles with his attempts at *bonjoo* (hello), *keef in-ti* (how are you) *yek yoj-bok* (please), *gratsee* (thank you) and *sahha* (goodbye).

There were three more cases of 'Twins?', one potential pair being so close to arrival that the Sergeant declared, 'If she starts any tricks on my X-ray table, I will really lose my temper!'

'Marvellous thing, X-ray,' George said, smiling at the agitated patient, and they got her off the premises without mishap and with a confirmed double blessing.

'That report turned up, you know,' the Sergeant told him as they switched plates.

'Really?'

'Returned to the Hospital Office. Been dispatched now – correctly addressed. Man there couldn't organize the proverbial.'

'Mmm.'

'Did I tell you I got a wire yesterday? The bloke at the P.O. says, 'Will I read this to you?' so I says, 'Go on then,' and he reads, 'Solution to all difficulties immediate marriage!' Last thing I want to see all morning's bloody twins!'

'I can imagine.' George could also imagine the laughter in the Post Office and how red the Sergeant's face had been, which was enough to restore their working harmony.

This included the Sergeant telling George to 'Scram' although there were four patients. Obedient as always, George scrammed, bumping into the Office Sergeant, also on his way home, and keen to offer George something as near an apology as dammit. So all the little sergeants were quite pleased to keep their stripes as it turned out.

Sunday 3.3.40
Surely it can't be long till I get a letter from you now, Darling. Here's hoping. Love and kisses

Monday 4.3.40
Some of the lads got letters today so I expect mine will be on the next boat – I hope! Goodnight Darling

Just as I was putting this away I heard that all regulars are to go home next month! Well! Maybe yes, and maybe no – just wait and see!

Wednesday 6.3.40
Oh! Yes! I got a letter from Kennoway today, so if my parents'

letter reached me, surely yours just can't be long now.
Goodnight

Chapter 4.

An 'international police force' is not a police force and those who call it by that name are trying, consciously or unconsciously, to deceive the public. We shall never learn to think correctly unless we call things by their proper names... If you approve of indiscriminate massacres, then you must say so. You have no right to deceive the unwary by calling your massacre-force by the same name as that which controls traffic and arrests burglars.
Ends and Means

'X-ray department,' George answered the call, checking his watch. 8.20am and work going well. 'Who's speaking?'

Trouble. 'Private Taylor.'

'This is the Sergeant-Major and they're searching high and low for Sergeant Stanton. Where the hell is he? Do you know anything about those plates for White?'

'Yes, Sir! Ready as requested but they have to be reported on by Major Morris – he's due in at 9.30.' When George had last seen Sergeant Stanton, it had been 6.45am and the Sergeant had been relaxed in civvies, ready for a day on the town, after a cheerful reminder to George to see to White and Smith's plates first, as they were leaving on the hospital ship that day.

'There's a whole convoy waiting for those bloody plates! The draft's been held up for half-an-hour. Get them down here at once!'

'Yes, Sir!' George beat it down to the ship. Was this what it felt like to be Admiral Cunningham, the fleet waiting for you to arrive before they could set sail? He didn't have time to enjoy his VIP status as he had to hotfoot back to deal with the urgent X-rays which filled the morning, so many that they even kept Major Morris writing records until 12.30.

A cheery call from Sergeant Stanton to check that all was well made it clear why no-one had tracked him down or thought to wire in earlier; he'd bunked off 7.30am parade to get an early start to Valletta.

'It'll blow over,' George reassured him, unnecessarily. Stanton was in a Valletta frame of mind, when tomorrow could go hang. George could do with a Valletta frame of mind himself and he thought he'd maybe treat himself to the pictures, having been done out of his leisure the night before by a Night Police detail.

After a day's work, he had to check the detail board, where his name had suddenly become popular for fire picket – during which he could at least read or write, if there were no pretend fires, or God forbid! real ones – and the dreaded 'Night Police'. This consisted of patrolling from 5pm until 9.30pm (curfew), dealing with any 'incidents', and reporting every half hour.

Failure to report resulted in them sending a search party, often with good cause. Men steamed all day, drilled and detailed in preparation for God knows what, and in the evening the kettle blew, often at the sight of the special armband worn by the night's 'policeman'. Two nights earlier, a Regimental Policeman on duty had been conked by some maniac and was still in a coma. George was finding it useful to expand his knowledge of local phrases beyond 'please' and 'thank you', neither of which came up much on Night Police.

'No pictures for you tonight, Spoof,' greeted him at the detail board, as a luckier man left for a night in Rabat. George swore and put on his armband. This was the third time in eight days and it wasn't his problem that the man whose name had been down first was already on night duty. George had spoken to the Sergeant about it and he was supposed to be speaking to the Orderly Sergeant and it was pretty clear what would come of all this speaking to sergeants – the same as usual!

It was hardly reassuring to hear the story of the recovering Regimental Policeman. The last words he'd heard were, 'Stick a knife in the _____!'

The night started quietly enough, with George and his partner pinching four men, two for throwing stones and two for fighting, but this made him too confident. After Lofty and he had split up, George saw about twenty Maltese hanging around the picture-house and told them to scram. Twenty grins responded.

'So you don't understand English?' George asked and repeated his request in Maltese.

The twenty grins were unchanging and George realised that everything depended on just how careful he was.

'Two minutes or I'll run you in,' he told them. No change.

Then he picked on one, told him to get lost, then another one, and each man in turn realised he was vulnerable to arrest if he refused, so sloped off.

George took a turn around the block but when he came back to the picture-house, he found the same group, at a slight distance, in a circle, loitering – apparently aimlessly. George suddenly realised that there were only about ten minutes daylight left and he made for the NAAFI as quickly as he could, leaving it through the back door to shake off his followers. The next time he passed the picture-house, they had lost interest and dispersed. It certainly kept you awake.

Being kept awake was starting to cause George problems. Convinced that his promotion prospects depended on shiny buttons and a nod of approval from the CO, he was finding it difficult to maintain inspection standards after a Night Police detail. He had prepared his speech in case he was put on a charge, the proforma for an official reprimand, but, so far, even a full kit inspection resulted only in the instruction to George to number his kit. This took him two hours to individually stamp each digit of 7265587 on every article he possessed, so that the numbers were floating in front of his eyes by the time he had finished.

Wednesday 13.3.40
Today has been the 13th!

Just listen to this list: I broke my mug at breakfast! That was the start. The forenoon was so-so, busy – and tearing around, but no major catastrophe. Then at 12.15pm I read orders. Oh! Oh! and Oh!

1. Route march in full kit for GST at ten past two.

2. Blood tested in the forenoon.

3. Night Police from 5pm to 9.30pm and

4. Fire picket from one o'clock till lights out. And of course I have to see that the X-ray dept. is run as well! I think I may have a slightly busier day than usual! It was also up on the board that I have another kit inspection on Sat. morning at 7.15 am.

What a 13th!
This afternoon I have cleaned up my brushes, washed my feet and a pair of socks in readiness for tomorrow. In the process I knocked a bottle of Brylcreem on the floor – what a mess! What next? And that's what I've been saying all day too.

I've just heard that the Amsterdam (the one we crossed in!) has been sunk by a mine. It's funny to think that a bunk we once slept in lies at the bottom of the sea.

Well! I got the first letter from you yesterday – since I arrived – since I left England. This last does not bring tears to my eyes because in spite of working day and night, half fed, calling everybody for everything, I am as happy or even happier than I have ever been before.

There is some quote about 'to have the love of a good woman' but I just can't remember it. Anyway, there must be something in it.

Here too! where I know it is impossible to see you I am not taking it so badly as when I was so near and yet so far. Well! that is nearly all.

Shortly, I am going to tea and then I will go to Rabat where I will post a letter to you in the 'civvy' box when it gets dark and I hope you will get it. This censor business certainly gets one down. Cheerio!

Thursday 14.3.40

I am writing this on a <u>Saturday</u> as I have been so busy that I have not had a minute to write – even to answer your letter.

Anyway, I will write as if it was Thursday morning as usual. Finished at 1pm. Ready at ten past two in <u>full</u> kit and steel helmet for the route march. It was some hike – over goat tracks – across the island. At 3.30pm we met the travelling kitchen and had a 'tin' of tea.

Then, until 4.15pm we did stretcher drill. The ground was so rough that it took one stretcher party about quarter of an hour to find the 'patient'. There was an ambulance there too and we were all asked if we were able to walk on then. Only one fellow dropped out.

I told the Company Sergeant Major that it was unfortunate that I was on Night Police after I got back and he said, 'We'll manage to excuse you tonight,' so that was O.K.

We eventually got back at 6.30pm, somewhat tired! The tea I got was worth it though. In fact, I had two teas, one after the other. The first was five slices of bread and jam and rissole. The second was three slices of bread, jam, two cheeses and onions. Accompanying this, I had four mugs of tea.

Now! I ask myself – do you think it would be cheaper to keep me a week than a fortnight? After that (no! I didn't go to bed!!) I tidied up my kit and went to bed, after attending to the remains of my feet. (Debugging today aussi.)

George didn't know what to do about his feet. Despite 'going native' with his first ever pair of light and airy sandals, which he wore whenever he could, and which did reduce the swelling, the constant sweating and route marches had reduced his flesh to peeling ribbons. There was more sticking plaster than flesh, just to keep him going.

As he became fitter, he could almost have enjoyed the route marches now, quite the way to see an island which was only seventeen miles by nine at its widest, but for his feet. It wasn't just the distance the men covered, nor the weight they carried, but the combination under the Maltese sun.

One route march turned into an evacuation of the wounded, when battle drill led to injury. George had to carry a man whose femur was broken, for three-quarters of a mile over ditches, walls and fields, the sweat trickling under his helmet at the rate of tears.

George's sandal

The wounded were not always the result of official skirmishes. On being discharged, one soldier immediately went on a Saturday-night spree, got half-canned, stole an army lorry and went for a run with a dozen mates. He hit a bus, killing the driver, five others and leaving all the rest casualties.

The operating-theatre next door to the X-ray department was working fit to burst, taking three hours to put one fellow together again. If they lived, they came to be X-rayed for broken bones and George had never seen bodies so battered and yet still alive.

Gradually the supposed limits to the working week were eroded, with more frequent preparations for air-raids. The whole island, soldiers and civilians alike, would man stations. The hundreds of churches rang their bells in warning, while all utilities were switched off and gas-masks were at the ready.

During one such exercise, George was the sentry, patrolling the hospital with the rattle to signify 'gas'. Such simulations left even less time to complete the work of the X-ray department, which had the extra pressure of a VIP patient.

'They've stopped the buses from Rabat,' had been the first hint that something was up. Then Lofty had told George that there were police on duty to prevent anyone using the stairs at one end of the hospital, even wearing their duty sandshoes, so there was obviously some big cheese on one of the wards.

It didn't take long before the word got around that Governor General Sir Bonham Carter, Malta's designated ruler since Britain had suspended local government, was not only in hospital but critically ill.

When he was brought for his X-ray, the stretcher bearers were Staff Sergeants, and the Governor was accompanied by the CO, the D.D.M.S., three majors and one lieutenant – George and Sergeant Stanton definitely lost amongst the pips.

Like the king unbending to his public, the Governor-General asked George, 'How long have you been out?' and on hearing the reply commented, 'You're from Scotland.'

It was a shaky foundation on which to build promotion hopes but the X-ray had gone well, despite Major Morris visiting them later that day to pick fault with Sergeant Stanton, his special-occasion monocle wiggling precariously.

When he'd gone, Stanton turned to George, 'Who rattled his cage?' Over seven hundred X-rays had now been completed since George had joined the department and no-one's mood was reliable.

Friday 22.3.40

This is <u>Good Friday</u> – we had two hot cross buns with our breakfast. I went over to the hospital at 9 o'clock to write up some films but, as I couldn't get a key, I just came back. Then, until dinner time, I played football. In the afternoon I had a rest and then went on Night Police at 5 o'clock. It had the effect of spoiling the day slightly. I was asked to go bathing and had to decline. There was also a huge procession (Catholics with all the dooh-dahs) in Rabat about 5 o'clock and I was really sorry to miss it. I am on Night Police alone now and am on every 6th night. Debugging today!

Saturday 23.3.40

Worked until 12.30. Then I flitted to another barrack room to make room for a new draft arriving next week sometime. In the afternoon I played football. At night, table tennis and draughts.

Sunday 24.3.40

Wrote home, my Grandmother and David – quite a good bit of work. I worked until 12.15pm. Sat in the sun all afternoon and went to church at six o'clock – quite voluntarily! Nor was it a guilty conscience! Later I played table tennis and draughts. I have been beaten at tennis but so far am unbeatable at draughts. When you get old, you must try draughts!

Monday 25.3.40

Easter Monday! This has been a lovely holiday weekend for me! Worked this morning till 11.15am, lay on bed till dinner time. Played football all afternoon. Then I had a bath and cleaned my locker for CO's inspection tomorrow. In all my off times I just wear shirt, pants, socks and sandals – boots when I play football of course. Imagine the hottest summer day you've known – and that is what I play football in. Already I'm browner than I've ever been before.

Today I got a letter from you and one from Taffy which I hope to answer sometime. It's all right for you to complain about my letters but if your letters had to be censored by your 'boss' then you would probably be pretty careful what you wrote too! All tonight. Cheerio.

In his increasingly rare time off work, George would listen to the radio, a Rediffusion system with one switch; middle – off, top – BBC overseas, bottom – Malta station. When reception was good, it was excellent but those moments were few and far between. The Malta 'station' seemed to consist of a wireless set which picked up other stations and slung them out, seemingly at random, and certainly switched to music as soon as any talk came on.

He would be listening to dance music one moment, the William Tell overture the next. He could hear his father's scathing comments on modern rubbish switching to reverent approval; his father, the choirmaster, whose young singers, including George's brother David, had won first prize in the Kirkcaldy Festival; his father, the pianist, who, although he could read music on sight, played by ear so well that he reckoned he could play non-stop for two days without repeating anything. He could accompany any singer or instrument so long as he was provided with the music.

His moral stance vis-à-vis dance music had been compromised when he couldn't resist correcting David's chords, but neither brother had dared accuse him aloud of actually listening to the dangerous rhythms.

Tuesday 23.4.40

Saw 'Four Feathers' at night – and although everyone admitted that it was good – the trouble was that it hurts even to look at a scorching sun on the pictures. They should show scenes on icebergs here!

Oh! I got a pair of sun-glasses – I thought they were only for show before – but not now! Even my pen will hardly write as the ink is drying on the nib so quickly.

Station Malta, the heat... so much that had seemed strange was becoming familiar beyond comment; the red and white flags flying side by side with the Union Jacks; the women's strange head-dresses, called faldetta; the huge lilies by the hospital entrance; the summer hail-storm which had frozen in the gutters, blocking them; the butter-coloured, limestone houses with their flat roofs; the stone balconies with pots of basil – one for each unmarried daughter; the strange sibilance of Malti, a language derived from the Phoenician, with Semitic and Arabic layers added, as in the buildings themselves. Working alongside the locals of the Royal Malta Artillery, George heard stories of Gozo tomatoes the size of melons, of goats which could tell your fortune; and of firework displays at fiestas which lasted for days – all in the past.

There was little doubt among the men that it had been a 'thieving native' who carried out the perfect wholesale crime which caused a real shindy in the barracks. When George awoke at six o'clock one Sunday morning, he found quite a stir going on. The veranda outside was lined with clothes and gradually it was revealed that every barracks had been turned over in the same way, all clothes being taken outside and the pockets emptied, with an estimated total of fifty pounds going missing. The Sergeant was lucky and found that his trousers, shirt and bible were all outside, a ten shilling note still tucked in his shirt pocket. George too was lucky, having kept up his cautious habit of sleeping with his belt on. It was his turn to mock those who accused him of Scottish habits.

Punctuality was as ingrained within him as love of steamed puddings and both were heightened by army discipline – from surfeit of one and lack of the other. His every minute governed by orders, he was bemused by the Mediterranean sense of time, and swore at it when it interfered with his careful systems. Like the occupying Romans before him, he wanted to impose order on the barbarians. How could a Presbyterian man of science be patient while waiting for an entire family to light three candles to a plastic saint before they would allow him to X-ray a child? How could he cope a fortnight later with a small mistake of timing?

Thursday 2.5.40

How this island continues to exist is a mystery to a great many, I'm sure. It's a military island almost and you would think that it would be the last word in efficiency. It is however the reverse. This putting off, carelessness and inefficiency seems to permeate everything. There was a typical example this morning – it would make anyone swear. On Monday a child died in the Military Families hospital, with Pneumonia.

Yesterday (Wed.) there was a post-mortem. The funeral was today and the Mother, Father, Priest turned up sharp at ten o'clock. The father went in and here was the child still on the slab after a completed dissection. Arrangements had been made for the coffin to arrive at eight o'clock and everything to be ready by ten o'clock and that was what happened!

That is typical of everything they handle.

Well! that's all this time. Cheerio.

His ears still ringing with the father's sobs, George sat on his bed, creasing the regulation folded top-sheet and aimlessly smoothing a small sheet of paper, the certificate of attendance for his radiography lectures. He pulled out the small box in which he kept his diary, his personal collection of letters and his certificates. He lifted his Highers' certificate and the testimonial from his employer, Forrester's the Chemist, and was about to file the new scrap of paper in its insignificant place, when he hesitated and pulled out a forgotten oddity. Part of George's job as a trainee pharmacist had been to offer a quick, chemical death for pets and his quiet kindness had so helped one lady part with her much-loved cat, that she had insisted on writing something for him.

To whom it may concern
  This is to certify that Mr George Taylor is of a courageous disposition, punctual, trustworthy, and extremely smart, a good grave digger, and the best cat killer in Gallatown and district.
  I can fully recommend him to anyone requiring his services.
  H Nicholson
  This day Dec 17th, 1935

George carefully placed the testimonial back in the box with its fellows. The cats of Gallatown had been better served than the children of Malta.

Children appear in George's photos as poignant figures in the landscape, absorbed in their friendships, lost amid the barricades on a beach, usually unaware of the quiet soldier taking their photo: childhood in wartime.

Possibly Mistra Bay

Chapter 5.

To be in love is, in many cases, to have achieved a state of being, in which it becomes possible to have direct intuition of the essentially lovely nature of ultimate reality.

For many people, everything is beloved as it ought to be, only when they are in love with 'some one creature'.
Ends and Means

To reach George, Nettie's letters had to do the Malta run, facing 'Bomb Alley' off Crete, vulnerable to attacks on the British fleet, accompanying supplies to the safety of Grand Harbour. Only if a convoy had successfully negotiated these hazards, undergone any necessary repairs and received orders which led to the reverse run to British waters, would George's letters stand any chance of reaching Nettie – and it was still only a chance.

In the afternoon I actually wrote 4 letters – the trouble being that I would need to write about forty to please some people. I think that the Sergeant has got some news! He hasn't written for three weeks so he got a wire (as usual!) and he had to wire back. It costs a packet too. He has worked it out that it costs his girl twenty-five bob a week for communications. Even a letter from her is registered and by air mail. Quite frankly, I think it's driving him nuts.

When George heard that there was a parcel waiting for him, after weeks of hearing nothing from Nettie, he rushed off in the mid-day sun to Rabat Post Office, and ripped the brown paper open on the spot. He turned over its contents, disbelieving.

She had sent him empty writing pads and not a word but their white reproach. He dragged his blistered feet the mile back to work, where he spent two hours in a shirt which dripped sweat. Her little joke had gone sadly wrong. She couldn't know the conditions out here... and yet!

Things were hotting up; did the officers know something they were keeping to themselves? One Friday after tea, George had just finished washing his poor feet when Sergeant Dodds gave marching orders – full kit on, blankets too. Four of them loaded the lorry with medical panniers, stoves, lamps, benches, trestles, stretchers, food and coal, then tore off in ten minutes flat. They had barely driven three miles when a car caught up with them and they were ordered back to barracks. They unloaded all their stuff and were told there had been a clerical error.

'Don't put your kit away too quickly boys,' they were advised. 'The mistake wasn't *what*, just *when*.'

George fished in his pocket, lit up and asked, 'Well?'

'Italy,' was Lofty's opinion. 'That's why it was done so quick. Hush-hush business – they don't want rumours flying.'

'They don't want mosquitoes flying either.'

'It'll be in the night, you bet.'

'Where's the fun, otherwise?'

'You heard what the Colonel said when he heard we'd gone? 'Splendid! Splendid! But you'll have to send after them and bring them back!' Good joke, I don't think.'

'Good job he was pleased about something. Only, the thing is, all the food's still there for us to load and it's perishable.'

'Sod it.'

They finished their cigarettes and left their kit ready to

fall into in the middle of the night.

They were indeed called out in the middle of the night but it was by the night wardmaster, who needed help to bring back three drunken patients who had done a bunk. George was so tired that he rolled straight back over in his bed and fell asleep again, staying unconscious even when the others returned, swearing as they found their own beds.

The next morning showed what George had missed. One side of Lofty's face was purpling where he had been kicked before Ed had managed to shoot morphia into the enraged escapee.

Orders were changing by the minute, with George's name on all of them. He was moved to the Sanitary Department, listed for Night Police and cricket, then confined to barracks with all off-duty personnel as part of a general order to be ready to move at a minute's notice.

This clashed with the Corporals' Dance, *the* dance of the year, which was cancelled along with the cricket, leaving men to kick rumpled beds and fight over card games. The band's opening notes on the radio were confirmed by the honeyed lilt of lyrics which churned George's stomach back to butterflies in a Scottish dance hall.

'Well, what do you know, he smiled at me in my dreams last night

My dreams are getting better all the time…'

Was she listening to their song too? Dancing with someone else? She had promised him she would sit out the dancing while he was away, as she had done to please him, when he was there. He could hold her in his arms well enough, without needing to watch his feet, her feet, and keep a beat, he had told her while she twirled and laughed at his lack of rhythm.

'Oh, maybe tonight I'll hold him tight when the moonbeams shine

My dreams are getting better all the time.' She had promised him a lot of things.

Just by the way – as a correspondent, your letters are definitely few and far between – Cheerio.

Whatever his disappointment at not hearing from Nettie, it was for her that he took photos of the island, including whenever he could the wistful Maltese children who skipped round his heels, mimicking him with a soldier's walk or a pretend camera. George used the skills he had learned on his photography course, which he had added to radiography, first aid and electricity, to develop a spool of film for an officer, taking an extra print of one view so he could send it to Nettie.

Men were moved to outposts. At a given signal, the the outposts were manned, the hospital made up to more beds, the Barracks hospital moved. Navy and RAF patients would come in and all departments would be on twenty-four-hour phone alert. Snippets of information were pieced together by the men given them, to guess at what next, and there was clearly some hustle on. George was returned to X-ray and told he would be trained. If only people would make up their minds! He was ordered to enforce perfect blackouts while on Night Police – emphasis on 'perfect'. He was supposed to take a bed over to the X-ray department and sleep there, relieved only for meals by the Sergeant, but he talked his way out of that lonely vigil only to be summoned at night because all the lights had been left on. It didn't do to point out that the Major had left last, so he didn't.

George was left alone with all the cardiograph work, which came under the same department's responsibility, while the Major and the Sergeant set up another X-ray room, a field unit for use in emergency. What was it that everyone else seemed to know?

Confinement to barracks was lifted and George attended lectures on life-saving, after a day's work and with bread, butter, jam and tea as his only sustenance, nothing else being available.

A letter finally reached him from Nettie.

On Friday I received a letter from you — hence the blank. I am now continuing this diary for my own satisfaction.

Was it then that he met Violet? Later, he couldn't remember if he had even had that excuse. He had certainly gone to Valletta, and Lofty didn't have to ask him twice. If a soldier went to Valletta by day, he might wander among the poor quarters of the Manderaggio, the low-lying area of the town on the Marsa Mxett side, where boatmen and watermen lived. It had been half-excavated by the Knights of Saint John, to replace the lesser harbour they were accustomed to in their first stronghold of Rhodes.

It had been too difficult to keep quarrying below sea-level on this new island, despite the sixteenth century regulation that the houses of Valletta must be built only of Manderaggio stone and the attempt had been abandoned. The Greek 'mandra' or 'sheepfold' had been Italianized to Manderaggio, the only unfinished element of the Knights' grand design.

An educated soldier would remember schoolboy tales of Malta's great siege in 1565, where Grand Master la Valette faced an Ottoman fleet of 31,000 men and 181 sail, led by the old warrior, Dragut Rais. Elizabeth 1 had said, 'If the Turks should prevail against the Isle of Malta it is uncertain what further peril might follow to the rest of Christendom' and, as Malta was considered indefensible, Christendom held its breath.

A man in his seventies, la Valette said that the fate of the order, the oldest order of chivalry, was to defend the bare rock to the end. He defied the diktat of Suleiman the Magnificent, another septuagenarian, who decreed, 'Those sons of Dogs! I say now that, for their continual raids and insults, they shall be destroyed!'

When sixty knights saw that they could no longer hold St Elmo's fort and sent to la Valette asking if they could surrender, he replied that they should fight to the end and so they did, buying with their lives the time la Valette needed for relief to reach the island.

Every schoolboy knew that the Maltese took revenge for Turkish disfiguration of bodies, that 'St Elmo's pay' meant 'no quarter given' as they slit the throats of captured Turks; that human heads had been used as cannon balls in the cruel trade which la Valette had so impossibly won, earning him a place in the crypt of St John's Co-Cathedral.

No educated soldier could be unaware of the layers of history as he climbed the stepped stone streets, past Auberges which had housed the different Langues of the Knights; Provence, Auvergne, France, Aragon, Castile, Italy, Germany, England. An educated soldier might stop to mock-salute the small white statue of Queen Victoria, wearing Maltese lace and seated in Queen Square. Or pause by the Palace itself to decipher the Latin words below the Royal arms which translated as 'To Great and Unconquered Britain, the Love of the Maltese and the Voice of Europe confirms these islands,' and with which the Maltese declared themselves to be British.

By day, a soldier might spend his pay in the Strada Real on trinkets to send home; on embroidered Indian silks or white filigree silver; on spoons emblazoned with the Knights' coats of arms in enamel; on handmade lace handkerchiefs; on imported sportswear for himself; or on the Camilleri brothers' sweets – pale pink cubes of Turkish delight dusted with sugar and smelling of roses – for a local girlfriend. He would watch older Maltese men, in black suits and black hats, shouting at each other while they sat at little tables and gesticulated their explosive contempt for each other's politics.

By night, a soldier, however well-educated, went to Valletta with only one thing on his mind; oblivion in Straight Street, known to all as 'the Gut': that street which promised to turn your blood to beer, and if you still ran hot, there were always obliging bodies available.

So, it was straight to the Gut for Lofty and George, whose brain still burned from Nettie's letter, with its unjust accusations and pouting threats. A beer or two would cool him down. The drinking joints spilled men onto loud streets, easing newcomers into their first beers. In traditional manner, first a man took a drink, then the drink took a drink, then the drink took the man. If the River Styx had truly flowed through Malta, then the proof was here, in the Gut.

Lofty got the first ones in and their pay gushed into their turn-taking, flowing even faster with their generosity to two girls who materialised at a table in the third? fourth? bar – if it was even that night at all when George met Violet. You were unlikely to meet good Catholic Maltese daughters in the Gut, and you would not meet the army wives but you might meet nurses, or plotters and coders, who tracked aircraft and decoded enemy messages. They might just turn up with an off-duty glitter which struck sparks off the shards in your own heart.

Violet was glamorous, with a Rita Hayworth roll in her brown hair, displaying a classical profile above a dance frock as her long fingers languorously tapped her cigarette. It was of course the cigarettes that gave the men their chance, and Lofty was first there, with George in tow, as Violet's friend searched for a light.

Through the smoke, the music, a clumsy shuffle around the room snuffling in the scent of a woman's hair like a bloodhound on the case, George found out that she was Violet. He asked her if she came there often and she responded, 'Malta? Oh yes, whenever there's a passing convoy. And you? I bet you own one of the islands.'

'Only a small one. I'd like another couple of beaches – I get really browned off when the visitors use mine. Upsets the tame turtles.'

Her eyes widened. 'Don't you just hate it when anything upsets the turtles. They must be finding it a trifle difficult at present.'

And so, George had not been George and Violet had been... something quite other. Lofty had been making good, if unsteady, headway with the friend, who called across, 'Violet, work tomorrow – remember?'

'Tomorrow.' Violet dismissed tomorrow beautifully, sending it into her cigarette smoke with one perfect pout.

'Work?'

'Tapping.' Her fingers tapped a dance on the table. Emma leaned across, speaking too loudly across the noise.

'We're listeners. Hush-hush.'

'Emma.' It was possible to miss the warning edge, so lightly was it given.

Emma's finger went, mocking, to her lips and she looked around. 'Walls have ears.'

'Can't be too careful, can we. Emma's always sooo dramatic but all I do is take calls – I'm a message girl – a thousand loaves of bread, ten thousand packets of tea and fifty thousand fillet steaks for Friday please.'

'A million jam roly-polys.' They all groaned.

'Please'

'Oh, if only.'

'If wishes were horses.'

'See her?' Violet pointed out a young woman talking earnestly to some servicemen and scribbling in a notepad. 'Times reporter, Winifred Cutajar Beck – she gets everywhere and tells her Editor everything.' Violet stared pointedly at Emma, who made a rueful mouth, silently acknowledging the reminder.

'Probably has her typewriter with her – look under the table.' Obediently they looked, but no typewriter visible. 'Rumour is, she's worried it will be stolen only she doesn't say 'steal', she says the Maltese are 'such pickers'!'

'Drink?'

Violet acknowledged the yellow concoction which arrived. 'Chin-chin.' Gin presumably but Lord knew what was in it.

If he had not drunk so much, he often wondered what

would have happened. He knew there had been some bet regarding his ability to waggle his ears and his eyebrows at the same time, and that it would be better not to think about where his wages had gone. He knew he had kissed her; kissing Violet was not something you forgot.

His wages had gone all right...not so much the wages of sin as wagers on. He couldn't vouch for Lofty's actions but whatever sequence had taken him there, George had ended up back in his own bed that night and atrociously hungover the next morning, almost too hungover to think of Nettie's letter, or of Violet.

What about his fiancée and his promises; more defiantly he wondered, what about his fiancée and *her* promises! What was it the Maltese assistant had said? Even Saint Paul was shipwrecked on Malta.

On 10th June 1940, Italy declared war on France and Great Britain – which included Malta. Sicily, where the Italian Regia Aeronautica had gathered, was only sixty miles away and Malta's only aeroplanes were four old Navy Gladiators packed away in crates somewhere on the island. Goats patrolled the aerodromes and almost everyone said that Malta was indefensible.

Senglea

Entry to Senglea

St Publius Church, Floriana, before severe damage in the 1942 bombing, when sixteen people were killed there.

St Publius Church, Floriana,

St Joseph's Church, Msida

One of the local children smiling for the camera

Chapter 6.

There are many people who believe themselves to be fundamentally humane and actually behave as humanitarians, but who, if changed circumstance offered occasions for being cruel (especially if the cruelty were represented as a means to some noble end) would succumb to the temptation with enthusiasm. Hence the enormous importance of preserving intact any long-established habit of decency and restraint. Hence the vital necessity of avoiding war.

Ends and Means

Until 1934, Italian had been, equally with English, the official language of Malta. The Maltese aristocracy – who could trace their forbears back to a time before Napoleon's occupation, before the Knights of St John, before Roger the Norman, before the Roman occupation – spoke Italian.

Catholicism was part of everyday life for the islanders; Roman Catholicism, with its Papal head and heart in Rome. Clashes between the church and the Maltese government, led by good Catholic, British Lord Strickland, led to a pre-election proclamation in all the churches that anyone voting for Strickland would be banned from receiving the sacrament.

Strickland was posted elsewhere temporarily in 1930 and his strident warnings against the Italianisation of British culture on Malta were ignored, along with his suggestions for aeroplane hangars and defensive barricades.

In the twenties and early thirties, Maltese teachers trained in Sicily, the better to teach Italian in their home primary schools. Mussolini encouraged his people to forge links with their Maltese brothers, whose Fascist Youth Party was growing, and the broadcasts from Rome were always conscious of the Maltese audience. There were however minor setbacks; a visiting Italian football team spoke their mother-tongue to their 'brothers' and were disillusioned by the stream of incomprehensible Maltese which was the reply.

There was also a major setback; Malta was British, by choice, and in 1934 Maltese, the language of the street, replaced Italian, the language of the palaces. Strickland, and his daughter Mabel, returned to the island to say, 'I told you so' and to dominate the press with the Maltese newspaper *Il-Berqa* (Lightning) and Mabel's new venture as Editor of *the Times of Malta.*

In 1940, Malta was still close to Italy in more than geography and Il Duce's declaration of war, from a balcony on the Palazzo Venezia in Rome, was broadcast and understood across Malta.

'Fighters of the land, sea and the air, Blackshirts of the revolution and of the legions, men and women of Italy, of the Empire and of the kingdom of Albania, listen! The hour marked out by destiny is sounding in the sky of our country! This is the hour of irrevocable decisions! The declaration of war has already been handed to the ambassadors of Britain and France!'

A premonition of the bombing to come shook the island. 'Mussolini ddikjara l-gwerra!' Mussolini has declared war!

The response of Malta's new Governor General, Sir William Dobbie, followed Mussolini on the loudspeakers, within minutes. 'The decision of His Majesty's Government to fight until our enemies are defeated will be heard with the greatest satisfaction by all ranks of the Garrison of Malta.

It may be that hard times lie ahead of us, but I know that however hard they may be, the courage and determination of all ranks will not falter, and that with God's help we will maintain the security of this fortress.

I therefore call on all humbly to seek God's help, and then in reliance on Him to do their duty unflinchingly.'

Private Taylor of the Garrison of Malta was delighted to have the reassurance of the Governor, a member of the Plymouth Brethren, that God was on their side. It seemed that He and George would both be busy. Military Hospital Mtarfa was now on a war footing. All ranks were confined to barracks, had to carry their steel helmet, respirator and field dressings in their respirator's haversack. The hospital became operational on 18th June 1940, seven days after the Italians had declared war on the island. As Mtarfa Military Hospital was elevated to No 90 British General Hospital, all military personnel were given acting promotion. Medical stores were in short supply, and the only antibiotic available on the wards was sulphonamide tablets, often ruined by sea water. These were crushed, and used as a powder on wounds, and there was no shortage of wounded.

The air-raid sirens wailed just before 7.00am on the 11th June and Malta's Italian brothers launched the first of eight raids that day. Ten Savoia Marchetti bombers accompanied by nine Macci fighters strafed Valletta. Their formation was old-fashioned, flying high at about twenty thousand feet, but it was efficient enough to defy the ear-splitting barrage of anti-aircraft guns.

No amount of Air Raid Precautions would have prepared people for the noise or the panic. No amount of drawing curtains, screening windows or planning to shelter underground would have prevented the destruction and deaths, mostly of civilians in the dockyards.

People thought it was another flight of bombers when

they saw four dark shapes overhead and few lifted their heads to see for themselves the first flight in defence of Malta. Rejected time after time in his appeals to London for aircraft, Air Commodore Maynard had unpacked boxes labelled 'Boxed Spares – Property of the Royal Navy' and turned their contents into four Gladiator planes.

Inevitably, the Fleet Arm had then demanded the return of its property, which had been re-boxed, re-requisitioned and rebuilt by RAF fitters and riggers, to become the only Air Force with which Rear Admiral Cunningham could respond to Italy's finest.

Three Gladiators took to the air, one truly being kept for spares, and their inexperienced pilots, who had taken off too late and were too slow to intercept, could only put on a chase.

Italy had two hundred planes; Malta had four. Despite that, 'Faith', 'Hope' and 'Charity' as the three in the air were nicknamed, caused such havoc that, from a declaration from Berlin on the 22nd June that 'the Italian air force has eliminated Royal Navy facilities on Malta', the AXIS view changed to the view that 'the defence is too good for Malta to be invaded – at present'.

That didn't mean any let-up in the bombing, not when Italy now viewed Malta as 'an unsinkable aircraft carrier anchored off the heel of Italy' and 'no longer an island but an infection to be cured'.

Editorial response to both the bombing and the rhetoric could be read daily in *the Times of Malta*, which had come out as usual on the morning of the 12th June. Its Editor had fired a worker for being late to work the day before; after all, she had warned them all plenty of times that anyone who did not turn up for work on the first day of bombing would be shot. *The Times of Malta* was not going to miss an edition, whatever happened, nor fail the people in expressing loyalty to Britain and the Empire. Small wonder that Italian broadcasts referred to Mabel Strickland, the newspaper's fierce editor, as 'the she-devil.'

George did not have much time to listen to the radio nor read the newspapers. He did not have time to think about Nettie, nor about Violet. When the air raids started, he wondered briefly about the latter, working somewhere in Valletta, and was glad to hear on the grapevine that she was fine. Apparently, she was regaling one and all with the story of how she had been on her way to work, getting a lift on some chap's motorbike, and they both dived into the hedge until the planes passed over.

George ignored the fantasies on sharing a hedge with her which accompanied the second-hand story, listening again when someone said she'd been moved underground, deep below Fort St Angelo, 'radio telegraphy or some such thing... totally boring, listening all day for German chit-chat. Jah, dis is der U-boat here, nein not your boat, U-boat'... crackle, crackle does your ears in'.

A miss was as good as a mile, his mother used to say, but Violet had been a near miss. Nettie's letter still hurt but, if she heard nothing from him, how was she to know better? How was she to know he cared, if not by accusing, threatening, hurting – and checking whether he was hurt? So, she was having a good time, dancing. Why would she say so, if not for the reaction? If not because she still cared? What a world where you checked how much someone cared by the measure of hurt you could cause them. George had far too much work to do to brood long.

Saturday 29.6.40

I have had no time since last writing but now I have a little time, I will try again to write a very short summary each day.

In the interval – Italy declared war – we have been working day and night. Short of food, too little sleep, too much work, too little pay. At the beginning of the month, I was taken out of X-ray and am now on B Upper – a ward having 98 beds. We have red crosses on our arms – and rifles. The company has been at the point of mutiny for about six weeks now (and it is still in the balance) because of the terrible conditions. Our worst day for raids – 9 through the day and 5 at night – usually about 25 planes.

No letters have arrived for weeks now – although I got your cable yesterday. Today I am on a long trot i.e. off duty from 10am to 1am, and on the rest of the day. If there are no special duties after I finish the ward, I am off at 8.15pm. I have roughly a half day a week but it is always used in doing work of some kind. Even if I get an hour or two off, I have quite often to go and help with X-ray work. That's all today.

Sunday 30.6.40
Fairly quiet – nothing much to say. Mortuary full up as usual – about 23 killed today.

Monday 1.7.40
Internal trouble again – one of our Corporals bayonetted a Malt. Yesterday one of our officers shot a fellow officer by loading his revolver when he wasn't looking. A Devon was also shot by a rifle. Not one air raid today and everyone is disappointed. I am just wondering how people will manage to settle down (if ever) to a life containing no thrills after living this rather strange life where bodies only mean more work.

Tuesday 2.7.40
Today's highlight was a mutinous meeting in which all our complaints were voiced in no uncertain voice. All the bulbs have been taken out of the lights and we are living like rats. Most of our clothes have been taken away some time ago – we have practically no clothes, and we have one shirt and one pair of trousers to last us a week in a country where a change at dinner time every day is necessary to keep one within comfortable sanity.

Nor are you allowed baths!! – shortage of water!! There seem *to be hundreds of these little things which accumulate to make this a hell on earth. That's all! – yes, enough!*

George was often alone on the ward, responsible for the routine admissions, drawing kits, taking temperatures, handing in kits, administering medicines, maintaining diet sheets, recording discharges and keeping the whole place clean to pass two daily inspections; all this for seventy patients.

In addition, there were a hundred and one extra jobs; lab tests, patients for X-ray, money being stolen, someone needing a pass to visit an ill relative. Just when he thought he knew all the answers, someone would come up with something else.

Wednesday 3.7.40
Nothing startling today. Air raids as per usual.

Friday 5.7.40
It was suggested last week that I become senior but I emphatically declined it as the other fellow is about forty and has been in a hospital before coming here. I scarcely think he would be pleased at having me for a boss after five weeks' experience!

Saturday 6.7.40
I've actually had a day off – the first since coming here. A very very quiet day. Lay in bed and read in the forenoon – (of course I was on the 6am and 7.30am parades as usual). In the afternoon I sorted out some films for my album and at night went to the pictures.

Then – we had our worst night raid so far. It was terrific! I suppose you have seen some 'war scenes' at the pictures – this was something similar – definitely hell let loose. It was more spectacular than anything else luckily. Just broken windows, mangled doors and a shambles was the result – few casualties. Incidentally I was out with my rifle looking for parachutists to shoot. I'm certainly not a nice fellow to meet on a dark night these days!

George was now bearing a rifle as well as the red cross of his name-saint, and it was not the first time Malta had seen men nurse the sick, then arm themselves. The Knights of Saint John had been called Hospitallers because of the requirement that each of them, including the Grand Master, give service to the sick on the day designated for his Langue each week. Their Sacra Infermeria, overlooking St Elmo, and famous for its Great Ward, the longest room in Europe, was one of the victims of Malta's latest attack. Luckier than the Opera House, the Infirmary – now Headquarters of the Malta Police Force – was damaged but not destroyed. Not so lucky was the Dental Centre, also in Valletta, where, two months after George had a tooth filled there, all inside were killed.

One of the R.A.M.C. corporals in George's barracks had been sleeping with a loaded revolver under his pillow for a week before he pasted another corporal and was placed in the Guardroom cells. Three corporals were on charges for inspection and other minor infractions, while yet another corporal faced a Court Martial. George thought it a bad time to be a Non-commissioned Officer.

Thursday 11.7.40

Well! I've been shaken at last! Since I arrived on the island I have been out to Valletta once and was with one of the nicest fellows I've known. It is with regret I have to say that he was killed in the last air raid yesterday (10.35pm)

At present, I just feel like going out and doing a spot of killing to make up for it. That's all I can write today.

Fireworks over Fort St Angelo,
where there would later be wartime 'fireworks' from ack-ack and bombers

Bridge into Valletta

Chapter 7.

There is one short-term policy which every individual can adopt – the policy of war resistance.
Ends and Means

There was no time to grieve for Lofty, no time for George to wonder if he would have gone with him, if…many ifs. The other ward orderly was taken into hospital himself for 'debility'; the Sister had a day off and George forgot to report for fire picket.

He read the consequent charge, stormed to the Sister and threatened to go to sick dock himself unless they were allocated another orderly. He'd had enough of covering for absence and mistakes, when he was stretched beyond his limits. He refused to take a kit to the stores. He narrowly escaped another charge for not sending in discharges, because he had to sit an examination for his Non-commissioned Officer promotion.

George warned the Sister he would go sick the next day and was put on iron and given a blood count. He was even visited by the Matron herself, who prescribed three days at rest camp. He survived the Friday, almost receiving another charge for a mistake Harding made with a kit, then he spent three days lying on the sands and swimming – and of course sheltering during air raids.

He returned to twelve-hour days on the ward. He sometimes had to physically restrain men coming round from chloroform, as they woke into their nightmares.

Sometimes they tried to leave, believing their world would be righted if only they got out of the ward, out of the sight of burns and bandages, out of earshot. George's ears suffered daily but at least he could still see, hear and swallow. Forget AXIS; the enemy was in every infected wound, every piece of paperwork, every temperature to take. Even the sterilising machinery was hostile, shorting out and turning a nurse into a patient with severe burns.

You took comfort where you could find it.

Friday 2.8.40

Worked till 1pm. Pay at two. I got a pass and caught the 4pm bus to Valletta (alone). I had a walk around and bought a new fountain pen – Conway Stewart and I knocked it down to 10 shillings. I also tried to get a wristlet watch but I couldn't get below 21 shillings for the one I wanted so I just gave it up. Then I had tea – iced lemonade first while waiting – then! (1) soup, (2) spaghetti, (3) chips, ham, poached egg, scrambled eggs – (all in one compound dish) – and bread and butter and a cup of tea. I then finished with fruit salad and custard and felt quite contented while having a cigarette after. I even felt that I had had good value for 2 shillings.

Then I resumed my strolling around and caught the 7 o'clock bus back – after adding a tin whistle to my purchases. I had a stroll around Rabat and then caught a bus for Durtorfa arriving home about 8.15. For the next hour I practised on my whistle. Quite a good day.

Already, you took for granted the dust, the streets blocked by ruins, the empty houses, abandoned by refugees who had fled Valletta to the villages or to the caves and old railway tunnels, now home to thousands. You took for granted the smell of overflowing cess-pits on the journey to Valletta; and in the city, cordite and choking dust.

Thursday 15.8.40

I went sick this morning with a rash on the palms of both hands – got the Medical Officer – he said it was due to sweating. Excessive sweating is still giving me trouble with my feet too. After a day's work with feet soaking wet, the skin is so soft that the slightest thing (I did it the first time drying them with a towel) takes off the outer layer and leaves red flesh. It then takes weeks to heal because one can't stop walking. Under constant treatment they are at present partially healed up although always painful to walk on. I was in front of the Colonel today to give evidence against the fellow who was absent from his bed yesterday. He was only admonished, because of insufficient evidence. The fellow who told them in Maltese not to leave the ward was discharged the same day and so could not be produced as a witness.

Fire practice at 3pm.

George eased his feet in the sea on a precious afternoon off. Blue skies, sunshine and swimming off Calypso's island... until suction on his arm and a squirm of tentacles made him carve towards the shore like a torpedo.

He took some photos, earning shy smiles from Maltese children and he wondered whether he would ever be able to point his camera at Nettie and their own children.

Lost in his musings, he was suddenly aware of a man standing close to him, holding an object at arm's length, his fingers about to pull the pin. Instinctively, he ran like the blazes until a stitch caught him. People were looking after him, puzzled, while the man who was holding a bunch of grapes offered them to someone else, picking one to show how good they were. There was no ease for George.

Saturday 24.8.40

Things are terrible!!! The wireless drums into us that the Navy controls the Mediterranean and yet – I have received one letter and I know definitely that you have received one in the last four months.

The one I got from you came by submarine. The one I posted on Wednesday last was on the destroyer sunk yesterday – and is now at the bottom of the sea. It does rather make one wonder if it's worth writing at all when they nearly all are 'destroyed by enemy action' as it appears in orders.

I lay in bed and read all afternoon and tonight I was at the pictures – Ritz Brothers 'At the Races'.

As nearly as I can remember, I heard this on the radio tonight:

> *There was a young girl they called Nettie,*
> *Beside Mussolini on a jetty,*
> *And there in the breeze*
> *He tickled her knees,*
> *And was strangled by her with spaghetti.*

Tuesday 27.8.40

Locker and barrack room inspection as per usual. Colonel Davidson's inspection of ward. These long days seem to get longer and longer. Still no word from home or you. For some time now, I have been missing you terribly, although the fact has gone unrecorded until now.

This sunburned rock is just hell on earth. Thank goodness the hottest of the weather seems to have been reached. Almost September now – it feels delightfully cool after what we have had. It feels cold at night – so much so that I have had to sleep with one sheet on!! I believe I forgot to say that I have been sleeping without a smile for some time. That is – you just put down a sheet and the bed is made. Then lie on top of the sheet and under the mosquito net and sweat the night away.

George knew that he was lucky to avoid night duty as long as he had, so it was no surprise when he read the orders. He moved his belongings to night duty quarters and started his new routine. Hourly temperature and tablet checks were much as before, complicated by the difficulties of seeing anything on a blacked-out ward. It was usually quiet between 12am and 5am then the rush started; temperatures, medicines, urines, swabs, sputums, treatments, bed baths and bed-making.

Tuesday 3.9.40
Received three letters today – one from home and two from you. And I wasn't pleased with yours. I still consider it a very dirty trick the way you got a bicycle – and of course now to hear that you have been in hospital is the last straw.

Not only had Nettie conned her older sister into buying her a racing bicycle, she had tested its speed on a steep hill, while delivering soldiers' pay, and come a cropper. It was typical of Nettie to make so light of breaking her collarbone and to be so excited about being the first patient in St Andrew's newest hospital, just converted from the town's best hotel. The food and the service still seemed to be keeping up to its five-star reputation.

George was not as lucky when he missed a step in the dark, fell down, then tested for damage three minutes later by running. Satisfied that no harm had been done, he returned to work until one in the morning, by which time the ankle was so swollen and painful that he had to knock on the floor to get the attention of Dusty, the orderly on the floor below. He was carried to the Wardmaster's where the Medical Officer insisted that George was admitted to General Surgery with 'injury to tarsals'.

George lay in bed, wiggled his toes and felt a bit better. He got up, walked a bit and decided that nothing was broken. He lay in bed for another couple of hours then he went to find the Sister and the Medical Officer to tell them he wanted out.

'But you only came in today!'

'You could put my discharge papers in for Monday...'

'We haven't got your papers yet so we can hardly discharge you! When you're fit, we'll do a special discharge, but it's back to bed for you.'

George was up at six-thirty on the Saturday. He washed, shaved, made his bed and checked his foot. It was definitely on the mend and he wanted out. Unfortunately, his eye had closed up completely. On the Sunday, he stayed in bed, getting up only to treat his eye and to eat.

Monday 9.9.40

Got up this morning and stayed up. Foot still tender but quite passable. Eye no better until 5pm when I performed a minor surgical operation and can with pleasure say that it is getting better already.

Polly, the Assistant Matron, looked the other way during his self-treatment and brought him first the good news that he was to get his special discharge; then the awful news that he could not be discharged at all, ever, because he did not exist. His records had gone missing and if he didn't exist on paper, he couldn't be discharged.

The temporary B178 form, which had replaced his lost original, had also gone missing and without a B178 he was going nowhere. Cheerful teasing that it would only take six months to replace the form added to his gloom; he knew from previous experience that it was, in truth, likely to take at least two months. However, for once, somebody sorted something out, and all George knew was that he was back on duty, this time on A Ward Upper, on nights as before.

George had been even more reserved with others than usual, after Lofty, but when Dusty Miller, from A Ward Lower, asked after his foot and suggested they could work together, he was quick to put the details into place. They both had to go into action to chivvy patients to shelter if there were an air-raid, but otherwise they could spell each other.

During the quiet time from midnight on, George would read and cover the wards while Dusty slept; then they would have a cup of tea at three, followed by Dusty's watch and George's sleep, until the five o'clock rush which needed both of them. Whoever was on watch would inspect the whole block. They even arranged cover from B Block so they could have supper together, ten until eleven one night, and eleven to twelve the next.

Official reports stated that there were thirty-one unexploded delayed action bombs liable to go off at any time. George's report would have added each and every patient on the wards. He would come on duty to find one man with a temperature of 103.8 and it was not the care needed to get it down to 99 by the morning which drained him, so much as the thirty-nine other patients needing routine care at the same time.

Wednesday–Thursday 18th–19th 40

Not so bad as last night but bad enough. One or two patients very ill and helpless makes it impossible to look after forty, so from 6am I have to take 20 odd temperatures give medicines, gargles, collect specimens of sputum etc and wash and make the beds of bed patients – and in between write the night report. This to be done by 7.30am.

So today is your 21st birthday. I suppose I'll have to admit you're a big girl now! I hope you got my cable and also hope to have an answer.

For once the notice board brought good news, via Dusty, who informed George that he had qualified as a Nursing Orderly, backdated six months – which meant six months backdated pay. Apart from working a twelve-hour day for two months without a break, in pitch darkness, it was a pretty cushy job. As long as Dusty was there. Oh, and apart from army regulations.

There was a baby in the Duty Room, the military

equivalent of a waiting room, when George went through it on his way for supper. It was obvious to him that it was in the last stages of pneumonia and the Duty Officer told him that they had been waiting two hours for an ambulance to take the little one to the civilian hospital. They were fifty yards from the operating theatre, oxygen, plenty of nursing orderlies.

'Why?' George asked.

'Red tape,' was the inadequate answer as the mother sat and watched her baby die without one thing being done to save it.

Then they moved Dusty. Matron was distraught at losing one of her best boys and told George she wished Seaman and Gates could be more like him and Dusty. Instead, she kept walking in on the other two, sleeping! Being caught sleeping on duty was worth fourteen days at least, any old time – but that meant being caught. George and Dusty planned a 'night' on the town before they parted company – the town now took as little notice of day or night as they did.

Friday-Saturday 27th–28th Sept 40

Routine night – unfortunately had six admissions. I don't know how it happened but anyway we got passes from 9am till 7.45pm. I slept 9 till 11.30am. Dressed and had some dinner – got a gharry to Rabat and then the bus to Valletta. Pictures from 2.30 till 4.30. Then a marvellous tea (same as last time I was down) and then we adjourned to Strada Stretta – otherwise Straight Street, otherwise the Gut – known all the world over and as it has it in the guide books 'frequented by soldiers and sailors of low morals,' so now I know the category I come under! We popped from one – joint, I think really expresses it – to another and viewed the scenery – I said scenery! I had three drinks and will admit that it was only because I had to go on duty at 8pm that I am alive now.

We got a taxi home at 7pm and I staggered on duty at 8pm.

Dusty went to the NAAFI and finished off what he had started, then staggered (just barely) into the bunk at 8.45pm. He immediately said, 'Lesh have a drink. Mush have a drink. I'll go to the NAAFI and get some'.

He sort of moved through the door and moved in again, in the same fashion, ten minutes later, and mournfully told me that they wouldn't sell him any. As he wasn't on duty, I made a bed in the ward and stuck him in it. Then I went downstairs and found that Corporal H was on and he had been out all day too. I put him in a small room so as he wouldn't be seen and he and Dusty slept and slept.

At 11 o'clock I 'got my head down' and the first thing I knew was that I was in darkness and someone was coming in holding a torch. It was allright though – just the Wardmaster's assistant – and the lights had been turned off at the main to effect some repairs. The time was 1.15am. He told me that clocks were changed tonight so I moved my watch to 12.15 and fell asleep.

I wakened at 3.10am and thought I would tell the Sister everything was all right as I usually do that about 3am. Anyway, when I went she looked at me as though I were crazy, I asked her if she had the correct time and she said twenty to five. Neither wonder she looked at me as if I was mad. Then I remembered and asked her if she had changed her clock back. She didn't know anything about it and wondered if he had played a trick on me as I was dopey at the time. Anyway, I went back to my bunk – and fell asleep!

I wakened at 4.20am (every time the door clicks I waken – Goody! Goody!) the Wardmaster on his round – and he confirmed the time question. A few minutes later, the Sister came and thanked me for telling her about the time and then – can you guess? – I fell asleep until 5.30am when I woke up Dusty and the Corporal. Not a bad night was it? 7 ½ hrs sleep with 3-5 mins 'wake-ups'.

Friday-Saturday 3ʳᵈ–4ᵗʰ Oct 40

Tonight, at teatime, Dusty tried his best to persuade me to go out tomorrow but I said No! I meant it. Quite a good night and had a shave before starting work in the morning.

Drew £5 pay this week and at 9am I walked to Rabat Post Office and tried to put it in the Savings bank. Unfortunately, there is none now. It seems that the Government scheme is the only one that money can be put in and as accounts etc are kept in England it means that permission has to be got from England (4 months maybe!) to draw money. I gave it up as hopeless. (The maximum one can draw is £3!! too!) So, if the Government is going to swindle me, I am as well to let the company office do it – I can at least draw any amount (if I have it!)

Got to bed at 10.30am. Awoke at 5pm. Tea etc. Some supper at the NAAFI. Then parade at 8pm. Gates and Seaman are missing. L.Cpl. Harland didn't turn up (and was blind drunk last night when he did) so I arrived to do two blocks alone – A Block lower and upper plus B Block lower and upper (about 300 patients!). At 8.30pm, Gates turned up and at 9pm a new fellow turned up for A Block lower (who had never even taken a temperature before!) Well!

Here is roughly what happened: Seaman is in the guard room – 'drunk on duty' etc. He's got 14 days and 7 days' pay stopped. Coming home, he bashed out two windows in the bus and Gates, in trying to help him, got into trouble. The police tried to arrest Gates and he bashed one – however he cleared it up and got a taxi back in time to start work in a reasonably sober condition.

Jock Mackay and Kilty (both Scotsmen) also had a fight in the NAAFI (fighting drunks, both of them) and Kilty is now in Hospital with a fractured skull and a magnificent black eye. Breakwell got into a fight down the Gut and his mother won't know him for quite some time. The senior Corporal in the company was in the Palace guard-room all night and was returned with thanks next morning – he had been found down the Gut with his 'stripes' in his pocket1 Rather a bad night for R.A.M.C. personnel! What!

Saturday-Sunday 4ᵗʰ–5th Oct 40

Definitely a lull today – everyone seems to be sleeping off the effects of bad beer.

Destroyer HMS Ivanhoe

Dreadnaught Battleship

The hospital in the background on Guardamangia Hill, is where Princess Elizabeth (later to be Queen Elizabeth II) was quartered when she was a naval wife stationed on Malta, 1949-1951

A hospital ship with its red cross symbols

The red cross should have guaranteed safe passage to such ships but that was rarely the case. In the early months of the war, casualties were evacuated by sea to Alexandria. Others were taken off when the first convoy reached Malta three months after the onset of the siege. The first hospital ship arrived early in 1941 to take the casualties of the aircraft carrier HMS Illustrious. Movement of casualties then became more irregular and averaged one to four a week. Casualties were transferred by bomber aircraft to Egypt, by flying boats to England, or by submarine to Gibraltar.

Chapter 8.

The patience of common humanity is the most important, and almost the most surprising, fact in history. Most men and women are prepared to tolerate the intolerable. The reasons are... ignorance... fear... a sense of kinship and social solidarity... mere habit and the force of inertia.... rationalizing these emotions in intellectual terms, is philosophical belief.
Ends and Means

When George arrived on duty at eight o'clock, he could see that one patient was very ill, the very bad throat merely an outward sign of much worse. George already knew what was coming but it wasn't until eleven o'clock that the Sister told him quietly that the man might not see through the night.

For three hours, through three morphine injections, George spent every minute with his patient until he lost him at 2.15am. After a brief visit from the Sister, confirming the obvious, George was left alone to prepare the body for post mortem at the Main Hospital. He worked all night, his only light a blackout candle lantern, which hid more light than escaped its metal case.

Bodysnatchers' shadows flickered across the wall as he shifted the dead weight. The technique which enabled George to turn and bed-bath patients worked less well with a limp corpse. There was no way of avoiding a danse macabre, the devil's breath reaching for George from that tortured throat. What help were his first aid notes? His classes on life-saving? He steadied his hands. Alive or dead, a patient's flesh was merely fabric, for rending, repairing or washing.

George was a kind cat-killer but when the cat was dead, it had to be buried. He focused on one domestic chore at a time and refused to see his own skeleton dancing in the romantic candle-light beneath the skin of his hand. He steadied his hands. Limbs would not stay where he put them, loosening slackly, sliding off the torso to swing and catch George's leg in a game of tag… 'you're it'.

It was like trussing a chicken to bandage the body neatly enough for George to transport it through dark corridors, trussing a chicken which looked very much like your own naked body, a chicken whose arms you had identified in the dark, by touch, like a lover.

The Post Mortem showed up Vincent's Angina, pneumonia, septicaemia, thickening of the mitral valves and scabies – he hadn't had a hope. He had been placed in a ward for minor medical conditions where one orderly looked after forty patients, rather than in the Main where it could be one to one. George slept all day and most of the following night, curled up tightly, but when he was awake, his hands kept shaking.

The Day Sister had left him a tin of pineapple and cream. In addition to the usual biscuits, provided by the Night Sister with tea, coffee, milk and sugar, that made quite a feast. George was happy to have a good report go to the Matron; less pleased to overhear 'Taylor's such a nice boy.' He was pleased at the gift of two blankets to make the night in a chair more comfortable but he didn't want to be tucked up in them.

Friday–Saturday 11th–12th Oct 40
Played tombola tonight but no luck!

Oh! Yes! It's my birthday today. 24! And honestly I feel like 12 tonight. I got two letters, (two excellent photographs) and one cable from you. I think it's almost too much at one time. The letters were posted in May – but that doesn't matter, does it?

I also wish to record that I have not celebrated my birthday with even one 'Blue' – otherwise known as Farson's Blue Label Pale Ale – beer if you like!

New Sisters came and went, which was fine by George as long as they left him alone and supplied their own tea. In sole charge, he did more nursing on nights.

Tuesday–Wednesday 15th–16th Oct 40

6 admissions – otherwise much as usual. This morning a fellow cut his throat from ear to ear – thank goodness he didn't do it through the night! Tonight, a whole bottle of sedatives has been dished out in order to put them to sleep.

Winter had finally arrived, playing wildfire lightning through the skies as a variation on the daily threat of bombers over the island. The lighting system was hit by every storm, leaving George to carry on with candles only, for as long as eight hours on one occasion, candles which greyed even living flesh with shadows.

Monday–Tuesday 21st–22nd Oct 40

Had third critical patient this evening and expected him to pass out any time during the night. Put on Serious Injury List at 10pm, and at 6am relations arrived.

At 7.15am I had him quite conscious for about two minutes. If they don't get him out before I come on duty again, it looks like another death for me.

I bought myself a new wristlet stop-watch this morning.

Tuesday–Wednesday 22nd–23rd Oct 40

Thank goodness – he's at the Main – with a special orderly and on Oxygen. Have had a quiet night. There is one consolation and that is that after a bad spell there is generally a lull. I have been very unlucky as I have had three bad lots – the first all recovered but I lost one out of the second and two out of the third. I have still three very bad throat cases but, barring complications, there's not much to worry about.

Callus passed this morning at 6.15am. and I was very sorry I didn't know early enough to get to the Post Mortem as it was a very interesting case.

Deaths had become 'interesting cases'. The man whose death was registered as the 24th October 1940 was Emmanuel Callus, a gunner in the Royal Malta Artillery

George went to Rabat, named after the Arab word for 'outskirts', and tried Maltese wine for the first time. It was like bitter port – a penny a tumbler and threepence worth would knock you senseless. An extra-special concert by the 'sherry girls', with seats reserved for the night staff, whetted George's appetite and when he returned to Rabat, he had only threepence left.

Greece came into the war and George was cheated of a day out. To ensure that the men slept during their designated 'sleeping day', he and Moore, the new Orderly on A Lower, were not told until the 8am duty parade that they had passes for two days off. Once they knew, they didn't have to think twice.

Undeterred by the lack of public transport (stopped because of petrol shortage) or even the air raid which delayed by over an hour the van on which they hitched a lift, they headed for the action.

Valletta offered business as usual, with new routes around ruins and a shop sign in English 'Bombed twice – back tomorrow'. The dogs and cats had mostly disappeared from the streets; abandoned by townspeople who had fled to shelters, they had run wild and become a problem to which someone must have found a solution. There were still a few tame goats left, nibbling at herbs on window-sills, sheltering in stone entrances, past which George and Moore threaded their way to whatever comforts were available.

A hungry soldier, missing Blighty, could still get lunch for two shillings and fourpence: tomato soup, spaghetti, lemon sole, chips, pancakes with sugar and lemon, and coffee. After lunch, George and Moore went to the pictures, ate tea with the same dedication as lunch, and then they arrived, inevitably, in Straight Street.

Was it the second bar or the third – she was never in the first bar – that he recognised the elegant flick of a wrist, the swing of shiny auburn hair and a glance that scanned you like an X-ray and moved on, leaving you exposed. George raised his glass to her across the room, she made the faintest gesture in response and drank deeply, smiling at the man beside her. No, Violet would not wait for a Faintheart.

'Know her?'

'Almost,' George replied. 'Almost.'

Her companion was leading her towards the door and she paused, touching George lightly on his arm.' Turtles fine?'

'Back in their shells,' he told her.

'Pity.'

'You?' he asked. 'how are you?'

'Like a mushroom. Permanently in the dark and all that manure dumped on one! You have no idea what rubbish men talk. It's driving me mad' She shrugged her elegant, bare shoulders. 'I swear I can hear ringing in my ears all the time and it's not my favourite dance tune.' She started to sing softly.

'Come on Violet, let's clear off.' Her companion glared at George and hooked his arm through Violet's, ushering her away.

'You take care of yourself.' George was undeterred and held her gaze, his Scottish accent stronger than usual.

'Not if I can find someone else who will,' she laughed at him as her skirt swished against the doorframe and she was gone. He wondered how blue his eyes were.

Someone backed into George and turned, either to apologise or to start a fight.

'Moore!' 'Petts!' They greeted one of their own, glazed with an earlier start to his drinking.

'Got a letter from home today!' Petts told them, bursting with his news. 'Going to be a Daddy!'

A well-trained orderly, Moore prescribed whisky for the new father-to-be while George counted on his fingers, calculated that this was good news, and joined in willingly with the medication. George kept to beer but enlivened this by drinking it through a straw and supping a further pint with a teaspoon, balking only at the request that he should take it standing on his head – and then only because he wanted to save a trick for another night.

Safely back at barracks, Moore could only be got quietly to bed by feeding bits of bread and cheese that someone scrounged from Ginger; Petts was asleep long before he hit his bed.

Having completed two calendar months on nights, George was transferred to the Seriously Ill Ward, as the Senior to a staff of eight. Air raids continued and Malta's response now contained a few more planes and pilots, courtesy of the aircraft carrier *Eagle*.

The anti-aircraft barrage was fired by gunners who included a thousand Maltese, and sometimes even their wives and children, handing shells into weary arms. Malta's war was a family affair.

Monday 4.11.40

Admitted an airman during the night. Two planes – crashed with 5 tons of bombs. Goodness knows how he is still alive and has been able to tell us all about it this morning. Blood transfusion and oxygen given but, in spite of this, he died this morning at 12 o'clock – appears to be internal haemorrhage. That for my second day has rather damped things down. Finished by 5pm and was in bed by 7pm.

Tuesday 5.11.40

Two more airmen in this morning – just been found! Just concussion I think – they'll pull through all right. Very busy day preparing for CO's inspection tomorrow. Shirt, shorts, boots, puttees, steel helmet, respirator and full marching order – and that's just me, never mind the ward! Finished at 7pm. Bed at 8.30pm.

Wednesday 6.11.40

Another airman in this morning – the luckiest so far – only a dislocated shoulder. He arrived on <u>Sunday</u> – has raided Italy and Germany 28 times since then – this is his first smash – and all six planes they brought out are smashed.

The dogfights during this week were so fierce that five RAF personnel died on the 3rd and 4th November 1940, all young men between the ages of twenty and twenty-eight.

Hospital regulations did not prevent the 'lucky' airman from being in a neighbouring bed to an Italian pilot shot down in the same battle, shot down by the very Officer who came in to visit one man and found himself unable to avoid the second.

George watched the Officer pause, brought face to face with his victim, and the lips tightened under a RAF moustache. The Italian's dark eyes flashed in his handsome, young face and he held up the accusing stump where an arm had been. Neither dropped his gaze until the wounded RAF pilot's soft 'Sir?' allowed the Officer to turn away from the pity of war and make the visit he had planned.

He caught George on the way out. 'Not good for

morale,' he said. 'Don't want that to happen to the men. Turn them soft in the air if they see too much of what it does to a man.'

George said nothing, knowing how 'seeing too much' turned a man hard in the army, not soft, unless of course it turned him plain bonkers.

There were rules. Once a plane was shot down, any airmen bailing out were to be picked up as prisoners-of-war. They were not to be picked off as sitting ducks on a dinghy nor shot in the dark, and they were to be rescued from over-patriotic Maltese lynching groups. Yet George had been called out, with his rifle, for parashots, just the night before, and mistakes had been known to happen.

It was best to concentrate on the basics of your own survival, especially as rations were becoming erratic, not only petrol and food but a soldier's essentials of beer and cigarettes so it cheered George up to be issued with fifty Woodbines. He was also delighted with his toeless, made to measure, light boots with rubber heels and lined ankles, which cost him nineteen shillings. They helped his poor feet but not enough.

Monday 11.11.40
I don't know whether I've mentioned it or not but I have had a slight rash on my face for a few days now – and the sores on my hands – and still got two rotten patches on my foot.

Friday 15.11.40
Went sick this morning. The Medical Officer wanted to put me in Hospital. Refused to go. Work as usual.

Grand Harbour, Valletta, showing British fleet

Pinto Wharves Marina

British fleet in Marsamxett Harbour. You can see the lighthouse on Fort St Elmo (on the horizon, to the right) which was demolished in 1940 so it did not serve as a landmark to enemy aircraft.

Chapter 9.

The good citizen feels a thrill of delight when his country 'takes a strong line', 'enhances its prestige', 'scores a diplomatic victory', 'increases its territory' – in other words when it bluffs, bullies, swindles and steals.
Ends and Means

George was sent to hospital on the seventeenth of November and kept in. He read Malta's *Times*, caught up on the news and worried about bread and ammunition – the stuff of life.

It was all very well for Churchill to show concern, saying, 'Whenever the Fleet is moving from Alexandria to the Central Mediterranean, reinforcements should be carried to Malta, which I consider to be in grievous danger at the present time.' However, it was the Fleet that had to deliver the goods and it had been months since a convoy had last reached Malta.

Hospital wards had always been good watering-holes and, listening in to the conversation, George had a good idea how far belts had been tightened. On a personal level, that meant men who were at full physical stretch and always hungry; on a strategic level, that meant rationing not only food but water, fuel and ammunition.

The walking wounded swopped stories and pooled information; for the time being, George was one of them. So was Bedford, an able-seaman who had been caught by

Italian gun-fire as his minesweeper, *Abingdon*, swept the Mediterranean south of Malta. He spoke out of one side of his mouth and his face looked ingrained with the engine oil of his coal-burning 'Smokey Joe'.

'What you've got to understand,' he told George, poking his stubby finger in mid-air to make his point, 'is that they know just as well as we do, that Malta needs supplies. How many mines do you think the Eyeties have laid out there? And just one will do for you.'

'Dinnae know. Twenty mebbe?'

The finger stabbed the air. 'We swept nine before I got caught and word is, M3 – that's our minefield – has 174 mines in it, all your basic contact mines, There's the five hundred-pounder, now that has a safety switch operating off the moving spindle and the old lead horns. Then there's the standard seven horn job. If you see a metal hedgehog on the beach, you'd better move fast, son!' He chuckled throatily at his own joke, choking on his laughter and reaching for a spittoon.

The pilot contributed, 'Saw one hit a rock once, blew itself to smithereens. I was flying over the drink, lacing into them – just missed one blighter. He must have thought his number was up when the sea exploded and instead it saved him – he changed his course and it was up, up and away.' Errol shook his blonde head. Probably younger than George, he was raring to get back to his Hurricane, and spoke of 'dog-fights' and 'a good show' as if he were describing a rugger match. Living up to his glamorous film-star nick-name, he was missing his local girlfriend as much as his plane.

'Terribly grateful if one is a bit thoughtful, the Malts,' he told the others, who included three Maltese gunners, from the Royal Malta Artillery. 'I mean, it's awfully good being able to go to one's own billet and know your bed's made, dinner cooked, home comforts, what?' He smiled disarmingly at the locals 'So I pick up a little something… that tasteless pasta your lot seem to like, or some kerosene or even some soap – that seems very popular, don't you know – and if it gets me a smile from a pretty girl so much the better.'

'You get some kerosene, Johnny,' Paulo told him grimly, 'you give it to us and we might give your plane a chance to have your bitch-fight.'

'Dog-fight,' Errol corrected him, ignoring that he'd been called 'Johnny', the universal name for any airman. 'And I'm not complaining, old chap – you do a damn fine job and all hours – but we do sometimes wonder if it's us you're trying to hit with all that noise and fury…'

Paulo's grin was fierce. 'You'll know about it if we are.'

With that sudden, young honesty which made it impossible to treat Errol to the put-downs he often deserved, and probably wouldn't notice, the pilot mused, 'Always try to put the record straight, you know? I mean, sometimes there's a bit of a do because two pilots are claiming the same hit and that's just not on. One always knows… and if I can see it's you chaps have got the blighter – and Lord knows we'd have no chance without the barrage – then I say so, every time.'

'You'd better ask the Lord to send us more ammo or we'll all find out what it's like without the barrage.'

'Ask Father Christmas, more like.'

'What do you want for Christmas, Bedford?'

The grizzled sailor sucked in his cheeks and blew out slowly. 'New minesweeper.'

'Thought you loved *Abingdon*.'

'I do, like a wife.' He shook his head, regretful. 'Like a first wife.'

He hushed the catcalls and whistles from the others. 'She was great when she was built, twenty years ago, and she's solid enough now for standard minesweeping – not one ship has been lost getting into your Grand Harbour and that's down to *Abingdon* and *Fury* – but the Italians were laying the old favourites and that's not how it's going to be in the future. There's new types of mines and the Smokey

Joes can't deal with them. And if the Harbour's mined…'

'No Christmas presents for anyone. What do you want, George?'

A sweet dream, a letter, the scent of a woman's hair. 'A pay rise,' he told them and then he smiled through their jibes of 'tight-fisted Scot.' The running joke continued with the smallest excuse. He only had to be seen with a key to prompt 'Wallet secure, Spoof?' just as Errol talking to a nurse prompted comments that made her blush. What else was there to do?

The men also talked about whoever was not there, the Maltese in their own language, the others with easy prejudice against the missing force. It bonded them all to mock the Italians, encouraged by Errol's analysis of the old-fashioned flying formation as 'too high to do serious damage but give one the quickest escape route'; encouraged by the newspapers' traditional stereotypes of the 'cowardly Eyeties', 'Hitler's jackals'; encouraged also by Bedford's tales of the Italian fleet, which never fought at night. If they had known the Italians' disadvantages of equipment, lacking radar in ships, lacking training and modern planes in the air, would they have shown any more charity? Or was the only Charity left a fighting aeroplane, still struggling through the air with the other survivor of the original trio?

In the same way, when Errol was not there, the men laughed at the RAF slang, moustaches, upper class expectations and, most of all, short term posting. Errol would be on his way home long before any of the others. If he didn't buy it in the air of course and of that, they didn't speak. They never talked about the percentage and youth of dead pilots, the daily risk expressed in boyish tales of derring-do, the likelihood of Errol growing into manhood.

When the gunners were not there, the men spoke of the natives, their religious superstitions, their fierce loyalties and family feuds.

When Bedford was elsewhere, it was the Navy's turn to be slated for its odd mix of criminals and coronets, its even more mixed reputation for womanising and woman-despising.

George was not surprised to overhear this sort of conversation and often feigned sleep, sometimes slipping off in earnest. Although he shuffled around to the end of his bed, checked his notes, his temperature chart and prescription, he remained unable to convince the staff that he should not be here and he frequently had to accept medication he did not want. His sleeping, like the rest of his life, seemed to be slipping out of his control.

It was while he was half-dozing that he heard, or thought he heard,

'Bomb-happy. You can see it in his eyes.'

'Looks perfectly normal to me.'

'That's what I mean. Look at you, look at me – that crazy look in the eyes – that's normal, what we're going through. And he's been here, on the island, being bombed most days and nights for six months, working stupid – you know the Army.'

'They say it does that, bombing.'

'Quietly mad I tell you, like my Uncle Bill. He came back from the first World War and you could hear him at nights, bashing around. And all day long, nothing would bother him, like nothing could bother him ever again. Bomb happy I tell you.'

'I don't know. Anyway, he's quiet when he sleeps – just a bit more quiet than when he's awake.'

'So why do you think they're keeping him here then? He might buy that story about his skin peeling off but there's more to it, you mark my words. I bet they gave him all sorts on that ward he was on. Have you seen him checking our charts? He can't stop himself.'

'His skin is peeling off you know, rashes and what have you, saw his feet when the nurse was putting some cream on them. Seen raw steak better.'

'I'm not saying he's not got what he says – I'm saying that's not all. You watch him.'

George worried sleepily about the poor chap they'd been talking about, told himself Bedford couldn't diagnose a black eye after a fight, and that it would be all right in the morning, if you could work out when morning was, in a hospital bed. He must check the temperature chart of the patient, back right, third bed, check up on him and let the nurse know. What did he want for Christmas? He drifted off again.

He was running away from home, not for the first time, and he always knew where to run to. His grandmother always held out her arms when she saw him, the black stuff of her high-buttoned dress starchy, crackling as he squashed it into folds. She gave George milk and home-made strawberry jam on small bread triangles, or boiled egg with toasted soldiers for dipping. She would say, 'Who stole your scone?' or 'The wind will change and keep you gurning like that' and he would tell his troubles, while she clucked and fussed.

He needed warmth and fussing; he was cold from the smooth precision of his father's discipline, his mother's distant beauty, and the exclusivity of whatever the two grown-ups shared.

He knew he could not stay with his grandmother and she would say, 'A sweetie afore ye go?'. George had a sweet tooth and in their ritual he would say, 'One in mouth and one in pock,' and she would smile, giving him the two sweets and watching one vanish into his shorts, for later.

When he was back home, when someone asked, 'Been at your grandmother's?' – if they had missed him at all – when they just made their assumptions, he would retrieve his second sweet and let the sugar fizz round his mouth.

He only really felt at home with his father in the school science room, where George and David were allowed to experiment at weekends and discover how to make patterns with iron filings on magnets and how to split light into rainbows through magic glass. Father did not like the word 'magic'.

Science was his passion – that, and his music. When he became the Headmaster of a school for children who would not go on to High School, or to Highers (the certificate for seventeen-year-olds), he made a science room to show them how the world worked. He was also proud of the school garden and the Home Economics room for the girls, but it was in the science room that he showed George how chemicals fizzed, bubbled, turned blue, grew into crystals or vanished. Father did not like the word 'vanished'. George learnt to say, 'prisms' and 'evaporated' but he still felt the fizz of a sweet in his brain and wanted more.

Christmas Day at Kennoway Drive was stiff as Sundays with church clothes and frowning looks at George and David, in case they were even thinking about games they dared not play. They must have had as many visitors as Baby Jesus but twice as boring, with no chance of kings or camels. The boys would sit on footstools, willing themselves invisible until there was a chance they could disappear in earnest from the over-warm room, the fire stacked high for the special day. When he was older, he would walk out with Nettie in the afternoon, their cheeks glowing.

New Year was something else. After his first ceremonial toast of a wee dram at midnight when he was seventeen, George had entered the adult world of all-night dances, an accordion skirling eightsome reels, a piece of cake and a drink at every house you cared to first-foot. Tall and dark, George had been in demand with his piece of coal, to be first over the threshold after midnight, in the Scottish Hogmanay custom, to bring good luck. Being accompanied by his vivacious girl added to the welcome he received. Even his father preferring to start the year with good omens. In George's memory there was always joy and snow on the ground.

On December 17th it snowed on Malta, to the disbelief of all. George had forgotten cold although he had known damp and dust since the summer, as moisture trickled down the walls of every stone building, and constant bombing choked the air. George looked out the hospital window. He had certainly forgotten the promise offered by virgin snow; here you could place your footprints, here you could start fresh. The gunners said their families had called the children and held up babies to see the precious stuff, and that it was a miracle.

Errol was either home or back in the skies, men had come and gone but George was still in hospital on December 21st when the news came that Admiral Cunningham had brought his flagship *Warspite* back to Malta the day before, for the first time since May. There had been quite a show, the band playing and guard paraded on the deck, every vantage point packed with cheering crowds and the dockers singing 'Rule Britannia' and 'God Save the King' as they mobbed the disembarking sailors.

'Wanted to be first in their pockets,' was the ward verdict.

'Whatever they brought won't go far enough – we need a full convoy.'

'The only packet we're getting is on its way.' The siren summoned them to shelter and the Regia Aeronautica performed its ritual pass overhead. You could set your watch by the bombing raids. Although there would be spells without any, sometimes days, when they did come, the waves were predictable and could almost be incorporated into work routines. Almost. No-one could ever get used to the noise, the ear-splitting response from the gunners or the exploding bombs which shattered Valletta flight by flight.

Then, a second miracle: the flight of bombers snowed Christmas cards over Malta and the Regia Aeronautica kept a Christmas peace for a week. Air Raid wardens and members of the Special Constabulary gave parties for the children. The men sang Christmas carols in their hospital ward, led by an army padre, and they did not yet know that the Tenth Fliegekorps had been deployed to Sicily. The German High Command, frustrated by the inefficiency of its Italian allies, had ordered Kesselring to 'neutralise Malta'.

J.M. Gray (Nettie) in her ATS uniform at the start of the war. The Auxiliary Territorial Service was the women's branch of the British Army. Nettie threw herself into her work with characteristic enthusiasm.

Nettie being inspected by The Princess Royal,

Countess of Harewood, Glasgow 1941

Nettie (front row, 2nd from left) in her P.T. class (Physical Training)

Nettie on the famous bicycle. Her job was to deliver soldiers' pay.

Prank 'charge sheet' filed against Nettie at Bendarroch Camp in 1943. Her alleged crimes were G.B.H. (Grievous Bodily Harm): wounding a colleague in the temple by throwing a teaspoon at him during dinner and throwing a cup of tea over another male colleague.

CHARGE

Army Form B 252
(See King's Regulations)

.... A.T.S. .... Regiment

{ Battery
{ Squadron
"J" Coy. .... { Troop or
{ Company

Refused to
CHARGE against No. give number. Rank Sgt.

Name ~~Mary~~ GRAY J.

Place In the Field .... Date of Offence 10th April, 1943.

OFFENCE1 W.O.A.S. using violence against a superior Warrant Officer, i.e. in that she on the date stated did throw one tea spoon, the property of the Sergt's Mess, Bendarroch Camp, at a certain Warrant Officer (C.S.M. R.H. Temple, 195 Coy., P.C.) whilst in the execution of his duty i.e. eating his dinner (to which he was rightly entitled), the spoon causing a deep wound in his temple, thereby constituting an action of inflicting grevious bodily harm to the said Warrant Officer.
2. Attempting to pour one jug of tea on a/n Warrant Officer, in an effort to scald him to death.
Names of Witnesses :—

1.
C.S.M. R.H. Temple.
S/Sgt. Bert (I.W.T.) Sgt. Derham, Blackman, Lee and Pollard.

Signature of O.C. Battery, }
Squadron, Troop or Company } ....

Punishment }
Awarded } ....

By whom } N.B. Practical Joke at
Awarded } ....
Bendarroch Camp
.... Adjutant.

30005. Wt.W34670/1406. 1,500,000. 10/41. K. & H., Ltd. G657/47.   P.T.O

Sergeant J.M. Gray (Nettie). She worked hard and was an officer by the end of her time in the ATS (to George's chagrin, as she outranked him)

Chapter 10.

Technological progress has merely provided us with more efficient means of going backwards.
Ends and Means

The airmen who found themselves on George's ward in January 1941 told him that the Stuka 87 was a pure dive-bomber, the Junkers 88 a shallow dive-bomber and the Messerschmitt 109s were damned good fighters – not as good as a Spitfire of course, but then the Spitfires hadn't reached Malta, had they, whereas the German planes had. The Stuka sounded like a siren when it dived, guns flashing. Sometimes, on the ward, a man would scream in his sleep like a Stuka.

George re-read Nettie's letters, even *that* one. *'There are other men I could marry, you know.'* He drew the poison, dwelt on the words which hurt the most. At least the plural 'men' meant there wasn't another man. *'You promised you would write and I haven't heard a word from you.'*

All his words to her were leaching ink to the ocean, paper bleached like fishbones.

'If you cared, you would have written to say so.'

Thoughts of her were all that kept him going when the planes screamed overhead, when his feet shredded into carrot peelings.

'When you did write, your letters told me nothing and I could tell you'd stopped loving me so I'm going dancing, drinking and

smoking.'

She had been the one to volunteer, 'I shall even sit out the dancing for I know you don't like it and,' she had flirted a sideways glance, 'you don't like to see me dance with someone else, do you?'

'No,' he'd replied, 'and you should be careful about drinking and smoking. You don't want people to think you're that sort of girl.' She'd blushed and agreed.

Was she becoming that sort of girl? Like Violet? Or worse? George couldn't believe it. There was always an innocence about Nettie, an innocence that hurt her as she grew and understood better the relationships in her own family. She had run to George then, crying, telling him what she had discovered and he had not been surprised. He told her that it didn't make any difference to him, that she was his girl.

No, Nettie was too innocent to become that sort of girl. He imagined her dancing, drinking and smoking. She would look like a schoolgirl playing wicked, checking to see its effect. Like the letter, all for effect, to check what others thought, to check he cared. That was what it always came back to, that she wasn't sure he cared, or cared enough, and she had needed to hurt him to get a response, to judge his response. Like most of the previous letters, his response was sunk without trace.

Something must have reached her though, turned the tide of her trust in the next batch of precious beige paper.

My dearest George, how could I have doubted you? Tell me again that you love me and it still won't be half as much as I love you. The band played 'My dreams...' at the dance last night and I sat there with my toes twitching and I thought only of you.

Surely you're due some leave now and can come home to me. It's really quite bad here and although I do keep my chin up, it has been rather longer without you than I was prepared for. One man I took pay to only two weeks ago has been declared missing in action and Sue has lost her brother last week. It gets one down rather. It really has been long enough — you are entitled to leave you know, and must ask for it. Don't be backwards in coming forward.'

When the air-raid started, George opened his mouth in mute scream so that the planes and the guns could burst his ears voicing his frustrations for him.

He dreamed of when they first met. Or rather of the time they thought of as their first meeting. He got on the bus as usual to go home from work at Forrester's, the chemist in Kirkcaldy, and, the bus being rather full, he sat beside a pretty girl with black curls. They exchanged a few words, snatching glances only at each other's profiles, too close to be able with any politeness to look at each other, side-by-side in the intimacy permitted to strangers travelling together.

When they reached East Wemyss, he stood to allow her to pass, inhaled the young warmth of her perfume and smile as she passed him and he day-dreamed the rest of the way home to Kennoway. He was disappointed the rest of that week, despite ensuring that he caught the same bus each night, but he was rewarded exactly a week later, and the same smile welcomed him as he took the empty place beside her. She was attending night school to improve herself, and their weekly assignation was soon a routine, formalised on the night a weary lady tried to sit beside Nettie and she covered the seat with her hand, said, 'I'm sorry but this seat's taken,' and smiled at George, anxiously hovering in the background.

He had never met anyone so vivacious, so interested in everything about him and so determined to better herself. The bus journey was far too short and once a week too infrequent, so they found more time, and their courtship led to the bluebell woods and their engagement. Somewhere along the way, Nettie met David and gave a small gasp of recognition; for his part, George's younger brother taxed the lovers with selective memories.

A few years earlier, David and Nettie were in the same class in school, had even had one of those boy-girl romances, 'Nettie loves-David/David loves Nettie'. Such was their infatuation that George had asked to see the famous girlfriend and had been shown young Nettie by his besotted brother. If Nettie was amazed at finding that David was George's brother, George was equally amazed at finding that Nettie had been that young girlfriend, and no amount of cynicism on David's part ever shook that amazement.

Except perhaps in George's troubled dreams on a hospital ward, where, sweating and shaking off the sheets, he struggled to get on the bus from Kirkcaldy, shouldered out of the way by airmen and sailors; where his legs grew heavy and he had to lift them with his hands, picking up feet which had floated fins, like tropical fish, each foot a bomb's weight, five hundred pounds – he somehow knew this even in his dream.

He would struggle the impossible climb up the step, his money spilling out of his pockets, running like mercury between the seats. He could see the Maltese Cross engraved on the silver coins as they melted and slipped through his grasp. He could see Nettie smiling at him and he would reach towards her, only to be blocked by army khaki or air force blue, some other man getting to her first as she faded into mist, smiling at someone else.

He sometimes recognised that someone else, in his signals uniform, charming his brother's girl with heroic tales of escapades in France. Waking, George would wonder at his poor brain, question the medication, spare a thought for his brother, still missing in France, with a girl of his own worrying at home. George would read Nettie's letters again, and again.

Then, on January 16th, something happened. Rumours came of a convoy, the longed-for merchant ship, a badly damaged destroyer accompanied into the harbour by tugs, but there was something else. Before the news hit the ward, there was a scurrying of nurses, shifting of beds, blankets, urinals, an inattention to all the routines of the less seriously ill patients.

George became aware of bodies passing along corridors on stretchers, covered bodies, screaming bodies, crying bodies, hundreds it seemed. No-one said a word and into the silent speculation came the bodies to fill the newly added beds, cramming the men together, the smell of sweat and rank illness overlaid with antiseptic and the newcomers' singed flesh.

Once the dam broke, the words overflowed. A man whose arms were entirely bandaged – Ted – started the flood. 'God knows how we got here. I can't believe the bastards didn't finish us off in the harbour... not that it would have taken much. She's still there, still on fire, what's left of her.'

Piece by piece, the men heard from the seamen who could talk, that they had been on an aircraft carrier, *Illustrious*. She was providing air cover for two convoys, to Greece and Malta, consisting of four battleships, nine cruisers and twenty-three destroyers. She was also supposed to deliver the Fulmar and Swordfish planes that Malta needed.

Waiting for them in Sicily were over three hundred aircraft, Fliegerkorps X, dedicated to laying siege on Malta and to blocking relief. Eighty-five miles from Malta, a well-rehearsed attack aimed for the *Illustrious* with wave after wave of the forty Stukas diving in courageously low and fatally accurate.

They struck after the Fleet Air Arm Fulmars had taken off from the huge armour-plated deck, so they could follow up the bombs with machine-gun fire, pulling up at the last minute, almost from the deck itself. Hit, crippled and blazing, the *Illustrious* could not keep up with the fleet but started to circle madly, hoisting the signal, 'I am not under control'.

Once one had spoken, other voices joined in to tell *Illustrious'* story.

'Wasn't the fire burnt me, was the bloody metal. Crumpled steel, blistering hot, and God help anyone who was closer to it than I was.'

'God don't need to help them now – He'll just have some explaining to do.'

'Seven hours daylight to get hit again, thousands of tons of high octane fuel and ammo stewing below deck, what do you think we were like? Wearing asbestos suits, doing what we were told like always.'

'When the power went, that really was it. Equipment all bloody useless, jamming anyway it was so hot, petrol leaking into flames, and fire turning men... toast we were, toast...hoses less use than pissing on the flames, just steam everywhere... and the bloody planes were back. Half the guns out... but then, half the men were out too so I suppose it made no difference... and them what could look out saw what the rest of us heard – the other buggers wouldn't go and leave us. Every bloody man on every bloody ship like cowboy wagons round us, firing that blessed barrage against the Indians. Even the Fulmars came back – they just refuelled in Malta and turned right back round and there they were, weighing in to make life difficult up in the air for Jerry, knowing they'd never light on that deck again – scored a few times, too.'

'We got as close as forty miles to go, engines still working but you couldn't breathe in the boiler room with stokers fainting with the fumes and heat – sprinkler system jammed on so if it wasn't the fires that got us, we were listing so much we'd drown from the water inside the ship before outside.

Then we got hit again, and the whole bloody shebang started all over again, no bloody joke. We were crawling knackered and back to dragging wounded out the way... not that we could do anything to help the poor buggers...had to put the fires out.'

'But we did it, forty miles in two hours... a feather would have finished it, but they didn't come back with a feather...'

'They didn't come back.'

'Perhaps they thought they had finished her.'

'Have they?'

'Surely.'

'No,' the man was adamant.

'There's got to be a point to it all...'

'She's in Grand Harbour – French Creek, someone called it.'

'You can see why they'd want her – good catch for the Hun... the *Illustrious* did for half the Eyetie navy and we only lost two planes.'

'Till now.'

'You heard Captain Boyd, he was giving orders as we was carried off... I heard him asking estimated time to make ready for sea.'

'You think so?'

'She's not dead just because Jerry says so.'

'Heard the broadcast?'

'Aye, Jerry radio said they'd finish her off in the Harbour.'

'So where are they, then?'

'You don't want to believe everything you hear on the radio.' The old Malta hands could join in on this theme with enthusiasm. 'They said the British Naval Base in Malta had been annihilated. And they said H.M.S. *Angelo* had been sunk!'

'So?'

'St Angelo is a fort!'

'And the coal-mines, don't forget the coal-mines.'

'Yeah, they said the Maltese coal-mines had all been destroyed.'

'And?'

'We don't have any!'

Spirits rose – and dived again, with the memories of bomb-holes through steel and skin.

'All the cooks were killed.'

'Bastard, that.'

'You know the real bastard? First of her kind, the

Illustrious, and that flight deck could take 500-pound bombs – so they made thousand-pounders and we took six of the buggers!'

It was Churchill who ordered the Navy to take supplies to Malta but it was HMS *Illustrious* that lost one hundred and twenty-one men.

News drifted in. A merchantman had brought three thousand tons of seed potatoes and four thousand tons of ammunition: Malta's basics. Supplies had eased the situation but only till the next convoy, and rationing was still in place. More rock than soil, Malta relied totally on imports to survive; without the seed potatoes, Malta could not grow potatoes. It was an island which could be starved as well as bombed but it was also an island which had survived siege before.

The Harbour was bombed and the Maltese stevedores at Parlatorio Wharf went on strike, refusing to work in the hell-fire of diving planes and the wall of fire put up by the artillery in a deafening box barrage. *The Times of Malta* spat fury at the stevedores' lack of patriotism but they stayed on strike and many of the supplies bought so dearly, were lost.

Some of those on the docks lived to tell the world of the heavy guns in the fort, waiting till the dive-bombers were low enough to level off and their shots might reach them; of a motor-car flying through the air; of women's prayers shrill even through the madness of the anti-aircraft guns.

The *Illustrious*, camouflaged top-side by creamy yellow paint, repaired at breakneck speed, survived. Fourteen days after sustaining the most horrific damage, she left for Alexandria. The three cities around Grand Harbour were not so lucky. The attempt to finish off the aircraft carrier had cost the Germans ninety planes and the Maltese, their homes and relatives. Archbishop Caruana condemned the looting of the suburbs as 'a very grave sin' and the exodus from Valletta to the catacombs and tunnels was completed.

One bright, moonlit night in February, Bedford's prophecies came true and the Luftwaffe dropped magnetic and acoustic mines by parachute into the submarine harbour at Marsa Mxett, and into Grand Harbour. Three of the mines exploded on impact on shore, causing massive destruction, and the others closed both harbours.

Chapter 11.

Ordinarily decent behaviour cannot be expected of the National Person, who is thought of as incapable of... even common sense. Men, who in private life behave as reasonable and moral human beings, become transformed as soon as they are acting as representatives of the National Person into the likeness of their stupid, hysterical and touchy tribal divinity.
Ends and Means

George dreamed that he was marooned on an island like his great great great great uncle, Alexander Selkirk. He had told them the ship would sink but for his mutinous suggestion they had merely left him here to go insane.

Now, George must wait and watch for ships, good angels to rescue him or the avenging angels of the enemy.

But if he looked for ships, he would starve; he must catch goats, find fruits and fetch water. If he was seeking food, he would miss a ship and die crazy. He looked out to sea until he could stand the hunger no longer. He read his bible to the hobbled goats just to hear a human voice. He drank out of a coconut shell which already had the silver ring around its rim that George had seen when his mother took him to Edinburgh Museum.

George made clothes out of skins, stripping the skin carefully from his bloodied feet and sewing it with vines to cover his shame. He did not want anyone to see his body.

There was nobody. There never was any Man Friday.

When George awoke, he was indeed on an island, but a long way from the Scottish seaside village of Largo where Selkirk punched his brother and longed-for adventure at sea.

'What news?' they asked each new patient hungrily.

One newcomer, Spud, worked on the air crew at Luqa aerodrome. Or *had* worked – it was not certain where some of the men would work when they left the hospital. At least, from their ward, it was likely to be 'when'.

'They get them, the planes, when they're landing,' Spud told them. 'The Fulmars are great guns in the sky but our aerodrome is shot to hell, there's no cover for us on the ground to get the planes back in, repair them – no hangars – just blast pens for the planes and slit trenches for us, bombed every day, rebuilt every night – and they get them when they're landing, sitting ducks, however we try to camouflage them. Us too.'

'Why don't they just wait it out in the sky?'

'Fuel.' Petrol and kerosene were rationed. Virtually all transport at a standstill on the island, and the planes which kept the bombers at bay had to conserve fuel. No-one knew when or if another convoy might reach Malta. Meanwhile, the only source of supplies was from submarines or planes, in tiny amounts.

'Even thought the old Smokeys would have to stop sweeping – no coal.'

'Thought they were no use against these new mines?'

'There are still old ones out there but no, you're right, it takes the *Ploughboy* to sort out magnetic and acoustic. They tried bombing and gunning the mines – better than nothing but still too risky to get the subs in. Then they fitted *Ploughboy* with a magnetic skid sweep, so that helped, and then we got the SA hammer – that's acoustic equipment they fit on the bow.

Don't know why I'm so pleased. If we hadn't been sweeping a sub into Harbour, I wouldn't have been caught,' Jack shifted slightly in the bed. 'Can't even move the bloody things.' No-one looked at his legs. 'We'd lifted three mines, going sweetly I thought, then 'bang' and we were blowing so badly we had to beach her. Them bloody planes whining and diving at us all the time – bloody miracle we could concentrate enough to find any mines at all, got to concentrate you know. The *Ploughboy* got off and back to work. Not me, I'm beached proper. Call it a job?!'

Sometimes George heard Jack keeping lookout in his sleep, doing the half-hour watch for mines that was all a man could stand, scanning the sea for metal death. Jack would tell himself to concentrate, flinch as if ducking the planes, count the minutes he had left to survive the watch.

They read the account in *The Times* of the bombing of Luqa aerodrome and the nearby village. 'Almost all the houses and farms on the outskirts facing the fields bear marks of the shrapnel, which bit holes in the walls... these people, most of them miners, stonecutters and farmers, are among the most courageous and confident one can be privileged to meet. They have dug shelters, carried away to other villages the most valuable portions of their furniture and household goods, and they continue to live and work there, notwithstanding the severe punishment the village has had to submit to at the hands of the enemy.'

'Rubble,' confirmed Spud. 'and dust and craters. The work the boys put in to get the runway half decent again, you wouldn't believe.'

'Heard the latest, boys?'

'Well?'

'Two kids arrived by plane to stay with their auntie and uncle – some joker sent them here to escape the blitz!'

'We don't get the fires.'

'Stone don't catch fire.'

'Same bombs though.'

'More bombs.'

'One will do.'

'Shelters are pretty damn strong though.'

No-one said, 'so strong you could be buried alive, to die slowly, instead of exploding or going up in flames'. They did not talk about ways of dying, only of near-escapes.

'No shelters for the planes though.' Spud returned to his old theme.

'There would have been if Strickland had got his way.' Julio was an anti-aircraft gunner caught in Valletta by a Stuka. 'Our old government in the thirties wanted to build hangars for the planes. Strickland was always going on about war coming and danger from the Italians.'

'Well he was right then, wasn't he?'

'So why the hell didn't you do it?'

'Who wants to spend money preparing for war? What if that's what makes the war happen in the first place? Anyway, Strickland was not so convincing, he had some bad press.'

'Mabel print it, did she?'

Julio acknowledged the joke. 'Chip off the old block, that lady. I think she wants to be in government herself, like her father. It's lucky we are not too English in our laws.'

'What?'

'You let women vote and even join your government – crazy. What do they know?'

George thought of Nettie, twenty-one and able to vote at last, and she should be allowed her opinion. He smiled at the memory of those opinions. No, he didn't see Nettie as his M.P. She was born for motherhood if any woman ever was. Small children were drawn to her as to a sweetshop. He could picture her now, playing games with rhyming songs. No blue-stocking, not like Mabel Strickland whom George had seen striding about Valletta, tall and hatchet-faced. Look out Malta, if she could act on her politics!

'Some women would be better than what we've got.'

'A labrador would be better than what we've got.'

'You mean Holy Joe?'

'By God's help, Malta will not weaken'. Spud managed a passable imitation of General Governor Dobbie, quoting his words in a broadcast after *Illustrious* had left Grand Harbour.

'While he relies on his direct line to God, no-one down here is talking to anyone else. I tell you, I've found out more about the other forces lying in this bed than in all my time on Malta.'

'George is right. It's not just the men neither. The Admiral was hopping about losing those supplies after *Illustrious*. I mean bad enough the flaming Malts letting us down – sorry, Julio, but I mean, a strike on the docks? Give us a break, there's a bloody war on.'

'You think we don't know that? It's our women, our children and our churches the filthy Boche aim at!' Hits on the ancient Cathedral, which must have been deliberate, had outraged locals. 'And you need to eat – so do we – so why do we get paid half of what you do? Five shillings a day I get – try buying bread out of that! You live here, you pay the same as us, some of you,' Julio looked at Jack, 'even board in our houses while my people live in caves, so don't talk to me about *the Malts*!'

'Apart from the money,' Spud quickly rode the debate, 'it's a mess. I don't blame no dockers for scarpering. There's planes buzzing around shelling you to kingdom come and apart from Julio and his boys, what's to protect you?'

'The dockers are civvies too,' Julio pointed out. 'No sign of army boys on those docks.'

'Should have been,' they all agreed, 'military situation if ever there was. No bloody communication… it's Dobbie, he's losing it.'

'I've heard you can get smoke stuff to send up over the docks. Unload undercover of that.'

'So why the hell don't we have some?'

'Dobbie,' they all agreed, all except for the Maltese Julio, who murmured quietly, 'He is a good man, a godly man.'

'Never mind chaps, 'the eyes of Britain are watching Malta in her struggle.'

'Don't forget the whole 'British Empire', someone corrected the Churchill quotation and someone else completed it; 'and we are sure that success as well as glory will reward your efforts.'

'Here's to success and glory.' Spud mimed a toast then wiped his hand on his backside.

'Here's a good'un.' Jack had been flicking through the newspaper. 'There's a travelling theatre group stuck here so they're just going to keep on travelling round the island, giving shows.'

'Won't be as good as the Sherry girls.'

'Or the RAFfians,' and they reminisced about the shows, and about the men who looked surprisingly good dressed as women. They talked George into playing his tin whistle and he wondered if it was too late for rescue, if he were already stark raving bonkers.

February saw the return of conscription to the island for the first time since 1792 when the islanders had laid siege to the French in Valletta. Able-bodied men between sixteen and fifty-six could be called up for military service, with exemption for government employees, dockyard workers, farmers, quarry men and stonecutters. As soon as the law allowed, hundreds of nineteen to twenty-nine-year olds were called up, quickly turning to thousands.

Thanks to the farmers' work on the garden of Malta, its satellite island of Gozo, there were always fruits and vegetables, but the little gondolas, with the eye of Osiris painted on the bows of each, had to run the gauntlet of the mined harbour and the German planes to deliver the goods to the Supplies Managers on Malta. Produce brought over by day was carefully counted and allocated according to ration agreements; produce brought over by night was far more lucrative.

Sugar, coffee, tea, margarine, matches, lard, rice and soap were all rationed. Goats' milk was still available but no cows', and tinned milk was considered essential to sweeten the coffee which had replaced cups of tea for the locals. They missed their cups of tea, and were finding it increasingly difficult to get their usual diet of olive oil and bread with a little tomato paste; the Maltese had never been as keen on pasta as their Italian neighbours, and potatoes were a luxury. Seed potatoes had to be imported in order to grow them on, and the three thousand in the January convoy would not go very far.

All of this George heard from the Maltese patients who came and went from his ward. No-one ever had enough to eat and they all talked of food with nostalgia and reverence. George heard about pumpkins ripening in the sun on the flat roofs, about Zebbug olives – the town's very name meaning 'olives' in Maltese.

He heard that the winter 'gregale', the Greek wind, had finished blowing and that the spring herbs – thyme, rosemary, wild garlic – were sprouting in the high garrigue. It would be May before the dry, dusty southerly sirocco, the Xlokk in Malta, sweated men and buildings, providing cloud cover for convoys.

George practised his Maltese and learned about the island, across which prehistoric beasts once ran from icy Europe to the warmth of Africa, when Malta was still a causeway linking two continents, even then the strategic lynch-pin. The traditional two-wheeled cart, pulled by a horse or donkey, was still following the same prehistoric tracks rutted across the island, which sometimes even ran parallel or crossed like railway junctions. The Maltese too were still following the same track, repelling would-be invaders from this arid, stony British soil with a passionate nationalism. George would look the other way when a man, angry at the latest AXIS assault, spoke of the devil and crossed himself.

George was fascinated by the old stories of the island, of Fungus Rock which was guarded so closely by the Knights that a man needed the Grand Master's permission to be winched across, alone, and collect the black, medicinal fungus in a basket; of the ubiquitous 'Haxia Inglesa', the English weed, yellow Cape Sorrel, which had been introduced in the nineteenth century by a South African woman.

Then his Protestant soul and scientific brain would be repelled by a tale of miracles, told with superstitious zeal, St Paul banishing the snakes from the island or the Virgin sparing a child's life by warning its mother where a bomb would fall. George was uncomfortable amongst saints and would testify on the bible to the snake that he had seen.

Just when George was convinced they had mislaid him among their forms, a living wraith haunting the ward, in here by mistake and so unable to escape (if there had been nothing wrong in the first place how would they pronounce him cured?) just when he was giving up hopes of getting out, they signed his release papers, as inexplicably as he had been admitted, his skin still covered in rashes.

23.3.41

Came out!!! Uncured!!! And was posted to Murta – 'for a change of air'. There I was not allowed to wet my hands or do any work, so I was given to the store as a help. As a store there was nothing in it – but I made tea and painted notice boards etc. (what you call starting at the bottom!!!)

I went out every night of the week to Johnnie's and didn't half lead a fast night life for about six weeks till my money ran out. But luckily, before that, my hands cleared up and the lad who was on the job when I arrived was given the push and I was left there.

In March 1941, Malta was transferred to the Middle East Command, in recognition of its strategic position. The irritation caused by this small island in Rommel's North African campaign would later draw the wrath of the

Luftwaffe against it. Meanwhile, George set to work, finding some stores to organise and distribute.

Rabat Citadel, Gozo

Saluting Battery and view of Grand Harbour

Ta' Pinu Basilica, Gozo

Xlendi Bay, Gozo, and the Church of Our Lady of Mount Carmel

St Joseph's Church, Kalkara (skyline, central)
was completely destroyed by the 1942 bombing

Mtarfa Barracks

Chapter 12.

Life during war-time takes on significance and purposefulness, so that even the most intrinsically boring job is ennobled as 'war-work'.
Ends and Means

The sky over Malta was endless white and the dust lay thick or swirled through wind and bombs. The 15th Field Ambulance had been formed and George was on duty in the army stores at Murta, performing loaves-and-fishes miracles through inventories and rationing.

His Staff Sergeant lived out in what passed for married quarters so it was George, living in, who coped with the frantic requisitions, from eight in the morning until two in the following morning, days merging into each other. There was brief support from a Corporal who had trained as a Quartermaster but he was speedily moved elsewhere.

Then, to Sergeant Pitt's delight, a Lieutenant Quarter-Master joined them. George was promoted to Corporal, all in one jump, and allowed to keep a gofer, James, to help him at the stores. To match his new status, George bought his first 'blues', dress uniform; all dressed up and nowhere to go.

Supplies brought by the mine-laying submarines were known as 'the magic carpet' and word spread across the island when *Unique, Utmost or Upright* returned to their harbour at Marsa Mxett, which was also the minesweeping base. A returning submarine would be accompanied by local vessels converted to use as auxiliary minesweepers. For the crews of the submarines, these little ships became their friends, the last contact they had before they left on their dangerous mission, the first seen on return to safety.

Support was mutual and submarine captains would note the position of mines parachuting into the harbour and notify the sweepers. The minesweeping was no token gesture, with ever-increasing numbers of mines laid by Italian and German ships in addition to those dropped by aircraft. AXIS wanted Malta, cut off completely, and the minefields forced the Fleet closer to land and closer to the German air power. George was not the only one counting the goods in his store and the days until a convoy was necessary.

After a slight lull in May, when Crete was invaded, there was no relief from bombing – or from the summer heat. Beaches were banned because of the mines, so townspeople were unable to swim or fish. They lived in dust and on short rations. Policemen accompanied the kerosene carts to prevent black marketeering or violence. Kerosene was the only reliable form of heating and lighting so rationing was strict. If islanders, troops and Maltese alike, swopped jokes about the cowardly Italians, it was hardly surprising, but it became difficult to do so after the events of July.

A convoy of six merchant ships, with its accompanying destroyers and aircraft-carrier, had run the Mediterranean blockade to reach Malta in July, stores intact and ships no more than slightly damaged. According to the subsequent newspaper reports, Maltese radar had picked up an Italian ship, but George suspected that the listeners must have known more than that.

He imagined Violet, in the cold, damp dungeons below St Angelo, using her Italian or listening to the coded messages. She might have tapped one ear, to stop the ringing which had started to affect her – George had seen the little mannerism and recognised it, along with her habitual little cough. She would have passed on the message, understanding its importance and pretending not to, excluded from the small circle of decision-making, defined by her need-to-know, her position within Ultra.

Whisper the very words, but George heard things in bars. She, or others like her, might have used the new RF Type X machine cipher, or intercepted *en clair* radio messages, or plotted the bearings taken on ships and predicted their course. However, it had really been detected, the newspaper report told George that the radar had picked up the Italian ship *Diana* nine miles north of Fort St Elmo, when she turned around and headed back to Syracuse.

Even when placed on alert, how did Sergeant Zammit of the Royal Malta Artillery know what it was that he could see from his dawn watch on St Elmo, unless he had received certain information in advance? Just as the light was breaking, a small motor-boat was heading towards Zammit's battery at St Elmo. He sounded the alarm and the coastal gunners, who had never before had a target, rattled off their fire.

Eighteen small boats had been left by *Diana*, each one of them an explosive motor-boat, the bow a torpedo-head, an engine in the middle and a sailor in the stern. His job was to activate the torpedo, then eject before the explosion. If he timed it to survive the explosion, he was likely to drown or be shot; the best he could hope for was imprisonment for the duration of the war.

The first boat blew up the bridge spanning the two arms of the harbour's breakwater, blocking the entrance. If this had been part of the plan, the subsequent explosions certainly weren't, as the gunners sent red and green tracer bullets in the glare of shore searchlights, then picked off thirteen boats as they careered desperately around the harbour.

Hurricane fighters dealt with the remaining four as they attempted an impossible retreat and prevented any attempt at covering them from the Italian Macchi planes. One boat, three prisoners-of-war and a furry white mascot dog with a red bow, which was found on the empty boat, were retained by Malta as trophies.

The Decima Flottiglia Mas (10th Light Flotilla) had never really expected the return of its men. They considered it worth the risk to destroy the vital supplies on the convoy in the Harbour. If they had succeeded, what glory! Perhaps they should have used their other specialised craft, the 'maiali' or 'pigs'. These were slow-speed torpedoes on which two men sat in full diving gear, until they were just below the target, when they removed the detachable warhead, clamped it to the keel, set the time fuse and withdrew to safety on the 'pig'. It was very difficult for a while to make the old jokes about the cowardly Italians.

The convoy brought: two thousand tons of frozen meat; two thousand tons of edible oils; three months' supply of sugar, coffee, fats and tea; ten thousand tons of ammunition; spare submarine propellers; spare Hurricane engines; hundreds of anti-aircraft guns; a total of sixty-five thousand tons of supplies – and extra work for George. The convoy also brought fresh troops and the whole weary process of explaining Malta to newcomers, who stared open-mouthed at the old Maltese sitting outside cave entrances on wooden boxes which had once held foodstuffs.

The reinforcements brought by the convoy did not bring unqualified joy. Because of shortage of men, both 15 Field Ambulance and 161 Field Ambulance had Maltese RAMC Other Ranks serving with them. However, in Nov 1942, reinforcements arrived, and in order to prepare these medical units for overseas service, Maltese medics were replaced by British personnel. The casual use and demotion of locals created a simmering resentment, adding to the difficulties of integrating newcomers to 'how things were' on Malta.

George measured time in convoys and supplies, the

equation of survival, and September brought the *Imperial Star* with several hundred crates of bombs, five hundred tons of kerosene, five hundred tons of refrigerated meat, grain, flour, small arms ammunition and three hundred passengers. It would keep them going for a while but no-one lost sight of the next deadline. When a Daily Mirror reporter smuggled himself into Malta aboard a bomber, he was greeted by Governor-General Dobbie with the words, 'We would rather have had a sack of potatoes.'

There was certainly enough food to see them through Christmas, which was observed as a ceasefire on both sides. In the shelters, the priests used what had once been their travelling altars to celebrate mass, while the cavern walls streamed with damp. Even the walls of the houses glistened wet as Malta mopped up the rain and breathed it out again over the sickly yellow of the limestone. Unusually, it rained steadily over Christmas, adding to people's cold and hunger in what they called 'The Black Winter'.

On December 7th, 1941, Pearl Harbour was bombed and on the 8th, the USA declared war against Japan. On the 11th December, the Americans declared war against Germany and Italy. AXIS now had a new enemy but this made little difference, as yet, to the USA's new allies on Malta.

Parents planned foodless parties and repainted toys, which they passed from one family to another, to try to make Christmas special for their children. Those same children who had exchanged shy smiles for George and his camera in his 'landscapes', so that he could send photos home to Nettie, hinting to her of all he hoped would be theirs, now played 'chicken' with the mines dropped from the sky.

Soldiers, denied their own games of 'chicken', were bored, stuck as they were in groups of five or six in 'Elephant' shelters. The Commanding Officer of the Royal Artillery considered both issues and declared 'Gunners will make toys'. With the imagination bred of shortage, the

Gunners put on a show of over two thousand toys; innumerable model spitfires, but also cars, soldiers made from bully beef tins and one completely working model of a theatre interior. The Times carried the photographs of a child's face as he received his present; the gift was mutual.

George, too, celebrated Christmas.

Xmas 1941
A very good feed anyway – and I finished up the day by going with James to Nappa.

In Nappa, they sampled the 'jungle juice' and paid for it, with one bicycle missing in action. James had to fill in a variety of forms describing the circumstances in which his bicycle disappeared and, perhaps due to the omissions in his account, the adventurous article was charged to the public.

New Year 1941
Last New Year I spent in hospital – this I spent in bed!! It was one I just didn't see! I was put to bed unconscious at 19.45 hrs. And then New Year's Day I spent with a horrible hangover.

In his New Year broadcast, Governor-General Dobbie gave details of what to do in the event of an invasion. From this point on, church bells would no longer be rung as an all-clear after an air-raid but only when invasion was imminent. If this should happen, everyone was to stay at home and clear the streets.

In a country where the Archbishop was officially accorded the rank of Major-General, with the guard turning out to him every day as he crossed the Palace Square in Valletta, it was perhaps not surprising that the church bells were an essential part of military strategy. People prayed for them to remain silent.

The Christmas truce was over. By December 1941, there

had been about seventy AXIS aircraft attacking each week; this increased to two hundred. There were two hundred and sixty-two air-raids in January 1942. The continuing problems of mines were exacerbated by the air attacks on the sweepers, to such an extent that *Abingdon* was ordered to sweep only at night, navigating by means of a small light shown from points ashore at various fixed times so that a cross-bearing could be taken. To add further to the strain on Bedford's mates, new types of antennae mines appeared.

The usual feast of Candlemas, with all parish priests attending the Palace and each collecting the heavy wax candle when his parish was named, was not the only event cancelled, but *the Times* still came out every day. On one occasion, its indomitable Editor wired London, 'Heavy bombing interrupted reception. Please repeat Derby winners.'

Chapter 13.

The function of well-intentioned individuals in association is to live in accordance with those truths, to demonstrate what happens when theory is translated into practice, to create small-scale working models of the better form of society to which the speculative idealist looks forward.
Ends and Means

His promotion was not the only reason why George bought his 'blues'; one afternoon when they were alone in the stores, the Lieutenant had said to George, 'I hear good things about you, Taylor.'

'Thank you, Sir.'

'Your country does need men like you.' George waited to get some idea of the drift of this. It was an odd way to approach the topic of further promotion. 'There's a lot of us feel strongly that good men... and I'm not afraid to use the word 'good' although it's not terribly fashionable... that good men should unite... not just in one corps but across the forces, not just across the forces but across all sectors...do you take my meaning, man?'

'Perhaps you could give me some more detail, Sir?' George fished, desperately.

'The great and the good, Taylor, that's what it comes too, the great and the good. I think you'd be a damned fine Mason and I'm willing to stand up for you.'

George was speechless.

'So that's settled then. Next meeting's on the seventh – February that is – at 5.30, in Villa Blye, Pawla. Damned difficult getting chaps together and when we do we're quite likely to get the usual Gerry noise, but we get by. Wear your blues…you can go with Pitt. Now, bandages, where the hell did that last consignment get to? Mtarfa has been on my back'…

Pitt also being a Mason seemed the least strange aspect of this conversation and George met meaningful nods – which suddenly seemed to come from every chance contact – with a knowing nod in reply.

If only he had understood half of what he seemed to. With little more said than, 'You need to know this,' and, 'This might interest you,' George was given a pocket-sized book, with a totally plain green cover, entitled inside 'The 'Standard' Ritual of Scottish Freemasonry', and also a book written by Joseph Fort Newton. From the former, George swotted up on the Initiation Ceremony as diligently as he had ever prepared for his Ward Orderly examinations on First Aid, inspired by Newton's words:

When is a man a Mason?

When he can look out over rivers, the hills and the far horizon with a profound sense of his own littleness in the vast scheme of things, and yet have faith, hope and courage, which is the root of every virtue.

When he knows that down in his heart, every man is as noble, as divine, as diabolic, and as lonely as himself, and seeks to know, to forgive and to love his fellow man.

When he knows how to sympathise with men in their sorrows, yea, even in their sins, knowing that each man fights a hard fight, against many odds. When he has learned how to make friends and to keep them, and above all, to keep friends with himself.

When he loves flowers, can hunt the birds without a gun, and feel the thrill of an old forgotten joy, when he hears the laugh of a little child. When he can be happy and high minded amid the meaner drudgeries of life.

When star crowned trees and the glint of sunlight on flowing waters, subdue him, like the thought of one much loved and long dead. When no voice of distress reaches his ears in vain and no hand seeks his aid, without response.

When he finds good in every faith, that helps man to lay hold of divine things, and see majestic meanings in life, whatever the name of that faith should be. When he can look into a wayside puddle and see something beyond mud, and into the face of the most forlorn fellow mortal, and see something beyond sin.

When he knows how to pray, how to love, how to hope. When he has kept faith with himself and his fellow man, with his God; in his hand a sword for evil, in his heart, a bit of a song – glad to live but not afraid to die.

Such a man has found the real secret of Masonry and the one which it is trying to give to all the world.

George sat outside in the moonlight, smoking. Even in February, the air was pleasant, merely a cool tickle against his skin. He inhaled, deeply, glad to live but not afraid to die. Sometimes when he sat like this, he reached for Nettie, fixing on a star and believing she saw the same star and thought of him, but tonight the stars seemed to be a skyful of brethren.

There were other men who thought as he did; other men who recognised him as a brother; other men who would work through this war and afterwards, for what was good and real. Strange the way men buried their truest beliefs underneath the dirt of jokes and soldiery, pearls from grit, and yet here George had proof that other men wanted a better world. If the rumours held good, then these were powerful men too, higher again than the Lieutenant; men of action. Yet they considered him an equal, fit for their democratic world in which promotion was truly on merit and by anonymous ballot.

George imagined Nettie's pride in him, knowing how foolish he was being and that he could not even confide in his diary. In his initiation ceremony, he would swear fidelity, 'without evasion, equivocation, or any mental reservation whatsoever, under no less a penalty than that of having my throat cut across, my tongue torn out by the root, and buried in the sands of the sea at low water mark, or a cable's length from the shore, or the equally effective punishment of being branded as a wilfully perjured individual, void of all moral worth, and unfit to be received into this or any other Lodge, or any society of men who prize honour and virtue above the merely external advantages of rank and fortune.'

Not since he'd been a boy scout had he crossed his heart with other boys and hoped to die but he remembered the way a secret bonded and gave power. It was something just to know from the specific pressure of a handshake that another man was with you, at a higher level than this headless hurtling called war; to know that you had been recognised as the rational idealist that you are; to know you had brothers.

George wondered about his flesh-and-blood brother. Where was David now? The last his parents had heard, David was in a camp in Italy, probably eating better than George with all the Red Cross rations sent to prisoners of war. Some days George wondered if David were not better off than himself; other days he knew it for a fact.

The inevitable scream of a siren interrupted George's reverie and he sighed, stubbed out his cigarette and went indoors, disdaining the shelter in case there was a marked man in it. If your name was on a bomb, that was how it was, but you didn't want to be round too many other people and get caught accidentally in their fate. He realised that the logic was dubious but if he were going mad, it was only Malta-mad, like everyone else.

In preparation for his Masonic inspection, George polished his heart and soul, tarnished as they were by army ways and war. He re-read the leaflet which had been slipped to him, detailing venue, officers (with their names) and an agenda which included

'To Ballot for, and if accepted, and present, to Initiate:
Mr George Swan Taylor R.A.M.C.
Born on the 12th day of October, 1916 at Kirkcaldy, Fife, Scotland, of British Nationality, residing at Mtarfa Barracks, Malta.'

It was like reading your own obituary. It was good to be a 'Mr' among other 'Misters'; corporal was all well and good but not when idiots in other regiments were leapfrogging the ranks to officer and not when green recruits outranked him with their special-conscription-offer pips.

Not when Nettie's latest letter was full of her own promotion, her leading role as Physical Training Instructor of her 'girls' and her own recommendation to OCTU, Officer Training. She already outranked him and was shooting towards a commission.

Theoretically, he would have to salute her if they met. Now that did make him smile as he imagined her tossing her curls and flirting with him, in response. No, he really was losing his marbles if he was taking seriously the girls at home playing soldiers. Of course, they were having to make do, pretend to be everything from bank managers to mechanics while their men were fighting but things would soon get back to normal after the war when they all had babies.

When they were married, Nettie would know of him being a Mason, without him having to tell her. He would have mysterious meetings 'on men's business' to which he would take his secret parcel and she would know, without asking, that he was well thought of by other men and that he was part of a brotherhood determined to change the attitudes which led to war in the first place. Her eyes would shine with her pride in him and she would know that 'Behind every great man, there's a great woman.'

She needed him to be a great man. He imagined some future date, after long years with Nettie, and three? five? children, when he was called to meet with the being he was learning to call 'The Great Architect of the Universe'. Serious-faced men would visit Nettie, would explain how respected Brother George had been, would tell her that she and the children would always be supported, and they would give her the magnificent contribution that had been voted on after respects had been paid to a lost brother. He would protect his wife and family, far beyond the pittance the army might offer if he died in service.

George counted the days to his initiation. He also counted the daily air raids, the stores, and the days until those stores ran out. Bread regulations were introduced for civilians. Each family had to register with one breadseller and buy only there; no farinaceous foods (pastry, cakes or biscuits) were to be made and pasta was rationed.

The restrictions on buying their food staple, bread, hit the locals much harder than pasta rationing as the latter was far less popular than in Italy. The fresh white bread, which had scented the villages, deteriorated with additives of potato, maize or barley to a tough, grey lump which just about sustained the stomach but darkened the mood.

A half-day in Valletta showed George the latest damage. Street vendors no longer called their wares, having fled to the catacombs or the rural villages, with nothing legal left to vend. The black-market trade was not shouted in the streets but grew with every restriction. There were still gharry drivers offering a ride but their eyes never left their precious horses, doubly precious with the scarcity of meat.

George passed the 'First and Last Bar', without even noticing its familiar name, heading further up the Gut, ignoring the girls who called 'Good time in here, soldier boy,' finding a dive he'd used before and where he recognised some of the boys, and at least one of the girls.

'Got the blues, soldier boy?' Violet teased, swinging on the arm of a tall blonde man in a Devonshire uniform, with pips of course. 'Friend,' she told her partner, patting his arm as he eyed George.

'Celebrating,' George told her, bending one knee to relax the knife-crease in his brand-new trousers and forcing his sleeve elbow into a relaxed pose on the bar.

'My, my. Must be Colonel then.'

'Governor-General,' George told her.

'Time we had a new one.' Violet ignored the shushing of those around her and turned on Lieutenant Devonshire. 'What? Is this news?' Her laugh grated and turned into a cough. 'I tell you what's news. They're talking about us in London, yes, Malta has been mentioned in dispatches. I can even tell you what they said.' She shook off a restraining arm. 'It's not classified, you fool, just desperate. They're worried about us in London, what with the bombs and the lack of food, and Churchill has turned his splendid attention our way. Do you want to hear the piercing insight he offered our Governor-General? Do you?'

'Violet!'

'Churchill suggested to Dobbie that we might need to kill cattle for meat.' No-one needed to have it pointed out to them that there never had been any cattle on Malta or that, if there had been, they would have long since gone the way of pigs, rabbits, goats, horses and – some said – dogs and cats. If that was the level of understanding of those at the top…

Someone broke the silence. 'I say it's time for more drinks. What do we come here for?'

'A good time,' was the chorused reply, overlapping with a new verse of 'Roll over, Mabel', growing louder from one corner,' while the punchline, 'Thought it were a Wren in a duffle-coat – so 'e said,' could be heard from another knot of swaying uniforms.

'Flower?' George was being asked by a barefoot girl of about eleven? twelve? holding a wicker tray of blighted wayside posies, each tied with a scrap of wool. 'For the lady?' George dug out some silver coins and was rewarded with a smile and a hopeful 'Two for price of one?' as the girl rubbed one leg against the other. 'For bread, Mister?'

'Don't encourage her, Spoof. It just makes them worse if you give them stuff.'

George presented the wilted posy to Violet with an ironic bow, and the little flower-seller, seeing she had lost his attention, moved on.

Violet kissed his cheek, a hint of stale breath beneath the sweetness of her scent, 'You're a good man. Stay away from this.' Her arm swept the scene, then she was gone, glittering away from George, bones where she used to be curves.

'Flowers,' George heard a sailor saying, 'Do you remember old Gordon? Chief Petty Officer? Used to only take shore leave on Malta, nowhere else, just Malta. Watch used to take the piss when they saw him coming back from the Gut, sailors' dream this place and what did he come back with every time? Flowers. Not a poxy little bunch like these, a whole blooming bouquet of the things. You could hardly see this little bloke for the flowers. And what the watch didn't understand was why his men was so glad to see him back, one of them funny things they thought, must treat 'em good on rotas or something. Anyway – you've guessed it haven't you? – his men was so glad to see him because he brought back the biggest bloody bottle of Nelson's blood you've seen in your life – that's rum to you ignoramuses – hidden right there in those flowers and the Watch never knew nothing about it. Malta was something, then.'

George paused in the daylight outside the bar and tutted in annoyance. He would have his work cut out to get the dust off his blues before February 7th.

Upper Barrakka Gardens, Valletta

Command Pay Office was in the Palazzo Villa Rosa, hit by bombs on Easter Sunday, April 1942, with many casualties

Palazzo Villa Rosa Gardens and St George's Barracks.

Palazzo Villa Rosa Grotto

Chapter 14.

In almost every period and in every country private individuals have associated for the purpose of initiating desirable change and of working out for themselves a way of life superior to that of their contemporaries.
Ends and Means

George idly traced the insignia on his cap badge as the car swayed along a dust track towards Pawla. He and Pitt had been lucky to hitch a lift as petrol rations remained strict; there were, however, always carts and cars visiting the stores so it had been a question of co-ordinating a rations collection. He caught himself once more outlining the staff and serpent with his forefinger, and remembered signing up; *'in arduis fidelis'*, faithful through hard times.

He had certainly seen some hard times, and he had done his best, but it now seemed to him that the R.A.M.C. motto should have worked both ways. Had the Regiment stood by him in hard times? He thought of his slow route to promotion, the incompetence which was more of a battle than the daily madness from the skies, and of the way some men always managed to find what little luxuries were left on the island.

He looked again at the ancient symbols of medical power; the rod of Aesculapius, Father of Medicine, and the harmless snake used for healing throughout the middle east; Aesculapius, killed by Jupiter and turned god for his presumption in bringing the dead to life; and snakes supposedly banished from this island by St Paul. Neither the Greek god nor the snake – whatever the healing power of its forked tongue – was welcome on Malta.

What then of the crown above them? It was supposed to remind a soldier that the medics had become part of the forces of the crown, Queen Elizabeth – a good Scot – their Colonel-in-Chief. What did the Maltese think of the Crown now? As a good Dissenting Scot, George would not have placed loyalty to the Crown high on his own list of priorities. He traced the badge symbols again, slowly. He wanted to swear fealty to someone, to an organisation, that lived up to its emblems.

'Gin and tonic?'

'Aye, I will thanks,' George's accent broadened under pressure and though he leaned as if casually on the bar, he was grateful of the support as his brain parroted the initiate's responses over and over.

'New brother,' Pitt needlessly informed the man smoothly measuring the drinks and introduced George to Brother Massey and his wife, whose warm smile and scent of lavender reminded George of home.

Some fifteen men were gathered in a room reminiscent of a café interior, with chequered tiles on the floor, tables and chairs informally spaced out around a room luminous in its white paint, despite the lack of windows. A bar opened up two-thirds of one wall, with the closed doors of a serving-hatch next to the bar. Above the bar and on all the walls were regimental insignia, and the hatch lintel was topped with a pottery cockerel.

'You're wanted…'

Brother Massey smiled at his wife in what was clearly a routine hand-over as he responded to the summons and she fronted the bar, passing a motherly comment on the 'peaky looks' or 'new moustache' of her customers, who lingered around the bar to enjoy being teased.

George gratefully accepted the move to a table, letting the gin warm his stomach and numb his nerves. Mrs Massey was framed in the window of the bar, beneath the strip of red and white awning brightening the top frame, like in a punch-and-judy show.

The organ notes started, vibrating through the solid walls. George took another gulp of gin, amazed just at being there, where he could hear snippets of conversation that seemed invested with deep significance, whether it was '... can't train a dog for toffee...' or 'next convoy... could be as long as May... have to be prepared for surrender...'

Sometimes, George imagined surrender, him a prisoner-of-war like his brother, his illegal diary doubly dangerous. He had stopped writing anything much in his diary but he could not bear to throw it away and what was already written would condemn him, whichever side read it. He didn't rate his chances highly if Malta surrendered – strange how they all thought of Malta as a person, with powers and choices. Someone like him didn't count for much, not like the Governor-General or the big cheeses. The hoi poloi would sink or swim at random or by fate; no ransom for the other ranks, no quarter. It was ever thus – but not tonight, when he would join the great and good, by invitation.

A few of the men came over to their table, were introduced to George and moved on to another group. Then the organ notes repeated, insistently, and men rose quietly and left the room. George followed, waiting, as instructed, in a room off the Hallway, where he pulled his manual out of his pocket and imagined the ceremony to open the Lodge in the First Degree, the degree to which he would be admitted after tonight. In the future, who knew what might happen? If promotion were truly on merit, then no-one worked harder than G.S.T., and if rewards were just, unlike in the R.A.M.C.

After the single knock of the gavel, the Worshipful

Master would first say, 'Brethren, assist me to open this Lodge,' and all there would stand, then he would continue, speaking to the Junior Warden, 'Brother—'

George tried to recall the name of the Tyler, who had been introduced to him… yes, that was it, Dada.

'Brother Dada, what is the first duty of every Mason?'

After the response, 'To see that the Lodge is properly Tyled,' the various office-holders would follow the ritual dialogue to confirm with the Tyler that the Lodge was Tyled and none but Brethren present.

Now that would be something, to be a Tyler, your duty 'being armed with a drawn sword, to keep off all cowans and eavesdroppers, and see that Candidates come properly prepared'.

George prayed to the Great Architect of the Universe that this particular candidate would be found to have come properly prepared. He counted yet more black and white floor tiles, waiting for Lodge business to reach the stage that would admit him and just when he was calculating the largest number of complete black tiles inside any right-angled triangle, he jumped, as the door opened and Brother Dada told him it was time.

In front of the Tyler, George emptied his pockets, leaving keys and coins in a small basket, adding his belt as Brother Dada indicated the metal buckle. Jacket and right shoe were removed until George stood in trousers, shirt, socks and left shoe only. His shirt was unbuttoned to reveal his left breast, his right sleeve rolled up to reveal the elbow, his left trouser leg rolled up above the knee and a slipper placed on his unshod foot.

It took all George's army discipline to accept the stranger's touch but, once he had overcome the instinctive panic, there was a euphoric relief in letting control go. Never before had he placed himself so completely in someone else's hands, never had he given his trust so completely, and the leap of faith lifted him higher than the gin had.

It was to be blind faith indeed that was expected of him. George barely felt the rope placed around his neck in a loose hangman's knot before he was blindfolded and led to the door of the Lodge. He could feel the end of the rope swinging against his back as he walked. The Tyler stopped and gave the ceremonial knock on the door and George felt the swish of air as it opened.

The voice turned away from George as it spoke, back to the Inner Chamber. 'Brother Junior Warden, there is an alarm.' That would be the Inner Guard.

'Right Worshipful Master, there is an alarm.'

'Brother Junior Warden, you will enquire the cause.'

'Brother Inner Guard, see who seeks admission.'

The next words came directly at George. 'Who comes here?' but he knew it was not for him to respond. Others must speak on his behalf before he would be allowed to speak on his own, like Mowgli he thought, when the pack debated if he should join them, and it took the pledge of Baloo and Bagheera to make him wolf.

'Mr George Swan Taylor, a poor candidate in a state of darkness, who has been well and worthily recommended, regularly proposed and approved in open Lodge, now comes of his own free will and accord, humbly soliciting to be admitted to the Mysteries and privileges of ancient Freemasonry.'

'How does he hope to obtain those privileges?'

'By the help of God, being free, and of good report.'

'Let him wait till I make a report to the Right Worshipful Master.' The door closed.

George felt the déjà vu of hearing for the first time the formulae so often studied in his little green book. It ought to be different now that he was 'the cause of alarm' but it all seemed to be happening to someone else, some George who was a lucky blighter, becoming a Freemason.

Once more the door opened and the Inner Guard spoke directly to George, who was prepared for the cold point against his chest and suppressed the instinctive gasp.

'In the name of the Great Architect of the Universe, enter this Lodge of Entered Apprentice Freemasons on the point of a Sacred Implement pressing your naked left breast, and as this is a momentary torture to your feelings, so may the recollection of it prove an everlasting torture to your conscience should you ever reveal the secrets of Fraternity unlawfully.'

The pressure lifted from George's chest and he was led into the room, where another man, the Junior Deacon, took his right hand and directed him to the Master. As he answered the basic questions confirming his eligibility by age and belief in God, George could feel eyes burning through his blindfold as his brother wolves circled. Not one to seek attention, he could not remember ever having suffered its dizziness in this way and he dropped to his knees with relief when so instructed. He did not have to see the floor to know that it was chequered in black and white tiles, cold reality through the weave of his blue trousers. He had a moment's anxiety for the knees of his twice-worn blues but stifled such prosaic concerns in the ceremony.

'… while the blessing of heaven is invoked in aid of our proceedings.' Again, George felt the disturbance of air rather than heard wands crossing over his head as the Deacons followed their set pattern.

George heard the Brethren moving around him and he shut them out, pretending he was alone with the voice, using his blindness to focus his mind, as if he were alone with his god. This made it easier to speak a faith in public that had always been concealed in church by his bowed head and shared murmurs.

'In all cases of difficulty and danger, in whom do you put your trust?'

'In God,' George replied, as the air raid warning started to scream.

The Master merely raised his voice but George felt the words from memory rather than heard them above the familiar wail.

'Your trust being in God, your faith is well founded. Relying on such sure support, you may safely rise and accompany your conductor with a firm but humble confidence, for where the name of God is invoked we trust no danger can ensue.'

George suspected he was not the only Brother invoking the name of God as the thunder of bombs and answering ack-ack drowned the Master's words.

George felt arms supporting him to rise to his feet, where he swayed a little, disoriented by blindness and kneeling, uncertain whether the shudder through the floor was his or from the nearness of the bombing. As far as he could tell, no-one had diverged from the ceremony although they must all have known that they should take shelter.

In whom do you put your trust? The room and George shook as he was supported clockwise on procession through North, East, South and West, to be viewed by the Brethren.

At one point, George was stopped, and his right hand taken and guided to tap a Brother's shoulder – that would be the Junior Warden. Again, George was questioned, and pledged his faith, then the taps and responses were repeated with the Senior Warden. Finally, George returned to the Master.

'Mr George Swan Taylor, do you seriously declare on your honour, that, unbiased by the improper solicitations of friends against your own inclination, and uninfluenced by mercenary or other unworthy motive, you freely and voluntarily offer yourself a Candidate for the mysteries and privileges of ancient Freemasonry?

'I do.'

'Brother Junior Deacon, it is the Right Worshipful Master's command that you instruct the Candidate to advance to the altar by the proper steps.'

Then the Junior Deacon's voice. 'The method of

advancing to the altar is by three steps irregular as regards length. Take one pace with the left foot, bringing the right up to it.' He paused for George to carry out each instruction. 'Then another longer pace with left foot, again bringing up the right.' Pause. Pace. 'Then a third, longer still, with left foot, bringing up the right as before.'

'Mr George Swan Taylor.' As suddenly as it had begun, the bombing stopped and George heard his name shouted into the silence. His ears still rang with gunfire and it seemed that his name rolled round the invisible skies, seeing off the Hun with the courage of the Brotherhood.

In whom do you put your trust?

'Let me assure you those vows are not incompatible with your moral, civil or religious duties. Are you willing therefore to take a solemn obligation, founded on the principles I have stated, to keep inviolate the secrets and mysteries of our order?'

'I am.'

'Then you will kneel on your left knee, your right knee in the form of a square, place your left hand under, and your right hand upon this Book, which is the Volume of Sacred Law. Repeat your name at length and say after me…' The Master gave one knock, echoed by all the Wardens and George heard the movements as men stood to witness his Obligation. His right hand was guided onto the Bible and he repeated the phrases after the Master.

'I, George Swan Taylor, in the presence of The Great Architect of the Universe, and in the body of this Chartered and Right Worshipful Lodge of Ancient, Free and Accepted Masons regularly assembled and properly constituted, of my own free will and accord, do hereby and hereon solemnly swear that I will always hele, conceal, and never reveal any of the secrets of or belonging to Ancient Freemasonry.

I likewise solemnly pledge myself to support and maintain the Constitution and Laws of the Grand Lodge of Scotland, and promise strict obedience to the Bye-Laws and Office-Bearers of this Lodge of St Andrew, Number 966 on the Roll of the Grand Lodge of Scotland. So help me the Grand Architect of the Universe and keep me steadfast in this the solemn obligation of an Entered Apprentice Freemason.' George sealed his oath by kissing the Bible.

'Brother George Taylor, having been kept for some time in a state of darkness, what in your present situation do you most desire?'

'Light,' was George's heartfelt response and the gun-crack of one handclap by twenty men made him jump as someone removed his blindfold. He blinked at the light, temporarily blinded indeed, then the faces swam into focus, along with the square and compasses, the goblet, the dagger, all placed in relationship to the three pillars according to the Tracing Board of the First Degree.

'The Sacred Writings are to guide our faith, the Square to regulate our actions and the Compasses to keep us in due bounds with all mankind, more particularly our Brethren in Freemasonry.'

George was shown how to make with his fingers the sign of the Square, by which he could make himself known as a Mason or recognise a Brother. He was presented with the cream lambskin Apron to wear at future meetings, edged in the tartan of the Lodge but otherwise plain, as befitted his degree.

'I shall immediately proceed to put your principles to the test, by calling on you to exercise that virtue which may justly be denominated the distinguishing characteristic of a Freemason's heart – I mean charity.

In a society so widely extended as Freemasonry, whose branches are spread over the four quarters of the globe, it cannot be denied that we have many members of rank and affluence; neither can it be concealed that among the thousands who range under its banners there are some who, perhaps from circumstances of unavoidable misfortune and calamity, are reduced to the lowest ebb of poverty and distress.

On their behalf it has been our usual custom to awaken the feelings of every Initiate, by making such a claim on his charity as his circumstances in life may fairly warrant; whatever therefore you feel disposed to give, you will deposit with the Junior Deacon, and I assure you it will be thankfully received and faithfully applied.'

George confirmed that he had been stripped of all coin or he would have given freely.

'I congratulate you on the honourable sentiments by which you are actuated, likewise on the inability which, in the present instance, precludes you from gratifying them. Believe me, this trial was not made to sport with your feelings.

Far be from us any such intention. It was done for three special reasons: First, to put your principles to the test; Second, to evince to the Brethren that you had neither money nor vulgar metal substance about you, for, if you had, the ceremony thus far of your initiation must have been repeated; and Thirdly, as a warning to your own heart, that, should you at any time meet a poor and distressed but worthy Brother who may claim your assistance, you will remember the circumstances of your admission into Freemasonry.'

George privately thought it more likely that he would be that poor, distressed but worthy Brother, but he had no problem in accepting the principle.

The Charity box was circulated and George knew that its contents would support war victims, widows and families whose regiments provided little. He would not leave Nettie without provision.

'I now present you with the working tools of an Entered Apprentice Freemason, which are the 24-inch gauge, the Mallet and the Chisel.

We apply these tools figuratively and in a moral sense. Thus, from the 24-inch gauge, we learn that accuracy and precision are necessary for the proper conduct of our affairs in life, and, as it is divided into twenty-four equal parts, it reminds us of the twenty-four hours of the day, and directs us to apply them to their proper objects, namely thanksgiving to the Great Architect of the Universe, labour for ourselves, our dependents, and our Brethren, refreshment and enjoyment of the good gifts which Providence has bestowed, and sleep, nature's great restorer.

The Mallet teaches us that skill without exertion is of little avail, and that labour is the lot of man. From the Chisel we learn that education and perseverance are necessary to establish perfection, that the rude material receives its fine polish but from repeated efforts alone.

And from the whole we deduce this moral, that knowledge, grounded on accuracy, aided by labour and prompted by education and perseverance, will finally overcome all difficulties, raise ignorance from its native darkness, and establish happiness in the paths of life.'

The final homily passed George by in a total blur, he was taken to his own position in the scheme of things, in the North-East and he sat there during the Closing Ceremony and the Untyling, without taking in a single word or gesture.

'Drink, Brother Taylor?' were words he did understand and cheerfully accepted. Baloo and Bagheera had vouched for him, he had been accepted as pack and he was very thirsty.

'Word to the wise, Taylor,' Dada, the Tyler advised him, 'Freemasons are a real no-no amongst the natives. Just the rumour of it lost old man Strickland the election, so they say, so be doubly careful, eh?'

George just nodded. He had probably sworn secrecy fifty times during his initiation, in as many variants of wording, so what was once more?

The Master, now an egalitarian Brother Woods, seemed distracted as he waved away offers of a drink and summoned his caretaker. 'Thought it was close – it was closer than that this time. Let's go check out the bloody damage, see what we can cobble together as repairs.'

George's Certificate of Membership of the Caledonian Arch Chapter, held in Senglea, Malta.

The dates in the certificates are some time after George's various acceptance ceremonies, presumably when central administration in Scotland caught up with membership details. They also refer to different lodges. When a Freemason cannot attend his own lodge, he can join a 'sister' lodge, so George attended various Lodges, all under the umbrella of Scottish Freemasonry

*1826 Headstone at Msida Bastion Cemetery, Floriana
for the founder of the Masonic Lodge of St John and St Paul at Malta*

George's Mark Master Certificate, endorsed 15ᵗʰ June 1944

Chapter 15.

Optimistic theorists count sport as a bond between nations. In the present state of nationalistic feeling it is only another cause of international misunderstanding. The battles waged on the football field and the race-track are merely preliminaries to, and even contributory causes of, more serious contests.
Ends and Means

'Why are the Malts so against the Masons?' George asked Pitt when they were alone together, sorting what was left of their store of tinned goods.

'Prejudice.'

George mentally reviewed the Brethren present at the meeting; it made sense that they would be Scots – it was the Lodge of St Andrew after all, daughter of the Grand Lodge of Scotland.

'Suppose someone nominated Julio or Matieu,' George named two of the Maltese artillery who regularly made up numbers on the football team, which was flagging from injury and fatigue, 'would they be eligible?'

'Don't see why not.' Pitt reflected. 'Few good chaps joined us in India, locals... I remember one, Vijay, became a judge... the man was more English than if he'd been born there. Totally open society, the Masons... true democracy. Whole point of the thing isn't it, respect for the country you're in and all that.' He shook his head.

'Different in Malta – suspicious mob, even when you're sweating cobblers for them. Look at that strike over equal pay – I mean, have they any idea what it costs to live back home?'

George felt a pang of guilt. He had been full of good intentions regarding his wages but his careful records of money saved and money spent, his accounting for occasional nights on the town had stopped long since. If it took a night in a bar to quieten the bombers screaming between his ears, if he could buy a loaf of bread without black flecks in it, then he would spend what it took to get him through the day. Saving to be with Nettie was a dream from his younger days; staying alive to be with Nettie was as much as he could aim for. Sometimes he forgot what she looked like and he would take out her photograph, panicking until he recalled some little mannerism or her laugh. It was as if he had rubbed the shine off his memories so that they could no longer light his life; her letters were too few and he had read them too often. Recent letters spoke of compliments she had received, of promotion prospects, of people he didn't know – one of them, he sometimes thought, being Nettie.

Even the soreness of their separation had grown scar tissue, become a mere condition of existence. George had a fiancée, Nettie, and he wrote to her telling her he loved her and of course that he planned to marry her as soon as he could, but none of this was now, or on Malta. He even fretted less at censorship; as Nettie could have no understanding of what he was enduring, there was no frustration in not being able to tell her anyway. As for expressing his feelings, he no longer cared about the Censor reading of George's love for his girl. He hardly wrote in his diary any more. Perhaps, whatever words he continued to use, he no longer cared.

A few day later Pitt passed him a sheet of paper. 'This went round in India – very popular. Thought it might answer your question.' George put the folded note in his pocket and waited till he could sit alone on the wall, smoking, before he pulled out the verses to read.

The Mother Lodge

There was Rundle, Station Master, an Beazley of the Rail,
an' Ackman, Commisariat, an' Donkin of the jail;
An' Blake, Conductor-Sargent, our Master twice was 'e
with 'im that kept the Europe-shop, Old Framjee Eduljee.

Outside – 'Sergeant! Sir! Salute! Salam!'
Inside – 'Brother' an' it doesn't do no 'arm.
We met upon the Level, an' we parted on the Square,
an' I was Junior Deacon in my Mother Lodge out there.

We'd Bola Nath, Accountant, and Saul, the Aden Jew,
an' Din Mohammed, draughtsman, of the Survey Office too;
There was Babu Chuckerbutty, an' Amir Singh the Sikh,
an' Castro from the fittin' sheds, the Roman Catholick.

We 'adn't good regalia, 'an our Lodge was old and bare,
But we knew the Ancient Landmarks, 'an we kept them to a hair.
'An looking on it backwards, it often strikes me thus,
There ain't such things as infidels, excep' perhaps it's us.

For monthly after Labour, we'd all sit down and smoke,
(We dursn't give no banquets lest a brother's cast were broke.)
An' man on man got talkin', Religion an' the rest,
an' every man comparin' of the God 'e knew the best.

So man on man got talkin', an' not a Brother stirred
till mornin' waked the parrots, and that dam' brain-fever bird;
We'd say 'twas highly curious, an' we'd all ride 'ome to bed,
With Mo'ammed, God an' Shiva,changin' pickets in our 'ead.

Full oft on Guv'ment service, this rovin' foot 'ath pressed,
An' bore fraternal greetings to the Lodges, east and west.
Accordin' as command, from Kohat, to Singapore,
but I wish that I might see them, in my Mother Lodge once
more.

I wish that I might see them, my brethren, black an' brown,
with the trichies smellin' pleasant, an' the hog-darn passin'
down,
an' the old Khansamah snorin' on the bottle-khana floor,
like a Master in good standing, with my Mother Lodge once
more.

Outside – 'Sergeant! Sir! Salute! Salam!'
Inside – 'Brother' an' it doesn't do no 'arm.
We met upon the Level, an' we parted on the Square,
an' I was Junior Deacon in my Mother Lodge out there.

Kipling, of course. George smiled at the thought of
Sikhs and Mohammedans leaning on the bar at the Villa
Pawla and he for one was not daft enough to discuss
religion or politics – wasn't that what led to wars in the
first place? All he had wondered was whether the Malts
were excluded. His own Maltese was coming along nicely
and he would have had a chance to try it out, although, on
second thoughts, English – or Scots – was the natural
language of the Villa Pawla and he could not imagine
anyone speaking anything else there.

In some ways it was just so much easier to be Scots
together, without those worries you had around foreigners,
when you had to watch what you said all the time. It was
even 'not done' to say 'Malts'. I mean! Still, the important
point was that the Maltese could become Masons and
George felt happy with that. If the fellows didn't like the
idea, then that was their choice. He, for one, was delighted
with knowing that someone would not only notice, but

show some thought for his family, if he died, and he had every intention of working his way up through the degrees – a damn sight quicker than he was working up the army ranks.

February: 42

Made Lieutenant Sergeant on the 18th. About this time, I was doing a spot of boxing and other rough sports! On the 23rd I was about kicked to death on the football field – leg broken in three places – and plastered on the 25th.

By the way all the time there was never a day without air raids. You just get so used to it that you just don't bother!!

On the 27th I sent my crutches back to Imtarfa and on the 29th Musta got its packet. That morning the Royal Engineers had finished a new store just next to the one I sleep in and as we had a supposed underground operating theatre just opposite, I moved lots of equipment for the theatre to the new store. About one o'clock, the fun began – in came the bombers after the air strip at Tal Kali – every gun on the island seemed to be letting loose – a few odds and ends were dropped on Musta – then there was a lull.

Fred Williams (the dispenser) and I were in the new store getting all the dressings etc. to the theatre when the second lot started.

Well! I went! – as fast as my pin leg would let me – Fred a minute after. When I stuck my head out five minutes after – there wasn't any new store!! And all the equipment gone for a 'ball of chalk'. Fred was just out of the store by about 15 seconds! We lost old Jock and a Lieutenant Corporal over that. Both went to the shelter for every raid too – but they were just unlucky – the bomb got the shelter.

The next day I was sent to St. Angelo and all clothing was sent there and that was all I had to do for the next six weeks.

Most of my time was spent watching the dive bombing of Skinna, Valletta and the Harbour – a really magnificent sight

*to watch 100 dive bombers go to it – if only it wasn't killing
people and blowing the place to ——!*

George was dizzy with bombs. Fred had carefully
locked the front door of the new stores before walking
away, then running. He had given George the keys and
when they looked out at weeks' work turned to rubble,
George was still swinging the keys on his fingers.

It was long after the door had been blasted to
smithereens that George took in how useless the keys were
and told himself to chuck them, but he couldn't. The keys
had to go safely in the place where the keys were kept, in
the tin on the second shelf. He should have wept for the
waste, especially when he heard about Jock and the
Lieutenant-Colonel; instead, he put the keys carefully in
their proper place, noting clinically the slight shake in his
outstretched hand.

Watching the bombers was better than waiting for them.
Put Guy Fawkes' Night and New Year's Eve together and
you still wouldn't begin to imagine the firework display.
George had a ring-side seat as he learnt to distinguish
between the sharp bang of an anti-aircraft gun, pointing
the position of an enemy aircraft, and the echoing
'whoomph' or whistle of a bomb.

The Junkers 88s came low, shooting streams of red
glowing cricket balls at the Bofors guns. It was difficult not
to join in, shouting out encouragement as a Hurricane
chased a Messerschmitt 109.

George thought, but did not speak aloud, the words he
heard escaping from other men around him.

'Good show – now you've got him!'

'Turn, man, for God's sake, turn!' and every heart soared
with the plucky plane, only to dive again with another as it
trailed a column of black smoke. Everyone knew that the
old Hurricanes, the Gladiators and the Navy Swordfish
were fighting a desperate and, however protracted, losing
battle against the Luftwaffe's finest. Everyone had heard

the rumours of hundreds of Spitfires bound for Malta on an aircraft carrier – and everyone had heard that the surrender plans included a motor launch to carry off key dignitaries so that they could continue to 'plan strategically'.

The spectators saw one thousand bombs fall on Malta in February 1942.

When you were not working and there were no air raids, there was still time to kill – perhaps the most difficult killing of all in a war.

Football was out, due to what had been filed on report as a 'sporting injury'. George himself had not considered it to be very sporting at all and found the plaster doubly irritating in the heat.

He found order in the ancient tradition of Masonic practice, three pillars against change. He longed for the next meeting and he studied to progress by a degree, comforted by the invisible fellowship represented by his little green book. There were others who thought like he did, who would bring this war to an end – if needs be, despite the incompetence of the armed forces.

As if to confirm this, he received an anonymous missive, handed in by a private collecting supplies with the usual cart and complaints.

'What do you think we're running here?' George responded. 'Beaumarché?'

The private smiled wryly at the sarcastic reference to the well-known department store. 'All I'm saying is we're desperate… basics are rock bottom.'

'I know. We need a convoy.' The soldier responded to George's tone and shut up. Bombed to bits or starved wasn't much of a choice. He passed over the blank envelope to George without further comment.

Copied in a careful, unidentified hand was an article from *The American Mercury, Volume LII No 206*, published in February 1941

The Annihilation of Freemasonry
by Sven G. Lunden

There is only one group of men whom the Nazis and the Fascists hate more than the Jews. They are the Freemasons. In Italy, indeed, the anti-Jewish feeling is of recent vintage and largely artificial, whereas the Blackshirts hatred of Freemasonry is old and deep. In their own countries Hitler and Mussolini inaugurated their respective reigns with outrages against Masons and Masonic institutions, and they have never relaxed the systematic persecution. Now Nazi conquests of other European nations – whether by invasion or forcible 'persuasion' – are followed automatically by hostile measures against Freemasons. From Norway to the Balkans, the progress of the Swastika has brought outlawry, and often vandalism and death in its wake for all Masons. The anti-Semitic excesses have been widely reported, the anti-Catholic outrages have had considerable publicity, but the merciless totalitarian assaults on Freemasonry have not received a tithe of the world-wide attention they richly merit. They are practically an unknown chapter.

Nazi and Fascist publications leave no doubt of their belief that all the evil in the world, from the high mortality rate among the dinner guests of the Borgias down to the Versailles Treaty, has been the work of Freemasons, alone or with the help of Israel. In 'Mein Kampf', Hitler merges his twin phobias:

'The general pacifistic paralyzation of the national instinct of self-preservation, introduced into the circles of the so-called 'intelligentsia' by Freemasonry, is transmitted to the great masses, but above all to the bourgeoisie, by the activity of the great press, which today is always Jewish.

George noted the implied syllogisms – the press is Jewish, you are in the Press, therefore you are Jewish. He wondered what Mabel Strickland would have to say when Hitler told her she must be Jewish. Pleasing as the image was, with odds against Hitler surviving, he thought it more likely that Miss Strickland would be one of those with a place on the escaping motor launch – she had friends in high places.

More syllogisms: the Masons want peace (and in Nazi terms are against their nation), you want peace, therefore you are a Mason.

George shook his head over the logic which was still swaying nations, including some Maltese Italians locked up in cells and even some prominent Englishmen back home, although they were keeping pretty damn quiet about their views now. No Scots of course, George reminded himself. As far as he was concerned, Hitler was bad; if he was persecuting Masons, a Mason was therefore a good thing to be. George was pleased with his Q.E.D.

In the summer of 1925, Mussolini got around to dissolving Italian Freemasonry. In an open letter to Il Duce, the Grand Master of the Grande Oriente, Domizio Torrigiani, had the courage to stand up for democracy and freedom of thought. The price he paid was exile to the Lipari islands. After nearly going blind there, he died soon afterwards. Hundreds of other prominent Masons shared the harsh Liapri exile with him. At the peak of the anti-Mason agitation, in 1925 – 27 Blackshirt strong-arm squads looted the homes of well-known Masons in Milan, Florence and other cities, and murdered at least a hundred of them.

The Nazis acted more swiftly. Immediately on Hitler's rise to power, the ten Grand Lodges of Germany were dissolved. Many among the prominent dignitaries and members of the Order were sent to concentration camps. The Gestapo seized the membership lists of the Grand Lodges and looted in their libraries and collections of Masonic objects. Much of this loot was then exhibited in an 'Anti-Masonic Exposition' inaugurated in 1937 by Herr Dr Joseph Goebbels in Munich.

The Exposition included completely furnished Masonic Temples.

The persecution was carried over into Austria when the country was captured by the Nazis. The Masters of various Vienna lodges were immediately confined to the most notorious concentration camps, including the horrible living hell at Dachau in Bavaria. The same procedure was repeated when Hitler took over Czechoslovakia, then Poland. Immediately after conquering Holland and Belgium, the Nazis ordered the dissolution of the lodges in those nations. When France fell last June, the Vichy Government caused the two Masonic bodies of France, the Grand Orient and the Grenade Loge to be dissolved, their property being seized and sold at auction.

The summary does not begin to convey the full terror of the Calvary to which Freemasonry has been subjected wherever the Totalitarians took power. Murder, imprisonment, economic looting, social outlawry have been the bitter lot of individual Masons. Rapine has been the fate of their organisations, their treasures, their institutions of charity.

Why does this implacable and fanatic hatred of the Order obsess the totalitarian mind? The answer is in the whole history and temper of Freemasonry. For more than two centuries its leaders have been consistently on the side of political freedom and human dignity, reaping a harvest of persecution at the hands of tyrants.

Freemasonry is made up of Masonic bodies: lodges, Grand Lodges and other groupings. All of these scrupulously refrain from meddling in politics or any other subject not directly related to Masonic matters or charity. The Constitution of the Order stipulates that every member must be a loyal citizen of his own country, and it professes adherence to 'that religion in which all men agree' – that is, a belief in a Divine power, in morality and charity. In contrast to narrow Nationalism, it believes in serving Humanity as a whole. That is all that the Masonic

Order itself professes and is interested in. What individual Masons as citizens of their respective countries to serve the ideals they personally believe in, is their own business.

It is clear, consequently, why the Nazis and the Fascists and Bolsheviks must hate an organisation so steeped in humanitarian traditions. The totalitarian hatred for the Order is not merely emotional. It is clearly defined in the fundamental divergence between their creed and the Masonic ideal.

The Nazi Dr Rosenberg writes, 'Without doubt the masonic dogma of Humanity is a relapse into worlds of the most primitive conceptions; everywhere where it is put into practice it is accompanied by decadence, because it conflicts with the aristocratic laws of Nature.'

Thus in his own dogmatic terms he indicts Freemasonry for what is its greatest pride, its ideal of equality.

In 1938, Hitler's own publishing house issued a volume on 'Freemasonry, its World View (Weltanschaung), Organisation and Politics'. The Preface is written by Herr Heydrich, second in command of the Gestapo, and hence an expert on oppression and violence, and hints openly at the seizure of libraries and property of German Freemasonry. The book itself, by one Dieter Schwarz, says

'Nordic is the Nazi conception of the world, Jewish-oriental that of the Freemasons; in contrast to the anti-racial attitude of the lodges, the Nazi attitude is race-conscious...'

'Masonic lodges are... associations of men, who, closely bound together in a union employing symbolical usages, represent a supra-national spiritual movement, the idea of Humanity...a general association of mankind, without distinction of races, peoples, religions, social and political convictions.'

I have read several hundred books about Freemasonry and scores of original Masonic documents but I have never seen masonry's basic ideals expressed more clearly than by its mortal enemies in the passage above. Herr Heydrich and Herr

*Schwarz are right – the gulf between their 'Weltanschauung'
and the Masonic Ideals can never be bridged.*

George was a little bemused by the talk of Jews as a
nation, of 'Israel', when his own experience of Jews had
only been the sight of men with funny hats, long hair and
black clothes when he was visiting his aunt and uncle in
London. He was also puzzled by references to
'concentration camps' although there were rumours of all
kinds of treaty breaches by the Hun.

Sometimes, George and his fellows dismissed the
rumours as officers' tactics to maintain fighting morale. At
other times, they wondered, and George worried about his
brother, imprisoned, somewhere in occupied territory.

The article left George fired with a sense of righteous
indignation and he burned to act. The Champion of
Democracy ticked his name on the list, crossed his own
name out on the envelope and replaced it with the next
listed name, then replaced the article in the envelope, re-
sealed it and placed it with the completed – or rather as
complete as it was going to be – order for Mtarfa, as
instructed. After that, he returned to the routine loaves and
fishes miracle of fulfilling a requisition.

George's younger brother, David, who joined the Signals Regiment, was captured in France and spent 4.5 years as a Prisoner of War

Chapter 16.

Confucianism, to quote Max Weber, 'prefers a wise prudence to mere physical courage and declares that an untimely sacrifice of life is unfitting for a wise man.' Our European admiration for military heroism and martyrdom has tended to make men believe that a good death is more important than a good life, and that a long course of folly and crime can be cancelled out by a single act of physical courage.
Ends and Means

George was in the open near St Andrew's Barracks when the bombers came for him. He heard the sirens scream then the usual engine drone and anti-aircraft guns spitting fire but there were no explosions and the noise continued to grow until it dawned on his deafened brain that they were diving at him and he hurled himself into one of the dusty trenches which had been dug for protection. It didn't seem so protective any more.

April 42
Then! – St. Andrew's was dive bombed! Just one day! and there was about half a dozen buildings not touched! The Advance Dressing Station was one!

I reckon that I had the worst experience of my life that day. – I stood in a slit trench – watched the bombers come in – dive – the bombs leaving – and the nearest of one string was 20 yards

away – believe me when these bombs left the plane I thought my
name was on all of them!

George stood shaking in the trench for a lifetime, his
lifetime, his ears still ringing and phantom planes still
diving long after the last echoes of ack-ack had died out.
Then he ran. He pumped his arms and legs and hopped-
ran for his life, across the dry scrub and around the bomb
craters, feeling nothing in his plastered leg as he forced it
onwards. A stone ruin stopped him, sheltering him from
the skies and he sank to his knees, unable to take another
step. It took four attempts to light a cigarette and as his
ears replaced explosions and gunfire with the pounding of
his own blood, he took a deep drag and traced the solidity
of the stone with his free hand. His fingers found
unexpected patterns and he looked more carefully at the
stone, reading the old lettering:

NON GODE
L'IMMUNITÀ
ECCLESIATICA

'The church cannot offer you sanctuary.' George looked
at the remains of a Maltese church, bombed some time ago
to a few crumbling walls, and at the carefully chiselled
words of warning. He saw no reason to hurry his cigarette,
so he took another drag and stayed exactly where he was
until he could face dragging himself back to the stores.

He found that St Andrew's was hit by the Luftwaffe had
been virtually demolished. The hospital became non-
operational and its staff were transferred to 45 General
Hospital at St Patrick's, which was also hit. St Andrews'
Barracks, where most of the families of the 2nd/Royal
Irish Fusiliers had been quartered was also bombed.

George could not shake off the sensation that he
personally had been targeted. Places he'd worked were
now rubble and instead of feeling lucky that he'd survived,

he kept thinking of those who hadn't. He could easily have been in the position of one private, who was later awarded the British Empire Medal. What would George have done? He hoped he would never find out.

The report from his superior officer said that, 'On the morning of 25th April 1942, Private Lupton was a nursing orderly on an acute surgical ward, when the first bombing attack took place on the hospital. The only shelters in the hospital area were slit trenches unsuitable for bed cases. Private Lupton immediately set about protecting the bed patients by placing them under beds and covering them with mattresses and by his example greatly encouraged these helpless men. The ward received a direct hit, and the roof and a wall collapsed. Three patients were killed but Pte Lupton's work undoubtedly saved the lives of several others. Pte Lupton was himself buried and pinned down by a steel girdle, but although suffering from an extensive laceration of the scalp, when he was rescued, his first thought was for his patients. He showed a fine spirit of self-sacrifice and devotion to duty.'

Pitt was in a filthy mood and it didn't take long before he told George that orders were out to evacuate forces' women and children.

'Course I want her to be safe – although you know what Jane's like, she's muttering hell-fire at the thought of being sent off – and she's not stupid so she knows that things are pretty bad for them to have to go, then that just makes her worse about leaving me here. Devil of a tangle and we end up rowing. What makes it worse though is not knowing when... or how. If it's bad here, then there's no bloody guarantee of getting anyone safely away. I mean, if we can't get anything in, doesn't exactly cheer you up to think of trying to get your wife out?'

'Any idea at all about when?'

'As soon as they think there's a place – boat, plane, sub – you name it – everything but trains and balloons! – they put you on standby, so we've had six hours' notice that she would be going – imagine, George – me at work and she was told she had to go, no chance of good-bye even. Then it all fell through and when I got home she was sitting there in a right old state just staring at the wall.'

'Are they getting any of them out?'

'Slowly.'

'So it's bad then.'

'Going to get worse.'

'Bombs or starving?'

'Both.'

'Pity the poor bloody Maltese. Who's going to get them off?'

'Save it for us, George. We're going to die on this bloody rock and what for? Jesus, there it goes again.'

George could no longer tell whether sirens were inside or outside his head but Pitt was right – it was another raid, which meant there was no point talking for a while so they just carried on shifting boxes. There was no sanctuary anywhere any more.

March saw two thousand tons of bombs dropped on Malta in two hundred and seventy-five air raids, ninety at night; in April there were another two hundred and eighty-three raids, with ninety-six of them at night. The supplies and reinforcements so desperately needed were supposedly on their way. The convoy bound for Malta was heavily bombed and of its six cruisers, host of destroyers, and one battleship, only two ships, the *Pampas* and *Talabot*, reached Malta, and subsequent bombing of Grand Harbour destroyed much of the remaining cargo.

The Maltese stevedores refused to work through the raids and by the time the Cheshires were called in to unload the ships, it was too late. Forty-seven Spitfires did arrive, thanks to the US aircraft carrier *Wasp*, but were bombed within ninety minutes of landing, in the inadequate shelter of the stone blast pens; only twenty-seven survived and were refuelled quickly enough to return straight to the air and take on the Messerschmitts.

By the next day, only six Spitfires were still operational. Hard enough to reach Malta; harder still to be sitting ducks on airfields and in the docks, bombed, burned and picked off at the Luftwaffe's pleasure. A crashed German pilot, told the hospital nurses – who told George – 'Today I prisoner – in two months, you, you and you prisoner – I free.'

Malta was within AXIS grasp and the talk on the streets was of mistakes in high places. Why had the Germans been better prepared for attacking the planes and ships than the Allies for defending them? Why was the Navy doing one thing, the RAF something else and the army something else again? Why did they have no smoke canisters, a simple measure to protect incoming ships and reinforcements? And what was the Governor doing?

Increasingly, that last question was on men's lips, and the answer terse. Word was, the Governor was spent, worn out by his responsibility for a bombed and starving people, three hundred thousand most loyal British subjects. Well, who wasn't worn out?

Everything on the island – communications, fuel supplies, transport, essential supplies – was all breaking down or worn out. Dobbie's impassioned public references to God's aid struck many as more plea than conviction these days. 'God didn't unload those bloody ships, did he!' If they were down to asking for God's help, then God help them indeed.

The Times of Malta still brought the news daily but one of the casualties from the bombing had been the newsprint so recently unloaded and the paper went to press with singed edges, surviving the presses in that condition, to its Editor's relief. She had suffered enough criticism over wasting valuable cargo space with her precious newspaper – it would have been too bad to lose it.

The stores on the wharf had been hosed down with salt water to put out the fires and the rescue of the newsprint involved wrapping it in wet blankets to ease the paper and printing on a 'Dead slow' setting with fingers firmly crossed.

One Brigadier was convinced by the singed edges that *the Times* was black-marketing cigarettes and had to see the print run in action to be persuaded otherwise.

As far as Mabel Strickland was concerned, if Malta was running on empty, then the morale boost which she provided with her daily accounts of heroism, and which could reach every soul on the island, was as vital as a limited amount of flour or diesel. Those tales of heroism inevitably soared into the skies.

The Spitfire became the symbol of hope and its pilot a national hero. The sight of wings on a badge, or a flying jacket and boots, would bring out grins and thumbs-up signs from Maltese farmers or shopkeepers, who lodged pilots in their homes and shared in their lives and deaths. Omens were ignored by the heroes – a cloud crossing an airman's shadow or the rosary bead which broke off when he entered the room – and the pilots 'scrambled' when ordered.

George did not try to hold back his admiration of the airmen in their element. No-one could have watched a Spitfire rolling over, diving or chasing, without a kick of pride in the young man who took those risks. If you needed a reminder of the risks, you only had to watch as a plane flew into a bomb, or was hit by allied anti-aircraft as it chased too far.

You would see it thrown into the air, bank at 60 degrees, out of control, and wait for the flash of white that meant a parachute was opening and that a man might live. You would murmur a prayer and hope for more parachutes, as the plane itself crashed in flames, its ammunition going off in the heat. Even without a dog-fight in progress, the sight of a squadron in its special Malta formation, lifted the spirits. No, it was on the ground that George had a problem with airmen.

If he'd been asked why RAF men got his back up, the answer would have been a long one. They were automatically officers, they 'did a tour' then went home, they swaggered and behaved like the schoolboys they so nearly were, making bets on 'hits' and creating petty squadron rivalries, they talked about 'having fun' and 'adventures' – they even borrowed the Maltese word for 'finished' and talked about an aircraft being 'spitchered'.

They cracked incomprehensible jokes, putting on phoney German accents to imitate a Jerry pilot about to take off. They lived in tents in an olive grove, or with Maltese families, showing off for the beautiful daughters. They worshipped 'characters', who broke the rules, such as the commanding officer who wore the most bizarre outfits to fly, his favourites being thigh-high sheepskin leggings, which he had acquired in Crete and wore with army battle-dress and air force stripes; who preferred an Ascot cravat to a tie, had shoulder length ash-blonde hair and wore a grease-stained cap, even on top of his flying helmet. He also smoked as he flew, which was strictly against regulations. Women could not resist him and he lived with a beautiful cabaret artiste in Valletta, driving himself to work in an old car.

George was not impressed. Neither was he impressed by ridiculous moustaches or cigars. Without the Inniskillings and Manchesters working nights by arc-lamp, filling in holes to get airstrips operational, no-one would be up in the air at all – but there was no glamour to ground-workers, was there. If the pilots suffered from their rations, cramped by 'Malta Dog', and depressed by the lack of alcohol, then George found it difficult to be too sympathetic as he reluctantly fraternised in the bars, the shops or at the stores.

It was however an airman who captured the mood of Easter 1942 and George pinned up a copy in the stores of the verses which had first appeared on an Officers' Mess Notice Board:

Kesselring's Easter Hymn

Tis Holy Thursday, let us snooker
All the bloody Spits at Luqa
Forward Messerschmitt and Stuka
Halleluja.

Hail Good Friday, Hal Far's turn,
Prang the crews, the aircraft burn,
Will the blighters never learn?
Halleluja.

Now Kampfheschwaders, rise and shine
Make Takali toe the line
Here a rocket, there a mine
Halleluja

Christ the Lord is risen today
Let's bomb the harbour, bomb the bay,
Bomb the bloody place all day
Haleluja

Easter Monday so ply the whip
Smite the island thigh and hip
Tear it off a Safi strip
Halleluja.

On the ruined walls of houses, you would now occasionally see *Pace* chalked up but more often, *Bomb Rome*, despite Italian radio broadcasts appealing to 'our Maltese brethren' to come out from 'under the heel of British domination which has been forced on them under the threat of guns and bayonets.' Worse than guns and bayonets was bread rationing – less than fourteen ounces per person – which Dobbie had to introduce in April as the black markets and fighting queues worsened, despite increasing the numbers of communal feeding kitchens, renamed 'Victory Kitchens', where one hot dish or one meatless soup was provided. The potato crop was now bought by the government and redistributed.

George heard for the first time the term *Zero hour food*, to describe the projected moment they would run out, and he was not the only one to wonder if anyone back home knew the real picture of what was going on in Malta. After all, Dobbie determined what the Censor allowed out, so it depended on what Dobbie wanted the world to know, as to what was known. If you read *the Times of Malta*, you couldn't help wondering what was going on, or not going on, in London. It was reported that Dame Irene Ward had put a question in the House of Commons as to whether it was Churchill's intention to hold Malta or not. She did not get a satisfactory answer and she did not give up on the Malta question. George was too busy shifting his stores again to consider the matter long.

April 42

Next day I sent all clothing to Gargur as fortunately Mr Damon had taken over a church and caves there. I left St Andrew's at 5 o'clock and on arriving at Gargur a raid went. As we had just been going to inspect the caves we carried on – and a good job we did – five bombs screamed down right on top of us!

I almost thought the blighters were following me!

Well! We got settled down and have turned the church into what I am sure is the finest store on the island.

Three weeks before my plaster was due to come off, I got a bit browned off trailing it around so I cut it off with a pen knife! which goes to prove that the army has no system because to this day no-one has enquired about it. So far as I know my B178 may show that I am walking about with a plaster for the rest of my life.

Would George have been reassured if he'd heard that Malta was about to get a new Governor-General? That this was so, was thanks entirely to Mabel Strickland using the freedom of the press to write directly to Lord Mountbatten, expressing the same reservations about Dobbie which had been muttered on the streets by those without connections in London.

General Lord Gort V.C. was appointed to Malta as Governor-General and Supreme Commander, with the news that it could only survive for another six weeks, and with the terms of surrender in his pocket.

St Luke's Hospital ('the new hospital') Gwardamanga

St Luke's Hospital

(Rare photo) Chapel Floriana Bastion, part of the early fortification of Malta. It was used to celebrate mass for those confined in quarantine in Lazarretto (opposite) The chapel was destroyed during the war.

The Blue Grotto
Even in war-time, famous landmarks were still worth photographing.

The Sanctuary of Our Lady of Mellieha

Chapter 17.

Up to the end of the last war non-combatants, except in countries actually subject to invasion, were not in great physical danger. In any future war it is clear that they will be exposed to risks almost, if not quite, as great as those faced by fighting men. This will certainly tend to diminish the enthusiasm of non-combatants for war.
Ends and Means

Word reached George and Pitt that Villa Blye at Pawla, battered in the March bombing, had been finished off in April. As if the Masons had been clearly in the Germans' sights, four bombs had fallen simultaneously on the building and its immediate surroundings, blowing out most of the walls.

'Anyone caught?'

A head shake. 'Brother Massey was out. And his missus. Brother Lane wasn't far off and organised a working party. Hardly ten minutes before they got to the Villa and the thieving bastard were already in there, looking for loot. Chased them off pretty damn quick, I can tell you. Found the Charters, the Warrants, the Regalia – gave 'em all to Poole for safe-keeping. Regalia case has got the dints in it to tell the story. All the minutes destroyed though.' This time all three men shook their heads.

'A little bit of history gone.'

'They found a load of empty beer cans in the Inner

Sanctum. Know what they were there for? That's what was under the Union Jack to make the Altar. What we're reduced to, eh.'

'Next meeting?'

'That's three of us homeless now, the Irish and Scots Lodges of course, and the English had moved in since their place was written off. Talk is, someone's home, or perhaps a cave or friendly church – I'll let you know.'

'Never say die, eh?'

'Speaking of which... there's another one coming.' The visiting Mason stood bemused, then copied George and Pitt in standing to respectful attention, eyes cast down, hands clasped in front of them, as a procession followed a coffin into the churchyard where the army stores was now based. The Priest intoned, and women wailed, as the soldiers feigned invisibility and the funeral sobbed its way past them.

April 42

One slight disadvantage is that the churchyard is still used here – our record so far is three in one day. It's quite different here. The vaults are stone, with five more stones over the top. All the lad does is to lift the stones, pull out old pieces of coffin and smash up everything else with a pick. Then in goes the new one. He also quite proudly took us on a tour of inspection and showed us all his prize exhibits by pulling up stones here and there. One fellow was brought down from Imtarfa one night and, as there was no coffin, they just chucked him down. And now, after three years, the policeman (Maltese) that was with us still recognised him. Another man fell down and died – so they just left him there!

Well! To change the subject – when on my rifle course I had bulls first four shots and an inner the fifth, and I <u>was</u> annoyed because I got the inner!

When he found the chance, and the privacy, George

looked at the copy of the letter from his Lodge; they had not been slow to write to the Mother and Sister-lodges appealing for contributions. The restoration fund had been started already. Never say die.

'Local brethren and companions feel assured that they are not appealing in vain for a help which will not only give back to those who have been in the forefront of hostilities, a home worthy of our great profession, but a home which will be a lasting memorial of world-wide Masonic appreciation of the pride felt by all in the defence of Malta; a tribute to those of the brethren who took part therein and in privations of the siege and of those who gave their lives, and that this hope is real, is shown by the response already received.'

George contemplated his 'pride in defence of Malta' and found it wanting. On the other hand, the 'privations of the siege' were all too clear, in the daily strain on Pitt as he waited for news that his wife could leave the island, and in the raised voices of men as they disputed their requisitions from the stores.

'But we can't survive on that!'

'I know,' George would say.

'How can I tell the men that's all there is?'

'I don't know,' George would say.

'There must be something you can do!' George would say nothing.

Along with all the others who watched the Malta skies, George noticed that the RAF were sending out squadrons regardless of whether there was an enemy attack. When his rare excursions brought him into contact with airmen, he picked up more news than he was ever likely to get through *the Times of Malta*.

'*Wasp* might be on its way back with some more Spits.'

'And Father Christmas is bringing me Marilyn Monroe on the same ship.'

'You came out with the first lot, didn't you, Mac?'

'Aye, I was there.' This aroused raucous laughter as they all imitated the words with which Air-Marshall Sir Hugh Pugh Lloyd had greeted the new young Spitfire pilots when they arrived in May. 'In the future, after this war, when the name of Malta is mentioned, you will be able to say with pride, 'I was there.''

It had become the stock phrase after every near-miss to be told, 'Well, at least you can say, 'I was there'!'

'Sure was there,' Mac drawled.

'See, the man speaks fluent American.'

'Doesn't drink like a Yank. You should have seen his face when they told him he could drink coca cola or fruit juice but there's no alcohol on US navy ships.'

'So unlike the policy of our own dear king.'

'Wilted my moustache, dammit.' Mac stroked a magnificent bristling handlebar.

'Great food though.' No-one wanted to follow that thought further.

'Lloyd wants us going after them. Bit tricky without fuel and ammo what?'

'I nearly bought it last week. Soon as we were scrambled, I estimated the fuel, filled up, chased one blighter till I could see the guns on his side of the drink, then, blow me, it turned cloudy, I lost my way a bit getting back home and the fuel gauge said, 'You're spitchered, boy,' just as I landed at Hal-far. Too close a call.'

'I know, all very well guessing the fuel for a mission but you chase a hairsbreadth too far, or the weather turns, and you've twenty miles of drink to play glider over.'

'Perhaps our old army mate can rustle up some extra goodies for us...' and they would remember George, listening invisibly.

'Specials for the RAF,' he'd tease.

'Go on.' He'd show them a pair of boot soles. 'Guarantee you won't die in the air if you wear these.' They were hooked.

'No...'

'Only one condition...'

'Which is?'

'You don't wear them in a plane!'

'Seriously, man...'

'I am serious...'

In May the American aircraft carrier *Wasp* did bring more Spitfires and this time, under Gort's overall leadership, with Air Marshall Lloyd commanding the RAF, the planes were landed safely and turned around within twenty-four hours, in time to protect the minelayer *HMS Welshman* as it battled towards Malta with crucial anti-aircraft ammunition and plane spares.

The 11th May edition of *the Times of Malta* was jubilant. George scanned the headlines first:

BATTLE OF MALTA; AXIS HEAVY LOSSES
'SPITFIRES' SLAUGHTER 'STUKAS'
BRILLIANT TEAM WORK OF AA GUNNERS AND RAF
63 Enemy Aircraft Destroyed or Damaged over Malta yesterday!

The last two days have seen a metamorphosis in the Battle of Malta. After two days of the fiercest aerial combat that has ever taken place over the island, the Luftwaffe, with its Italian lackeys, has taken the most formidable beating that has been known since the Battle of Britain two and a half years ago.

Teamwork has been the watchword during all these weary months of taking a pounding, with very little else to do than grin and bear it. For months on end, the gunners have hurled steel and defiance at the enemy. They have been subjected to probably the most diabolical bombing the gunners have ever known, they have been ceaselessly machine-gunned; they have suffered casualties, but others have taken their places. Never once have they faltered. The people of Malta owe them a debt which is incalculable.

Since the beginning of April, this Island has been pounded without ceasing but yesterday the boot was on the other foot. The Hun set out to liquidate our aircraft on their aerodromes but he got a shattering shock. Instead of being on the ground our fighters were in the air, waiting for his blood. At the end of the day he retired to lick gaping wounds which he had never anticipated.

During the afternoon's raids, the sky looked like the outside of some fantastic wasp's nest, with aircraft milling about in a breathless hectic rough house. The noise of cannon and machine gun was all the sweeter for the fact that half at least of them were for once on our side. That being so, nobody on the ground had the slightest qualms about the result.'

Then the Harbour barrage went up. An almost solid cone of Anti-Aircraft burst rose over the harbour from ground level to almost 7,000 feet. It put to shame all other efforts at flak that anyone had seen.

Reports suggested that, in that one battle, twenty-three AXIS aircraft were definitely destroyed, another twenty probably destroyed and a further twenty damaged. Those who listened to the radio broadcast from Rome could afford to whistle cynically when informed that thirty-seven 'had not yet returned' and that thirty-seven Spitfires had been eliminated; it was common, confirmed knowledge that three Spitfires had been lost and only one pilot, and that *the Welshman* had unloaded and left safely under cover of darkness.

In the general celebration, people were prepared to forgive Churchill his poor knowledge of natural history when he thanked *Wasp's* Captain with the much-publicised words, 'Many thanks to you for all timely help. Who said a wasp couldn't sting twice?'

It was a good time for leaders to boost morale and Gort even presented the bombing in a positive light, declaring, 'We console ourselves by saying that every bomb here is one less at home or against Russia; and I gather they say at home that every bomb is one less upon Malta.'

George's moonlight vigils were sometimes disturbed by sirens, the arcs of tracer beams and rattle of ack-ack fire as an attempt at a night raid was foiled. On one occasion he saw a small rapidly winking light for a second or two, which must have been a Beaufighter, the British night plane, and then a small glow just in front of it which grew larger as it circled downwards until the raider hit the water and splashed in flames, a falling star on which George could not wish.

Out of eighteen ships heading for Malta in June, two staggered into the harbour and were at least unloaded efficiently, protected by the recently acquired smoke cannisters and soldiers working the docks alongside the Maltese stevedores. The new Governor broadcast his thanks publicly; 'I congratulate all concerned on the speed and energy with which the ships now in harbour were unloaded. It was a most successful augury for the future,' but everyone knew that the future depended on more than two ships and Gort still carried the terms of surrender in his top pocket.

On 18th June, George was promoted to Sergeant and given five days leave. He spent it in his billet, reading and writing, knowing there was no point going out as there was no food anywhere. News came of the fall of Tobruk on 20th June and the resulting switch of German attention away from Malta brought some lessening of the bombardments; small compensation for the fear that the war had turned, spun on its Axis indeed.

2.8.42

Well! The past month has been a bit quieter so far as bombs go, but strangely enough our fighters have broken all records by shooting down 140 last month, beating the previous by 28.

During the heaviest blitzing if our fighters followed the Gerry bombers — our fighters used to be blown to pieces by anti-

aircraft while the bombers carried on untouched. Last December, the Mediterranean Fleet under a new commander ran into one of <u>our own</u> minefields — since which there has been no Med. Fleet!!

The last convoy was unable to get through, with the result that for the first time since the war started, we're feeling it a bit.

Cigarettes — 25 a week. No beer. No boot polish. No hair cream. No potatoes. No eggs. very little veg. No fresh meat — (the civvies are on goats). Bread very short. No lemonade. Water short. No electric light, very little coal, and paraffin extremely short. And the civilians are worse off than we are.

For the past month, they have been repatriating wives of soldiers by plane. The Regimental Sergeant Major's wife is still here and they (wife and kids) appear to be practically starving. Her name has been down now for a month and still she has not gone.

At the present minute there is considerable trouble being caused on the island by wives in England. Letters are received by husbands out here to the effect that their wives are having or have had babies. Well! It doesn't exactly make the bloke feel like going out celebrating does it?

Two Regimental Sergeant Majors on the island have been 'written off'. One with D.T.s a bit and the other so 'Bomb Happy' after the 39th blitz that he's almost mentally deficient now.

We had the misfortune to lose a Staff Sergeant last month — hit by an anti-personnel mine. I was one of the bearers at the funeral.

Well! that brings me up to date I think. From now on I'll try and write a couple of lines every day.

There were so many things you had to remember not to think about. You didn't wonder if a metal object would parachute down, brush against you and explode; the new technology of anti-personnel mines. You didn't wonder whether your buzzing ears and shaking hands were normal, nor whether your laughter had that note in it, which you had last heard in a Regimental Sergeant Major, just before two Military Police escorted him to a secure cell.

Most of all, you did not wonder what it was like to die of hunger, watching women and children, mostly Maltese, starving to death with you. You did not think about the daily impossible sacrifices which left some pink in the children's cheeks and none in their adults'.

Rations for a family of five were four tins of corned beef, four tins of fish, four boxes of matches monthly, and under 14oz bread per person daily. The Victory kitchens were as busy as the black market. Men, including the troops and Lord Gort himself, were surviving on 1500 calories a day, when the minimum considered necessary to lead an active life was 3000. Soldiers were encouraged to rest during off-duty hours, to conserve energy. Even the breweries could no longer function because of the lack of fuel so beer was no longer available.

Despite everything, the Archbishop ordered a special novena to be said for the nine days prior to the Feast of the Assumption, with all the celebration which people could manage. It could not of course be a full festa like in the old days, with fireworks, Turkish delight, halwa, iced orange and lemon drinks but there was to be a celebration – and that was an order. Although unmoved by the Virgin Mary's reception in heaven, George too was looking forward to the 15th August; he had been summoned to a meeting of the Lodge, in the crypt of St Paul's Anglican Cathedral, Valletta.

Lintorn Barracks, Floriana

*The Royal Naval Hospital, Bighi, and Rinella Creek,
showing beach defences.*

Harbourfront with variety of transport

The Marina, Valletta

Chapter 18.

My own nature, as it happens, is on the whole phlegmatic, and in consequence, I have the greatest difficulty in entering into the experiences of those whose emotions are easily and violently aroused... I don't know why people should be shaken by such tempests of emotion on provocation, to my mind, so slight. Reading through the Prophetic Books (of William Blake) not long ago, I noticed that certain words, such as 'howling', 'cloud', 'storm', 'shriek' occurred with extraordinary frequency. My curiosity was aroused; I made a pencil mark in the margin every time one of these words occurred. Adding up the score at the end of a morning's reading, I found that the average worked out to something like two howls and a tempest to every page of verse. The Prophetic Books are, of course, symbolic descriptions of psychological states. What must have been the mentality of a man for whom thunder, lightning, clouds and screams seemed the most appropriate figures of speech for describing his ordinary thoughts and feelings?
Ends and Means

The postcard was ripped up into tiny pieces but George could not work the images out of his head, however hard he strained his muscles. He knew that these postcards dropped from the droning bombers were just another form of weapon, slow-release poison, and usually he was immune.

He had seen a few of them; men showed them to each other, took the mickey out of the contents and shredded them. He had seen a scrawny British lion being fed blood and tears by Churchill; a Jewish puppeteer working the strings on Churchill, Roosevelt and Stalin; the German eagle and chisel-cut young Nazis in victorious poses of all kinds; even some stylish art nouveau from Italy declaiming 'Glory to our army'.

The Italian postcards had been the most dangerous as there were still some followers of Il Duce among the Maltese, particularly among the nobility, who were vulnerable to Italian propaganda. Only a fortnight ago, a spy had been caught and imprisoned, but even his execution would be kinder than what would happen if your average Maltese men in the street got hold of him. George had been able to consider all of these attempts at subversion coolly, analysing their potential impact on the people amongst whom he worked, troops and locals, but this latest had been something else.

'Help your fellow-men' the text at the top had read, accompanying a lurid picture of a burly, grinning American soldier, reaching out a hand to a British skeleton with a face. The coup-de grace was delivered in the right-hand side of the card which was indicated by the skeleton's hand offering all that was there, with a zig-zag line between the two halves; 'And help yourselves…' Beside this text was the obscene image of the American soldier's black rump, trousers round his ankles, bouncing on an enthusiastic Blighty girl.

Had George imagined the ball of paper beside her, the screwed up letter to her fiancé in Malta? He sweated and heaved sacks, churning with disgust. He thought of those babies being born in Britain to wives whose husbands had not been home for two years. Some of those babies must be coloured, although not as many as the soldiers' jokes going the rounds would suggest.

He only needed to see his reflection in the mirror to see

the British skeleton and every telegram with news of babies proved the rest of it. Just because you hadn't heard news of a baby yet didn't mean it wasn't going on with your girl too. He lunged viciously at a sack which split, spilling precious potatoes on the floor as George kicked the sack for good measure.

Not Nettie, he thought. Not Nettie, he pleaded. He thought of Staff Sergeant Johnson, growing increasingly desperate as he heard from his wife; first, ten months after the event, that the house had been bombed to bits but that she and the two-year old were safe; then, only two weeks later, that she had heard nothing from him and had been so short of money that she'd had to ask for help from this friend; then, only two weeks after that, had been the killer blow, how sorry she was, mixed-up with asking what he could expect when he'd left her alone to bring up a little one and she hadn't heard from him for so long, and her friend had been so good to her...

The black rump pounded through George's brain; there were a few women finding 'good friends' back home. Johnson had pleaded his case with every superior officer he could fight his way to, with the support of the sergeant and NCO It was obvious to anyone that the man had fallen apart and would be of no use to the British Army or anyone else until – or unless – he sorted out his personal affairs and it had been a relief to all when the orders had come to send him home on a submarine.

Usually, any request for leave was treated as a joke and, in his letters which often didn't even reach her, George could not get Nettie to understand that 'rights' and 'entitlement' meant nothing on Malta. What did the men say? *Everything's different on Malta.* Johnson being sent off on the submarine though – it gave a man hope that someone did care, when it came to the crunch.

George hoped the 'friend' would get what for. He pictured that black backside booted into a cartoon sky, he pictured it sprayed with machine-gun fire. Crazy. Johnson wasn't the only one. George shook his head to clear it and picked up a stray potato. Women! Nothing but trouble. Trouble when you were apart and trouble – he thought of Pitt's tension as he still waited for his wife to be taken to safety – when they were with you.

Having no choice, George got on with his war. Each time a cart arrived to pick up its requisition from George's store, now neatly stacked in the church and caves beside it, with full inventory, the exchange of information sustained the men as much as the supplies. The word had been out all week that a convoy was on its way and everyone was jittery with held breath, crossed fingers and, for those who still retained their faith, prayers. *Operation Pedestal* was muttered quietly between men who trusted each other.

The first news reached George on August 14th, the day before his planned visit to Valletta and a Lodge meeting.

'Three,' George repeated.

'Three,' the man, McKensie, confirmed. 'Three merchantmen made it into harbour yesterday afternoon, six o'clock, unloaded sweet as you please.'

'Aye, not too sweet I hope. Better it's not so well-organised but comes the way it should.'

There had been all too well-founded rumours as to where the black market goods had come from, last time a ship had made it through.

McKensie shook his head. 'I think you'll be O.K.'

George still found the Americanism 'O.K.' strange, especially in a Scots accent, but he supposed he'd be using it himself before long. He replied, 'Not that I'd trust any of them with my wallet but Gort seem to have the boys in blue working with the fly-by-nights so's we're not falling over each other all the time. '

'Once he does the big do in the Square, presents this wee medal to us all, he'll be the big face on all our cards, eh?'

The newspapers had made much of Malta being the first island to ever be honoured with the George Cross, and it was common knowledge that Lord Gort had carried the medal out to his new post with him, to be presented during an appropriate lull in hostilities. Which was rather the point, if you were one of those serving on Malta. There was *no* lull in hostilities and the George Cross remained as securely in Lord Gort's possession as the terms for surrender. If you were a gambling man, you'd find better odds on him using the latter than getting the chance to present the former, but that was, of course, seditious talk.

'Ay, it'd be rare to have a new face – we're all collecting them and I swopped yon big US General Doolittle, for General McArthur. We're bound to win, so we are, with the great pin-ups we have.'

'Like wee boys with their football cards… or happy families – I'm looking for Lord Gort of the soldier family…'

'That's what they think of us, wee boys. At least Lord Muckety-muck is fighting this war. Dobbie was losing it, you only had to look at his face.'

'For now. If we do O.K.' there, George had said it, 'then he's a good leader. And if we don't, who'll be left to care? So, tell me more. There's three ships in – more on their way?'

'Mebbe. The short of it is, we heard bits from the debrief and there was fourteen merchantmen set off from Gibraltar.'

'Fourteen.' There was a silence.

'They've definitely lost nine.' George groaned without sound at the flour, cans, potatoes – months of life for the people starving on Malta – that were feeding the sea bottom. Then, and he was ashamed at the instinctive order of priority, he calculated the dead sailors.

'So many. How did they lose so many?'

'Malta's prize of the year for Jerry, you know that. They can't invade straight off because of the landscape.' Both knew that the sea defences had made Malta difficult for centuries and, with the addition of barbed wire to the criss-crossing walls, the land was curled up like a hedgehog against invasion from the skies. 'They've got to bomb us or starve us.'

'Or both.'

'So they hit that convoy with every aeroplane, Italian, German, God knows what but they hit them for breakfast, dinner and tea.'

'You said nine down, three in?'

'Yes, hopes of two more.'

There was one vital piece of information missing.

'And the tanker?' There would have been an oil tanker. Without fuel for the planes, the other supplies meant little. If the RAF was grounded, they'd all be sitting ducks and the invasion plan would be on Hitler's desk for sure.

McKensie's grim face said it all. '*SS Ohio*, posh job from Texas Oil Company... well it was when it set out from America. I don't know, Spoof,' McKensie was one of the few people who still used the old nick-name. George's promotion had turned him into Taylor, or even George, especially when news of 'the wee medal' had reached the 'barracks'.

For weeks, the in-joke had been 'George, cross? He's raving!' because of George's unusually outspoken bitterness at Malta's fine public image. He wasn't the only one to say, 'Can we eat it or burn it? If not, what use is it to them – ' and his sweep included the wide-eyed, skinny urchins, stealing empty boxes outside the cave, ' – or us?' They didn't need a medal but they did desperately need the oil. George didn't dare ask, he just let McKensie tell what he knew.

'The way the lads tell it, she's not dead yet but it'll take ten miracles to get her here, and every damned Hun or Eyetie trying to finish her off... unless they think they already have?'

He continued, wondering aloud, 'Yes, that's about the only thing would help. She's been hit by just about everything in the sea and sky – sub, Stukas, Junkers, mines, torpedoes – all going for her. A plane even crashed on her deck. She was crippled and slow, staggering along with 150 miles to go then about eleven am, day before yesterday, the 13th, they finally blew her boilers and left her dead in the water. The lads said it was hell on earth. Guns blazing away, from every ship left there, all sitting around this tinder-box no-one could afford to leave. Then air cover arrived from Malta and the merchants made a break for home. And that's it.'

'Where is she?' George wondered how many miles lay between Malta and its only hope of survival.

'Seventy miles off, they reckon.'

Seventy miles, with no engines, and under constant dive-bombing. It wasn't difficult to assess *Ohio*'s chances and there was a silence.

'So you want twenty blankets?' George asked. Carry on as usual was all they could do.

McKensie knew the score too. 'Ay and twenty beds to go with them. We're kitting up one of the ships to take out some wounded.'

'And you'll want four-posters complete with floral canopies? What do you think this is, man, bloody Jenners?' All good Scots knew the Edinburgh High Street store that claimed to sell everything.

McKensie grinned. 'Better than that — you can never get the service in the High Street. Besides, I was told you were a genius. 'If you want something, Taylor's your man; there's not a tin of bully beef on the island that's not in his tally.' That's what they say.'

It was not the time to make the usual jokes about counting the rats for the next inventory. 'So you say,' was George's habitual response, whether to flattery or complaint. It took a war to fire his temper and even then it didn't last long. He was too much the rational idealist, with a spoonful of Scottish grandmother encouraging him to spare his breath to cool his porridge, and so he usually did.

It came as no surprise when he got the message later on the 14th that the Lodge meeting for the next day was cancelled. Another merchantman had reached the Harbour while George had been talking to McKensie and the word was that two destroyers were towing the *Ohio*, with the great tanker sandwiched between them, its precious and deadly cargo headed once more for Malta. The sound of held breath was so loud across the island, you could hear it over the jubilation at the ships already in, and George decided to take his day off anyway and go into Valletta.

Every man on the island who was not working that day was in Valletta on August 15th, 1942 – or so it seemed to George. He could not get there early, and it was already sweltering mid-morning when he reached the harbour-side, or rather the back of the crowds lining the harbour-side and he didn't have to see it, to know from the atmosphere what was there.

He took off his tin hat, waved it in the air and said, 'Well.'

A family beside him turned at the sound of English, smiled at him and he beamed back, repeating, 'Well.'

'Il-Konvoj ta Santa Marija' they reproved him, to which his response was another absurd 'Well' like some creature escaped from 'Alice in Wonderland'. Whether it was Santa Marija, whose day this was, or the strange Scottish god 'Well', McKensie's ten miracles had taken place and the impossible hulk of an oil tanker was resting in the Harbour. Its decks were awash, and crumpled metal rose in jagged sheets from gaping holes, but its precious cargo was safe and being unloaded.

George jostled his way nearer the front, found another R.A.M.C. man, who in turn knew a RAF mechanic, and between them they picked up on the gossip. The *Ohio* had reached home at 9.30 that morning, sandwiched between its two destroyers, with a third ship serving as rudder – that having gone in yet another bomber attack. The triumphant mine-sweepers cleared a channel and the crowds, waiting, hoping and praying for the Assumption Day miracle that they believed was foretold by their

Archbishop. His order to celebrate this Day with all their hearts was explained when they saw their miracle limp into Grand Harbour.

The bombers still chased their prize but, fuelled with hope once more, the air and anti-aircraft response was impenetrable. Even while George and his companions watched, the great wreck shrieked and settled onto the sea bottom, her back finally broken.

'How could anything survive that?'

George looked around him, at the ruins of bombed Valletta, at the gaunt people of the town, throwing dried or withered flowers, singing. The children skipped around, catching the mood without understanding it, and George picked up the words of their songs. '*Ohio* we love you! Oh, *Ohio*, we love you so.' and 'Mussolini are you blind? Or can't you see the navy, the navy, the navy…' Was this how children's nursery rhymes were created? In blazing sunshine, with a lump in your throat and a dirty oil tanker turning into legend before your eyes?

'Another bloody mess to clean up,' the RAF mechanic commented, looking at the grimy carcass blocking the docks.

'Used to love swimming in Kalfrana Bay – do you know it?'

'Great spot for bathing and pretend you're on your holidays.'

George remembered the octopus.

'Until the Breconshire went down there in April. Gives me the spooks it does. '

'Word was you can still get the odd tin of milk from it –'

'And bottle of gin –'

'If you dive down.'

'What's so spooky about an old ship?'

'Not the ship, the plane that shot it down was spitchered too. When the water's calm, you can see the pilot sitting in his cockpit.'

'No!'

'Honest to God. You can even tell the time off his wristwatch.'

It was late evening as George hitched a ride back to his metal bed and the sun, which he took for granted now, was warming the scrubland with gold. Perhaps it was the sunlit halo, perhaps it was the day itself, or even Santa Maria at work once more, but when a girl appeared on a path by the road, illuminated in gold and smiling at him, George half-stood in the jeep and saluted her, returning the smile. The driver gave him a sideways glance.

'Feeling jolly?'

'Well!' was George's only comment but he grinned.

Probably the waterfront police station, Floriana

St Paul's Bay

Rinella Creek

St Julian's Bay

Chapter 19.

Ideas of 'glory' and 'immortal fame' still ferment in the minds of dictators and generals, and play an important part in the causation of war.
Ends and Means

The celebrations after the arrival of the Santa Marija convoy lasted longest among those who knew least, encouraged by the announcement that the 15th August was to be an annual holiday and that men between 16 and 60 were to have an increased bread ration. Beer was available again, if not flowing, and seamen told their convoy stories in the bars of the Gut. The distinctive triangular caps of the US Navy were worn with pride and George tried not to stare, and not to recall a certain postcard, as he saw his first black man, speaking with a deep American accent.

'So she was holed to hell, shipping water, waiting to explode and all the crew taken onto the *Santa Elisa*.'

'Yeah, we got them off that tanker and let them sit on our gasoline drums!' chipped in another sailor.

'Larsen, Third Officer, was jumping around like a prairie dog sniffing coyote and he keeps looking at the tanker, has this thing about the guns, driving us all cracked with his ideas. 'They can be repaired, we can go back on… if we man the guns…I'll need four men.' So we're looking at this, like, giant time-bomb right by us and he wants us to strap it to our butts and I guess there's a few of were going to shout up–'

'Yeah, right, and a few of us stepping backwards to leave the volunteers–'

'–and you'd have bet your bottom dollar on it being Dale, for sure, keen as mustard and mad for action. Sure enough, Larsen got his volunteers and they goddamned made it, mended the guns, manned them, even got theirs in first with a torpedo boat, and then rode the *Ohio* all the way home. '

'Some bronco. The President's writing their citation speeches now this minute, you bet ya.'

'Jeez, Dwayne, the President don't write speeches, stupid.'

'So how come he says so many, then wise guy?'

'He got writers, don't he? Dwayne's right about medals though…coming their way for sure. 'For heroism beyond the call of duty.'

'How do they choose who gets them?'

'Now, that's the big question ain't it?'

'So, do we all get medals? Or the five on *Ohio* or what?'

They considered this around the table. 'Naa, probably not even five, can't afford so many medals, real gold you know? They'll do a draw or something.'

'I bet he writes some bits of speeches or re-writes so it's more his thoughts, you now. No way a Democrat President just reads what he's given. Why, you might as well vote in an actor.' Everyone ignored Dwayne.

'So, who gets the medals and why?'

After a long contemplation, involving some serious drinking, there was a tentative suggestion.

'It's a bit like dying then – no reason some gets it and others not.'

Further contemplation. 'I know – it's the maddest bastards!' This met with approval and a general toast, 'To the maddest bastards!'

'Anyone here a mad bastard?'

'Not me, mate, want to get home in one piece – worth

more than a medal.'

'Drink up boys, we're all worth medals.'

George pronounced, 'The job's worth medals.'

This comment excited Lewis so much that he yelled, 'Come on over here' at the dusty little flower seller, holding her tray of withered flowers in the hopes that the new optimism would produce some customers.

She was in luck as Lewis produced a few bills, took the complete tray off her and said, 'Take-over bid, gal, go buy yourself some pretties.'

She stared at him, confused but serious, responded formally, 'Thank you, Sir, it will buy some bread for my family,' and left the bar.

The moment's awkwardness passed as Lewis dumped the tray on George's lap, ordering him, 'You Brits do this stuff best, the old Buckingham Palace Brigade, heh what? What's your name again? yeah, Taylor, right... but we need your given name. VIPs always have loads 'a names. George? Even better... we have King George—'

'Saint George—'

'The George to end all Georges, of London, England. He's here and he's going to present us with our Jobsworth Medals.'

It made as much sense to George as any other medal ceremony and he tucked a withered flower carefully into each man's cap or button-hole, outdoing the US President by composing his own speeches, which were rendered less witty by alcohol and by the habit of placing the flower between his teeth within the presentation ceremony.

'And who's going to give George his medal?' Lewis demanded.

'Marilyn Monroe,' decided Dwayne, transforming himself into a pouting blonde and planting a smacker on George's cheek as he tried to tuck the 'award' into George's trouser band.

Who should have medals? Fourteen cargo ships had set off for Malta in Operation Pedestal and only six had arrived; nine of the escort ships had been sunk or damaged, including the aircraft carrier *Eagle* which had served Malta well; the cost in sailors' lives was over three hundred. Churchill said, 'I am of the opinion that the price was worth paying.' Malta had come within a fortnight of total starvation and the supplies which had got through were only a reprieve not a rescue.

At last, on September 9th, Lord Gort could present the George Cross to the people of Malta.

His predecessor, Sir William Dobbie, had been notified of the award four months earlier, in May, when George V1 had written to him, 'To honour her brave people, I award the George Cross to the island Fortress of Malta; to bear witness to a heroism and devotion that will long be famous in History.'

Dobbie had replied, 'By God's help, Malta will not weaken but will endure until victory is won.'

Headlines in *the Times of Malta* at the time had read, 'King sets his seal on living history' and the very person who had composed those headlines, the *Times'* Editor, had turned Dobbie himself into yesterday's news. It was now his successor who could boost morale with the public presentation of the award itself.

The Palace Square, Valletta, was deliberately chosen for the celebration, its stone still ringing from centuries of battle. On the wall of the guards' room opposite the Palace itself was the plaque recording the crucial 1814 decision of the Treaty of Paris that Malta would be British; 'To Great Britain, still unsubdued, these Islands are entrusted by the Powers of Europe at the wish of the Maltese themselves.'

Despite the petrol shortage and the skeleton omnibus service thousands gathered in the Square under the Union Jacks and Maltese flags, to hear Lord Gort declare, 'Battle-scarred George Cross Malta stands firm, undaunted and undismayed, waiting for the time when she can call; pass friend, all is well in the island fortress!' The cheering crowds watched Chief Justice Sir George Borg receive the case containing the King's letter and the Cross, the highest award for gallantry, on behalf of the people of Malta. Sergeant George Taylor did not attend the event.

The Times of Malta was still eulogizing on September 19th. 'This island is today an outpost of the United Nations. Its stand against aggression has embodied the combined efforts of the four pillars of Democracy: Navy, Army, Air Force and Civilians. By their united efforts all have won for the Island of Malta in which they were born, or in which they were serving, or had served, undying fame.'

'George – cross?' The old joke was revived as men presented dockets at the stores.

George just bared his teeth and growled. He knew exactly what provisions were on the island and he listened to the bluff being called daily. The increased bread rations for men were reduced back again almost as quickly. It was nothing to find sooty smuts in food, the cooking oil having come from crashed aircraft and if men's rations of fruit and nuts were full of maggots, they didn't even think twice before eating them. Weevil-infested chocolate was boiled in water and the bugs skimmed to create a hot chocolate drink, on which George, always one with a sweet tooth, commented, 'Goody goody.'

Whole suburbs of Valletta had been living in catacombs for two years now, sitting outside in fine weather on empty boxes or the luxuries of tapestry cushions or rugs, stitched in the traditional brown and yellow. Scavenging was a way of life and no soldier could allow pity to turn his back on precious stores, which were guarded day and night.

It was not only George's stores which were precious. Mabel Strickland's pet rabbits had disappeared long ago, eggs were rarer than diamonds and the staple goat's milk was disappearing with the goats. Gort's promise that goats would be replaced at London's expense put no food on plates. Queuing for half a day at Victory kitchens might lead to three thin sausages and fifteen peas to be divided between three people. When Lord Gort paraded the

George Cross, which was to travel to all the villages on the island, some men stood on street corners and looked at him, in silence, rubbing their bellies.

George worked in the midst of the villagers and the displaced, saw their ravaged bodies as they made processions to the church, called upon their saints. He saw the children covered in skin sores, scratching their scabies. George sometimes saw the Maltese waif he'd seen silhouetted in sunshine – hard to think of her as a woman, she was so slight, and yet weren't they all but shadows?

She always seemed to appear from nowhere, like the fées of the old tales, come to carry him away to Fairyland where a hundred years would go by in a minute and George would emerge still young while the world had moved on without him.

It would not be such a bad thing, for this world to move on without him... and so, when she saluted him, he saluted her back and they both smiled, and she vanished. A little pleasure in a day which held only the weight of knowing too much. He knew to the day when the food would run out and he knew that the sewage pipes were broken, the raw excrement flooding the fields where the 'Grow more food campaign' was mainly increasing the spread of typhoid.

The postponed Masons' meeting took place on Thursday October 15th at the crypt of St Paul's Cathedral, Valletta, at 4.30pm sharp' in a surreal mix of high ceremony and Sunday school drama. God's presence echoed through every stone of the beautiful old cathedral and even in the cave-coldness of the crypt, the words 'Your trust being in God, your faith is well founded' carried the ancient authority of the place and its chivalric origin as a knights' Auberge.

The Brothers were as safe from the world and all its bombs as anywhere on Malta could make them and the crypt had frequently served as an air-raid shelter for the cathedral chaplain and his flock. However, spiritual elevation was hampered somewhat by the blanket rigged up to divide the Masons from another organisation sharing the crypt.

The regalia, although positioned correctly, according to the Tracing Board for the First Degree, had clearly been placed on whatever surfaces came to hand. The improvisation was inventive but hardly awe-inspiring. It was impossible to tyle the Lodge properly so the Tyler kept guard beyond the blanket, using hand-claps as knocks, and the ceremony was delivered sotto voce. The ritual to open the lodge in the Second Degree mostly consisted of ensuring only those so passed were present and, although he 'withdrew', George could hear the whispers on the other side of the blanket.

'By what instrument in architecture will you be proved?'

'By the Square, Right Worshipful Master.'

'And what is a Square?'

'An angle of 90 degrees, or the fourth part of a circle.'

George's imagination ranged back to his schooldays, going over his mathematics homework with his father who made the instruments seem so exciting that their use as magical symbols seemed natural. Not magical of course, he heard his father's stern correction; *you are a man of science.* The Tyler interrupted his thoughts and, after following instructions, George ducked around the blanket and the catechism began.

George accepted the injunction to 'act upon the Square with all mankind' and pressed his nose against the Set Square he had been given. He stayed kneeling during the Chaplain's prayer and then he whispered his part of the ceremony which would pass him to the rank of Fellow Craft.

'Give me the password,' demanded the Senior Warden.

'Shibboleth,' responded George.

'What is the symbolic import of the word?'

'It signifies the Gileadite Spirit.'

'How is it usually depicted in our Lodges?'

'By an ear of corn in a field of wheat.'

'Pass.' The Senior Warden took George by his right hand, presented him to the Right Worshipful Master with further formalities, until finally George swore to 'encourage industry and reward merit; supply the wants or relieve the necessities of worthy Brethren; and on no account to wrong them or see them wronged but to view their interests as inseparable from my own.' He did, of course, also swear for the thousandth time to keep all the Masonic secrets into which he had been initiated.

In the final part of the ceremony, George was presented with a set square, a spirit level and a plumb rule. 'The Square teaches us to regulate our actions by the Masonic rule and line, and to harmonise our conduct with the principles of morality and virtue. The Level demonstrates that we are descended from the same stock, partakers of the same nature, and sharers in the same hope, and that although distinctions among men are necessary to preserve subordination and to reward merit and ability, yet no eminence of station should make us forget that we are all Brethren, because the time will come when all distinctions, save those of goodness and virtue, will cease, and death, the grand leveller of all human greatness, will reduce us to the same state. The Plumb Rule admonishes us to walk uprightly in our several stations, to hold the scales of justice with equal poise, to observe the just medium between avarice and profusion, and to make our passions and prejudices coincide with the exact line of duty. Thus the Square teaches morality, The Level, equality, and the Plumb Rule, justness and uprightness of life and actions. Thus, by square conduct, level steps and upright intentions we hope to ascend to a higher realisation of that Immortal Principle whence all goodness emanates.'

George was then given the chance to adjust his dress while Baker, the Worshipful Master, gave the long symbolic explanation, based on Solomon's temple, for the Tracing Board which set out the ceremonial positions required to raise the Lodge to the Second Degree. Signing his name on the right-hand pillar printed on the certificate, George suspected he was not the only Brother ready for a cup of tea.

The days of wine and banquets were long gone and a Brother thought himself lucky to be given a cup of tea with some precious tinned milk and one biscuit. The talk after the ceremony was even more important to George than being passed to the Second Degree, and added to his store of knowledge about the state of the island. It was not comforting information.

He learned that aviation fuel stocks, although replenished by the *Ohio*, were still low, that all taxi-ing was forbidden, to conserve fuel, and that Air Vice-Marshall Park had ordered the riskiest bluff of all. He had instructed pilots to fly out to intercept bombers, giving the impression that they could attack them as far as Sicily itself.

If necessary, the pilots were to drop bombs harmlessly into the sea because in reality, of course, they had insufficient fuel to go very far at all. The strategy had tragically backfired on one mission when the planes had fuelled up just enough to take them out across the sea and back home but a change in weather had given them a heavy head-wind, costing them too much fuel on the return journey and all had been lost at sea, unable to make it home.

Park had known the stakes and so had his men. If AXIS guessed how low the RAF planes were on fuel, all they had to do was call the bluff, but if they believed what they saw, they would be wary of increasing their attack, and their already heavy losses. As long as the RAF held the skies, there was a chance of another convoy, another reprieve.

There was also the matter of North Africa.

The fall of Tobruk had left British troops, in particular the eighth army, the 'desert rats', concentrated at el Alamein, and Malta was a safe harbour en route there while cutting off supplies to Rommel's armies. The Reich General's view of Malta as 'that scorpion in the sea' was taken as a compliment by Malta's military leaders. The new Allied General heading to North Africa to face Rommel, had sent a message to Lord Gort via a Canadian Flight Lieutenant, that Malta's heroics would make victory in the western desert possible and that with victory in the western desert would go the liberation of Malta.

With Lord Montgomery's analysis in mind, Park continued to send out his men with nerves on 'full' and tanks showing empty, and the Brothers of the Lodge of St Andrews were not surprised to hear of how a Maltese businessman had presented Old Eagle Park with a cigarette case engraved with the initials MTAP – Malta Thanks Air Protection.

George ate and drank news from his Brothers, valued as an equal. In the security of the Masons' oaths, there was true freedom of speech. Some of the constrictions in George's throat eased as he heard his own seditious thoughts not only said aloud by others but discussed calmly, factually – truths faced.

Monday 3.8.42

Well! To tell the truth – the date is now 30/10/42 – such is life! – In my work I always try to 'do it now' but I am afraid my private affairs are in a sad state. However I will do my best to rectify this. I will just stick things down any old how – as they come into my head.

Staff Sergeant Johnson, the Chief Clerk, has had wife trouble and left by sub a month ago – no news – apparently overdue now.

Mrs Pitt is still here – after almost four months waiting – She has been warned (6 hours) three times now but that's all.

The grub is now in a hell of a state. we can only last about two months, and the civvies are much worse than we are. The black market is terrible – Paraffin 15 shillings a gallon – cigs

2/6 for 20. *Eggs 24 shillings a dozen – if you can get them!*

During the past month air activity has been renewed and we knocked just over 100 planes out of the sky in a fortnight.

Somebody produced an 'Everybodys' news-sheet in the mess and it had one of these articles – 'I was there' and it 'didn't half give us a liver' – the main expression in response was 'the lying _____ *!!' along with a few other choice remarks regarding his propaganda towards the local population!*

This island is filthy, unsanitary, stinking and an absolute disgrace to the British Empire. It is to be hoped that after the war it is made a fit place for people to live in.

Disease will be rampant this winter – two R.A.M.C. Sergeants have already gone home with T.B. – Typhoid is on the increase – Diphtheria is with us – and the hospitals are always full up, even without battle casualties.

The only bright spot at present is that I am playing football again – not like a cripple either!! We've got a good team at present and hope to go places and do things this year.

Rations have now been cut systematically for 2 ½ years so you will appreciate it when I say that another cut will mean the end of football. At present we're not getting enough to do a decent day's work.

Transport is slowly being reduced to a standstill – petrol cut and cut and cut – and now this week it is mixed with paraffin!

You may think all these ravings are most peculiar but the case is this: so far as I can see, this island is in a bad way – food will last three months – no more – so unless something almost in the nature of a miracle happens – we pack in. Now that's serious – almost enough to make a bloke like me start thinking.

The answer is, 'Me for the next boat!!'

Well! It's late now and I'm off to the mess for cream cakes and beer!!!!!!

Sergeant George Taylor

As he feared, George filled his precious notepad, with no chance of getting another one, so he had to start writing on the reverse of the thin sheets of paper.

A page from George's diary, March 1940

27.

Thursday:- 7.3.40.

Debugging. Really, very little of note today. Just much as usual with, at 2.15, a drill parade, worked until 4.45 & then came back as I had an appointment with the Barber for 5 o'clock. Put my bed together etc, cleaned up & so to bed. The weather is a bit cooler than it has been, in fact there is a slight nip in the air. — Of course that is wearing only shirt & Service Dress only.

Friday:- Forenoon very busy. Pay parade 2.10, then we had a "fire" — hoses going & everything except the flames. Worked until 4. From 5 till 9.30 was on night Police. Quite a day!

Saturday :- 9.3.40

I am writing this by the light of the fire which is rather a job. Well! Work until 1.15. In the afternoon I wrote a "letter" home — had a bath — changed clothes & made up my laundry — cleaned my boots (new!) & chinstrap — cleaned the metal of my water bottle cork. About 10 past 6 it came on rain — at 6.15, when I was in the middle of cleaning my locker, the lightning started & at 6.20 the lighting system was struck & all lights were off. By the light of a candle, I got my junk away & I am writing this now. We have a fire & now I think its cold today although really the temp is about 65.

George with his three stripes, showing his Sergeant's rank.
He was promoted to Sergeant on 18.6.42

Chapter 20.

Modern war destroys with the maximum of efficiency and the maximum of indiscrimination and therefore entails the commission of injustice far more numerous and far worse than any it is intended to redress.
Ends and Means

By the end of October, there was a cautious view that the worst of the bombing might be over and on November 11th, 1942, the British government gave ten million pounds to assist Malta 'to restore barbaric damage'. Numbers were flying around and the more incredible they were, the more likely they were to be true. The bombs dropped in March and April alone exceeded the total for the 1940 Greater London Blitz, which covered a much larger area.

A hundred churches, built by the Knights of St John, had been destroyed since the beginning of the year – deliberately, the Maltese said, – and Valletta was in ruins. Bombers sometimes unloaded their bombs over Valletta so as to discharge their mission without facing the anti-aircraft barrage in Grand Harbour.

The increasing numbers of pilots who had met the instructions to 'Scramble' over Malta had taken the fight as far as their fuel would carry them, confusing Kesselring with their apparent strength and cutting the supply line of ships heading to North Africa, so that only thirty-five per cent of provisions sent to Rommel actually reached him,

Again, the numbers, published in *the Times of Malta*, were beyond belief. At the beginning of 1942, a total of thirty RAF planes were facing regular raids by any number of six hundred AXIS bombers. By November, thanks largely to increasing numbers of Spitfires, and their pilots, the RAF had definitely destroyed 773 enemy aircraft, along with another 300 unconfirmed. The costs had been 195 RAF aircraft and 106 pilots.

There was no doubt that some of the pilots qualified for the 'maddest bastard' medals and they were proud of it. Competition between squadrons was fierce as they notched up enemy hits and when new pilots arrived on the island, Squadron Leaders were even known to toss for them. In such a manner, Lord Douglas-Hamilton won George 'Screwball' Beurling who then scored 18 fighters destroyed by the end of July. By October when Screwball bailed out and his parachute opened only twenty feet above the water, he had claimed 28 hits.

It was Squadron Leader 'Laddie' Lucas who had lost the toss over Beurling and he himself ensured that 249 squadron, with all its extra experience, kept ahead of 603, whose Scots motto *Gin ye daur*, 'If you dare', was lived again and again. The airmen spoke of it in public as 'great fun'. In private, a man might be more honest, as cheerful friends disappeared and a numbed perseverance took over from the enthusiasm.

Who could really blame the airman who had flown the wrong way off the carrier, avoiding Malta and heading instead to Algeria, where he informed his consul that he was a lost civil aviation pilot in need of repatriation? That such a story was so rare says a great deal about the men who flew to Malta's defence. There had been 1660 bombing attacks in 1942 before the end of October, and 1386 Maltese civilians had been killed in them.

It was not only the men of the Royal Malta Artillery who manned the anti-aircraft guns but their whole families, without training or ear protection, armed only with a passionate desire to fight back. Against all odds, AXIS had not won the air battle over Malta, and had decreased attacks, but the island remained under siege.

Monday 2.11.42

Usual busy <u>Monday</u>. It is now 4 weeks since I had a birthday and I still have had no cable from J.M.G. – I think it is a disgusting state of affairs to say the least of it. Otherwise there is very little happening. At least there seems to be a push on somewhere in Libya – we are preparing ships with bunks – fixing up airfields – and rattling off guns all day long.

Actually, we are another day nearer starvation. Bread, jam and cheese cut again. Cigs are going down to 25 a week – which is just about the last straw.

George and Jock Wallace contemplated their bread and jam.

'Don't eat it all at once,' Jock said and George's boyhood had answered,

'Mary had a little jam

to spread upon her bread;

she spread it on her hands and face

and on her frock instead.'

'Those were the days,' Jock acknowledged. Their smiles faded.

'If Mary had been on Malta, she'd have licked her dress…'

'And then given it to the baby to suck.'

Jock was George's latest partner-in-crime, a big red-haired Scot from the highlands with a softer accent than George, that whispering hint of the Gaelic in it. No other softness was discernible in Jock though and his dry sense of humour appealed to George, who was already thinking that he would miss the man. That was the way you thought. The sheer intensity of the situation brought you close and a name on an order split you up by a thousand miles – or more, if there was a bomb with your name in it. A story started and you never knew the next part, never mind the ending. What exactly was going on in Libya? Was it good news? Would George get home and see Nettie by Christmas or was he heading for a POW camp for the New Year?

The last time you saw someone should be signalled, lit up with fireworks, full of omens so you could say something memorable, but it never was. It was only in retrospect that you knew that had been the last time you saw him... or her. George remembered Violet's elegant shoulders, too thin shoulders, as she'd disappeared out of the Valletta bar, how long ago was it? on some officer's arm. He'd been pipped to the post there right enough.

Was that the last time he would see her? Was she still alive? If she was, he would not know if that was the last time until one of them died. And he probably wouldn't know if she died. He wouldn't know if he died either... He shouldn't be thinking of Violet. Which train of thought led him back round to Nettie and he couldn't wonder if he would see Nettie again; that was his article of faith. She was all the sweetness of life, playing Officer somewhere, forgetting his birthday. He was twenty-five. A flicker of skirts jumped into his field of vision and he put an extra snap to the salute and smile he gave to his girlish admirer when she skipped around from behind a rock, curtsied to him and ran away.

Hearing from Nettie was sometimes more painful than her silences, into which he could read what he wanted – or more pessimistically, what he feared. Her exuberance over her officer status grated on him, however he ridiculed any comparison between them – which she certainly never made.

Worse were her descriptions of the jolly larks she was having. One time, she was horrified at being put on a charge. The very sight of that chit of paper with her name and the number of the charge jumping out at her, had prevented her reading the detail, until she finally realised she'd been charged with throwing a cup of tea over someone in temper and that it was all a big hoax.

George could tell that the hoaxer was a man. The very fact Nettie did not name him said as much, and George pictured the man, close enough to her to tease her and arouse the pink spots in her cheeks, the flash in her hazel eyes and a cup of scalding tea over him – preferably in his lap, George hoped. She hadn't changed and on that he pinned his hopes as well as suffering his fears. If there was still such innocence, somewhere, there was a home to go back to.

Friday 6.11.42

Went to the pictures at B'kara with Jock Wallace – at night – it was a very pleasant change – picture 'Ask a policeman'. Probably you saw it about ten years ago.

Mrs Pitt is still with us – there is still no news of Staff Sergeant Johnson, and we're wondering if his submarine made it.

Have just been reading the information bulletin – in it we are told we are heroes!! – At least that's what the rest of the world says – apparently. Well! I can assure you I don't feel so good as all that – I can always remember being told – 'Well ! You've had food now and it doesn't matter so much later' You don't know how true those words were. I reckon it will take me at least a year of non-stop eating to make up for lost time.

Saturday 7.11.42

Usual day – work 8 to 8.30. Incidentally I don't think I've given you the latest detail of a week's work so here goes
<u>*Monday*</u>: *Rabat , Wardia, Naxxen and Imjar pay a visit and draw all supplies and solve their little difficulties.*
<u>*Tuesday*</u>: *Morning: Sizzievri and Attard.*

Afternoon: Combined Ordinance, NAAFI and laundry trip
<u>*Wednesday*</u>*: Petrol-less day – but Naxxen comes again by gategart and conducts all business.*
<u>*Thursday*</u>*: Ordinance trip and CO's inspection*
<u>*Friday*</u>*: St Andrews, Kelluha, Ligue and Odds and Sods!*
<u>*Saturday*</u>*: Clearing up the mess in general.*
<u>*Sunday*</u>*: ditto and cleaning up the mess my kit and affairs have got into.*

In between the above stations' visits, all bookwork and other horrible jobs are pushed – with a result that we are always too darned busy! It's a case of – in the winter we say 'Right! We'll work day and night and have a quiet summer' – and then when summer comes we are forced to say, 'We'll work day and night now and have a quiet winter.' Anyway, the joke is certainly on us.

Tomorrow, the George Cross is being exhibited in Gargur 10am till 12 noon – so probably all the local bigwigs will be knocking about all morning. I am afraid I am not sufficiently interested to go and see it.

There is no electric light at all in the village and one of the things I miss most is the wireless – especially after having got used to mine at Musta – incidentally Musta is no more.

Without the wireless, George felt truly marooned on his island. He missed the songs with bitter-sweet reminders of home, *'Wouldn't you know I saw him in my dreams last night...'* and he had lost the BBC World news, his hope of guessing what was happening in Libya. A mere Sergeant was not privy to military strategy, except of course in Lodge meetings.

George counted the days until he could mix again with men who not only knew what was going on, but who *decided* what would go on. In this heady company he was gaining respect and fast promotion through the ranks, without the invisible obstacles that seemed to bar his way in the R.A.M.C. He did wish he could let Nettie know that he was to be raised again at the next meeting. Thank goodness that there were no women Masons or she might be charming her way higher than he was, there too! An absurd thought, quickly dismissed.

When his lieutenant asked for a word with George, he hoped against experience that he would be at least recommended for OCTU at some future date. He didn't connect the meeting at all with the vanishing black robes and tall, flattened hat of the local priest, the Kapillan. He was therefore totally unprepared for what he was told.

Lieutenant Harris had his hands clasped behind his back and turned away from George as he spoke. 'Don't know how to say this, Taylor–'

George had many years' experience of when to say nothing.

'You don't strike me as one for the ladies–'

George racked his brains as to whether he could have offended a nursing sister – what, by refusing to give her an extra gross of bandages? Or had he looked at a woman's legs or something? Fat chance! He had seen Jane Pitt the day before and he had certainly smiled and asked her how she was, but he thought if there was something wrong in that quarter he'd hear about it from Pitt in no uncertain terms. And what did Harris mean by saying he wasn't a ladies' man? Was George so ugly? So unattractive? So impossible to imagine with a woman?

'–and God knows we all get lonely but these local girls are easy prey, George, in love with a uniform and a hero, and too innocent to ask the right questions of a man's motives. That's why the Kapillan keeps an eye on them, more of a parent, you know? And of course these Catholics tell their priests everything in the confessional so whatever it is between you and this – Marija – it's not a good idea. I'm sure you don't need me to spell it out for you?'

At least he was 'George' now, for the man-to-man pep talk, 'I haven't the foggiest what this is about... Sir,' George replied but, actually, he *was* starting to have an inkling..

The Lieutenant sighed. 'I'm afraid George, that Father Pietro is concerned that one of his flock, a young girl called Marija, has rather fallen for you – and not without encouragement – and she has high hopes for the future based on this... contact.'

George shook his head, bemused, and enlightened his superior officer about the only possibility for 'Marija', his angelic waif, who brightened his days and had clearly indulged in fantasies. His heart ached to think of her 'confession', her hopes and the likely responses from the Kapillan, wrongly convicting George, in absentia, of dishonourable intentions.

'Well, that's an end to it anyway. Father Pietro has spoken to Marija about her 'unmaidenly' behaviour,' the Lieutenant tried to share a man-of-the-world look with George but the latter was too upset at the thought of such a child being weighed down with sins and guilt and fear of men, to return it, 'and to her parents. People have been passing remarks about her behaviour and I'm sure it will stop now, so you won't be bothered any more.'

The implicit order was clear enough. 'Yes, sir.' George turned to go.

'Oh, and George?

'Yes Sir?'

'They're break-your-heart-beauties at sixteen, but run to fat by twenty, not like our girls back home.'

'Yes Sir,' muttered George, seething.

15.11.42

Well! Things have been happening since I wrote last. They had a tossup which Field Ambulance would move! Anyway, they decided on 161 and posted 36 Other Ranks from this unit to make it up to strength. At present it appears that the 15th is going to 'take over' the whole island, if and when they leave.

For your information – this move coincides with the 'big push in Libya and Tunisia' Well! That's the position today – further developments will be reported later.

I'm not feeling at all secretive these days, at least not when writing this, because I feel that no-one will ever read it anyway so I will proceed to discourse on my fast sex life on the island. This, by the way, is not my fault but the fault of half-witted females who seem to get in my way. But, in spite of the thousands who are after me, (I don't think!) I have only fallen (softly – of course) for two in the two and a half years I have had to endure on this rock. The first one died a natural death after a L/Cpl asked her to marry him! He didn't of course – but he is <u>still</u> chasing round trying to make dates with her!!

The latest effort is still going full swing – if you can call it that. It consists of a very small and childish female jumping out of unexpected places – whipping up a small salute or a curtsey as the mood suits her and then as soon as someone appears she mysteriously disappears. And to help things it appears that someone saw her up to these tricks and the matter was duly reported to the parish priest so my reputation appears to have gone forever!!

Well! I'm going to give up soon – writing I mean!

The grub has not improved. Dinner yesterday – 3 spoonfuls' curried rice, two pieces tinned meat and 3 biscuits – Oh! Lovely!!! Roll on the boat! Still! we get a beer and a half per week – cigs down to 10 per week. That's all tonight. I'm off for a game of chess.

Our Lady of Victories Church, Floriana, which marks the victory over the Turks in 1566 and is the original burial place of La Vallett, First Grand Master of the Knights of St John

Chapter 21.

The history of ideas is to a great extent the history of the misinterpretation of ideas. An outstanding individual makes a record of his life or formulates, in the light of his personal experiences, a theory about the nature of the world. Other individuals, not possessing his natural endowments, read what he has written, and because their psychological make-up is different from that of the author, fail to understand what he means. They re-interpret his words in the light of their own experience, their own knowledge, their own prejudices. Consequently, they learn from their teacher, not to be like him, but to be more themselves. Misunderstood, his words serve to justify their desires, rationalize their beliefs.
Ends and Means

'Right Worshipful Master, at the door of the Lodge stands Brother George Taylor, a poor candidate in a state of distress, who has been well and worthily recommended, regularly proposed and approved in open Lodge, now comes of his own free will and accord, humbly soliciting to be admitted to the mysteries and privileges of ancient Freemasonry.'

The familiar phrases from the two earlier ceremonies eased George into the ritual for raising him to the Third Degree. It was only November and already he was on his way to becoming a Master Mason. He had memorised all the words of his little green book, revised the passwords and signs which he already knew, preparatory for learning the secrets of a Master Mason. Once more the crypt of St Paul's Cathedral served as the temporary home of the Lodge of St Andrew and, for this particular ceremony, nowhere could have been more fitting. George shivered in the constant cool temperature created by the old stone and his own undress.

Brother Lane, the Right Worshipful Master, was speaking. 'We acknowledge the powerful aid by which he seeks admission. Is he in possession of the pass-grip and pass-word?

'He is not but his Conductor has given them for him.' Brother Hirst, the Inner Guard, gave the reply.

'Do you, Brother Inner Guard, vouch that the candidate is properly prepared?

'I do, Right Worshipful Master.'

'Then let him be admitted in due form.' In due form, George was instructed to enter the Lodge on the point of the Circle, and to consider that, just as the most vital parts of man are contained within the body, so are the most valuable tenets of Freemasonry symbolically comprehended between the points of the Circle, namely Virtue, Morality and Brotherly Love. In the cathedral crypt, where the knights of Malta had knelt and listened to the word of God, George fell to his knees and wondered. Aloud, he pledged his fidelity to this over-arching brotherhood which included all his other loyalties. *Arduis in Fidelis*, yet again.

'Then I shall entrust you with the pass-grip and pass-word of this degree. The pass-grip is given by a distinct pressure of the thumb between the index finger and middle finger of your Brother,' and George felt the pressure in the designated places as the Right Worshipful Master took George's hand in his own. 'This pass-grip demands a pass-word, which is 'Tubal Cain' who was the first architect in metals. The import of the word is 'Life after death'. You must be careful to remember this pass-grip and pass-word, as they will shortly be demanded of you by the Worshipful Senior Master as a test of merit. Pass.'

George was then taken round the Lodge, stopping to give the different grips and tokens of each rank through which he had been raised. He approached the altar with the required seven steps, 'beginning with the left foot, the first three as if stepping over an obstacle, the other four regular'. George knelt and repeated his vows on the Volume of Sacred Law, and was instructed in the meaning of the Third Degree.

'It invites you to reflect on the solemn subject of your own origin and destiny, and teaches you to feel that to the just and virtuous man death has no terrors equal to the stain of falsehood. Of this great truth the annals of Freemasonry afford a glorious example in the unshakeable fidelity and noble death of our Master, Hiram Abiff who was slain just before the completion of King Solomon's Temple, at the construction of which he was the principal architect.' George could no longer take in the words. He had some idea of what was to follow and all he could hear was the blood in his ears as he was taken to stand in the west.

The dim light was reduced further to only one candle flickering in the east, projecting grotesque human shadows across the curved stone walls. A disembodied voice intoned the old story, telling of the fifteen Fellows of Craft who had supervised the building of the Temple and resented the fact that they did not yet possess the secrets of a Master Mason even though the Temple was not complete. They resolved to gain these secrets, by whatever means, but twelve backed out of the plans, leaving three to carry out their scheme.

George saw shapes, little more than shadows themselves, move to position; one in the East, one in the North and the third in the South. He himself was to play the part of Hiram Abiff and he swallowed, trying to ease his dry mouth.

The voice continued. '... whither our Master Hiram Abiff had retired to pay his adoration to the Most High, as was his wonted custom at the High Twelve.'

George jumped at the funereal beat of twelve slow strikes on a gong.

'His devotions being ended he attempted to return by the south door.'

George was ushered into place.

'Here he was accosted,' the shadows on the wall warned George as the upraised arm paused above his head, poised to kill. 'by the first of the conspirators who, for want of other weapon, had armed himself with a heavy plumb rule, and who, in a threatening manner, demanded from our Master the secrets of a Master Mason, warning him that death was the consequence of a refusal.

Our Master, true to his obligation, intimated that diligence and patience would in due time entitle the Fellow Craftsman to these secrets but as for himself he would rather suffer death than betray the sacred trust reposed in him.

This answer not proving satisfactory, the ruffian aimed a blow at the head of our Master...' George stood stock still although he flinched inwardly as the small leaden bullet swung near his head '...but, being startled by the firmness of his demeanour, he missed his forehead, and the weapon glanced with such force on his right temple...' the Worshipful Junior Warden touched George's temple with the plumb rule... 'as to cause him to kneel and sink to the ground on his left knee.'

George knelt, the first 'villain' withdrew and George repeated his walk to the north, where he was 'attacked' with a level, which was then applied to his left temple, and finally to the east.

'There the third ruffian was posted, who received a similar reply to his insolent demand (for even at that trying moment our Master remained firm and unshaken), and thereupon the villain, who was armed with a heavy maul, struck him a violent blow on the forehead...' the Right Worshipful Master touched George's forehead with the maul '... which laid him low at his feet.'

George was turned around to face the inner circle again and the shock hit him as the flickering candlelight challenged his senses. In front of him was a skeleton, lying in a grave, and he was being motioned to lie down beside it, to play dead.

His mind raced, converting what he saw into what was possible and as he slowly forced his limbs to the ground, he felt the flannel of the blanket, which created the illusion of a dark hole, and he lay on his side of the double bed, with death beside him.

The Brothers made a silent circle round his 'grave', with office-bearers making a symbolic triangle inside that circle. For an eternity, George was left to imagine his own death and his brotherhood with the white bones beside him.

The candlelight played over the stones, raising ghostly knights. The crypt had once been the basement of the Auberge d'Allemagne, and it was as if those ancient voices broke the silence and spoke to him personally, calling him to join the Hospitaller Knights. His imagination conjured up the first Grand Master of the Knights of Malta, Philippe Villiers de l'Isle Adam and to George it was as if he spoke those first words of the ceremony, from Ecclesiastes, and never had George heard the words of the bible with such intensity of understanding.

'... because man goeth to his long home, and the mourners go about the streets.

Or ever the silver cord be loosed, or the golden bowl be broken, or the pitcher be broken at the fountain, or the wheel be broken at the cistern.

Then shall the dust return to the earth as it was; and the spirit shall return to God who gave it.

Vanity of vanities, saith the preacher; *all is vanity.*'

Words floated over George as he lay in his 'grave'. 'This

I hope will make a lasting impression on his and our minds, and conduce to an equal fidelity and steadfastness should we ever be placed in circumstances of a similar trial.'

The two failed attempts to raise Hiram Abiff were imitated as first the Junior, then the Senior Warden used the pass-grips of the first two degrees and then finally the Right Worshipful Master, following in the steps of King Solomon, used the grip of the Lion to raise George, with the pass-word pronounced syllable by syllable, with George taking his turn.

'It is thus, my Brother, that all Master masons are raised from a false death to a higher life and a fuller knowledge of the teachings of our mysteries. Let the emblems of mortality which lie before you lead you to contemplate your inevitable destiny, and guide your reflections to that most interesting of all human studies, the inner meaning of life, the knowledge of yourself. Be careful to perform your allotted task while it is day for the night cometh when no man can work; continue to listen to the voice of nature, which bears witness that even in this perishable frame resides a holy confidence that the Lord of Life will enable us to trample the king of terrors beneath our feet and lift our eyes to that bright Morning Star of Hope...' the candle was lifted high and others lit to brighten the crypt '...whose rising in the human breast brings peace and consolation to the faithful and obedient among men.'

George's apron was now presented to him in full ceremony. The pure white lambskin with its tartan edging and flap had been decorated with two rosettes, when he became a Fellow Craftsman and it now had the gilt tassels and the Gimel – the letter G – between the compasses 'which typify the spiritual part of man' and which showed that George was now a Master Mason. George felt absurdly pleased at the sight of that initial G – his initial G – on his apron.

The story of Hiram Assib was then completed in detail

and George heard in full what he had read beforehand, guessing the blanks where secret words would become clear to him during the ceremony. He heard of the acacia twig planted by Hiram Assib's grave by the Brother who found the recently buried body and he heard the substituted secrets with which they tried to awake the corpse and which were part of his arcane knowledge as a Master Mason.

He was taught the five signs of this degree, especially that of the Grand Hailing Sign of Distress, which would enable him to claim the utmost support of any Mason anywhere 'to the risk of his own life'. He was even shown the variations in this necessary to be understood by a Brother from an English or European Lodge.

If George saw any anomaly between use of this appeal and the injunction to consider himself 'strictly on the level' with all his Brethren, he certainly did not comment. As a Master Mason he had also gained the right to recommend a man to the Fraternity and he was given a list of considerations that he should take into account before making such a recommendation.

'I now present you with the working tools of a Master Mason which are the String, the Pencil and the Compasses.' As George accepted the tools and listened to their symbolic importance, and then the ritual dialogue to close the Lodge, he felt rather pleased with himself but refreshment was definitely long overdue.

George need not have worried as to what he might say about his ordeal in the dark. He had known beforehand that the tracing board showed a coffin and he had been prepared for the idea of such play-acting but it had been more than that. A flickering candle had blurred more boundaries than George cared to think about. Luckily, this seemed to apply to his Brothers too and they turned with relief to the much safer topics of starvation and surrender.

St Anne St, Floriana, showing the lion fountain (top right)
that was destroyed in bombing 28.4.1942

Carnival, Valletta

Porta Reale, Valletta

Men collecting seaweed to fertilise the fields

Chapter 22.

Even the best human persons have their defects and limitations; and to these, if they happen to be dead, must be added the defects and limitations of their biographers. Thus, according to his very inadequate biography, Jesus of Nazareth was never preoccupied with philosophy, art, music or science, and ignored almost completely the problems of politics, economics and sexual relations. It is also recorded of him that he blasted a fig-tree for not bearing fruit out of season, that he scourged the shop-keepers in the temple precincts and caused a herd of swine to drown. Scrupulous devotion to and imitation of the person of Jesus have resulted only too frequently in a fatal tendency, on the part of earnest Christians, to despise artistic creation and philosophic thought; to disparage the enquiring intelligence, to evade all long-range, large-scale problems of politics and economics, and to believe themselves justified in displaying anger, or, as they would doubtless prefer to call it, 'righteous indignation'.
Ends and Means

George could no longer pretend that the sallow tinge to his skin was imaginary; the mirror showed the tell-tale yellowing of his irises and he sighed, went to see the Medical Officer and accepted the diagnosis he had already made. It could have been worse. The way things were on Malta, it could have been a lot worse.

In hospital 4.12.42
Came in last Saturday with jaundice – and I go out on
<u>Tuesday</u> – exactly 10 days – not bad at all for jaundice. The
disease on this island has reached a horrible state . Several of
our own lads had been boarded with T.B. The following is a
list of the usual – and on the increase – typhoid, meningitis,
malaria, diphtheria, jaundice, T.B., Venereal Disease,
dysentery (we lost a Major with it!), Rheumatism as well as the
usual and unusual skin diseases, sandfly fever, Malta fever,
and battle and other casualties. In fact, we don't miss much.

Since I wrote last we have managed to sneak in two convoys,
each of 4 ships, which has certainly raised morale on the island
although no material evidence is yet forthcoming. Still! we
should at least get a decent Xmas dinner.

6.12.42

The latest 'arrival' on the island is infantile paralysis and the
one iron lung at the 45th is in commission.

It was one thing to face death in a masonic ritual; it was
quite another to contemplate the ways of dying currently
on offer in Malta as a consequence of starvation, appalling
sanitation and lack of hospital resources. George's medical
knowledge was too detailed for his own good, leaving him
unable to watch someone cough in the street without
looking for the wasting symptoms of TB.

He knew that a bowel upset could become fatal
dysentery for a body lacking any defences; and that
sneezing and shivering suggestive of flu might be the start
of infantile paralysis, otherwise known as poliomyelitis.
This disease particularly affected babies and children who
were recovering from fevers but it was not too
discriminating to attack adults, especially those weakened
by other illnesses – or lack of food.

After giving the worst symptoms of flu, the polio virus

would attack the nervous system, particularly the vulnerable spinal cord, and would often causing paralysis of a limb or limbs which would then be permanently wasted – if the patient recovered. The usual cause of death from polio was respiratory failure, a result of paralysis of the intercostal muscles and diaphragm, and which could usually be prevented by the artificial aid of a respirator or iron lung.

This capsule, looking like Captain Nemo's submarine, left only your head outside its artificial support and breathed for you, keeping you alive. This was all very well if you recovered your ability to breathe independently but polio sometimes deprived you of that too so that your entire life would be contained within an iron lung.

With only one iron lung on the entire island, this particular scenario was unlikely to cause anyone a problem but it was a problem that there was an epidemic of the highly infectious polio virus, a likely death rate of 10% of those infected, and that this was an island under siege. George was no longer afraid of death but he was petrified of polio paralysis. Perhaps it would go away.

27.12.42

As you see – the gaps in my writing are horrible, still, I'll try and fill them in a bit.

On the 6th Dec I left hospital – after a stop of only ten days. Since then I have been eating my own meals and half of Jock Wallace's as well.

Convoys – 2's and 4's have been slipping in all this month and now (about 30 in altogether) the food position is no longer critical – and the scale of issue on some commodities has been raised. Sugar is now 3ozs – the highest for two years. On the whole though – the position is unchanged.

No meals available outside – very little of anything in shops – only 10 cigs per week from the NAAFI – 3 bottles brew per fortnight (up now!) – milk on the black market is 15 shillings a tin – potatoes £12 for half a bag. – paraffin 25 shillings a gallon – bread 7/6 a loaf – eggs 30 shillings a dozen – cigs 2/6 for 10 – whisky £5 a bottle – flour £36 a bag – sugar 7/6 a pound – many other things you can't get at any price but can only be swopped – e.g. cigs for milk, bully beef for potatoes – mostly, food one person has, that another hasn't.

As you realise, the main topic on the island for months has been (and still is) – food. The 'Target date' by the way was Dec 15th i.e. the date at which the island could no longer be fed. (We still had 10 days rations in reserve.) We only just made it – supplies were being delivered straight from the ships to units for immediate consumption!

The morale on the island is O.K. at present. With the good news from Libya and the convoys slowly slipping in, everything seems to be under control.

Well! That about brings me to Xmas – The Civvies had three slices of bully beef (cold) with peas. I must say that we dined very well. All food was excellently cooked – and the general remark was that each one wished that those at home in England were having as good a meal.

6.45 Tea
7.30 Porridge with milk (oatmeal tinned – milk tinned)
Scrambled eggs (egg powder)
Bacon – fried sausage (Tinned)
Pork roll
Bread and butter – marmalade
Tea or coffee
1.00 Soup, Croutons, Steak and Kidney Pudding
Turkey, roast Potatoes, cream Potatoes
Cauliflower Cabbage
Xmas pudding – brandy sauce
Custard Jam tarts
Biscuits and Cheese. Beer. Cigs. Tea

5.00 Luncheon meat. Fruit and custard
Bread, butter, jam, chocolate, tea
Sweet biscuits
7.30 Sausage rolls, bread, cheese
Cocoa

What was it about a slap-up meal that turned George into a five-year-old? To the others' amazement, he recited,
'A wonderful bird is the pelican
For its beak can hold more than its belly can.'
and he then promptly demonstrated the problems of bigger beaks than bellies, being one of the first, but by no mean the last, to exit, looking green.

Needless to say it has upset practically all of us. After living on a meagre diet all these years — a healthy diet of good food brings us 'out in a rush' — It will probably be months after this war finishes before I get used to decent food again. Last week's joke was about a lad Petts — he flew to Egypt for an OCTU Course — and went in hospital next day. He had no sooner got there than he ordered steak, eggs and chips — his stomach just couldn't take it!!

Last <u>Tuesday,</u> we entertained the Corporals in the mess — the main trouble being that it cost the mess members 16 shillings each — and of course all the Cpls were unfit for duty next day.

Now for a brief account of my hectic !! Xmas. Were very busy at beginning of week getting things cleared up. Just made it by <u>Thursday</u> — at dinner time. Quartermaster Sergeant Greaves and the Regimental Sergeant Major left after lunch for Shema — I pottered about cleaning myself up — had tea — pottered about store until 7.30 — went to the pictures alone — went to Naxxar after pictures — talked to Jock Wallace (on duty!) until 1.45 — walked to Gargur — went to Barrack room — all our lads incapable — went to bed. 20.00 hrs

Friday (Xmas Day)

Up at 6am. Served tea at Naxxar to troops in bed!! – Back to stores – to barrack room at 11.30 for a drink – then to Mess at 12 for C.O's inspection. On guard at stores from 12.45 till 2. Then went to Naxxar for lunch – back at 3.30 – had tea at 5 – mooned about alone till 7.30 – went to pictures but unfortunately – none! Went back – to bed!

Saturday 26.12.42

Another blank day – Gerry out – playing hockey afternoon – dance at night and drinking all night and all morning. Went to pictures alone at 7.30.
10.00 – to bed.

Sunday 27.12.42

Never in all my life have I felt so lonely. – I've lived and slept alone now for nearly two years – but this Xmas has been the worst three days I've ever had to endure. I understand why people talk to themselves.

Monday 28.12.42

Work again – thank goodness! Something to occupy my mind.. Just the usual routine.

The usual routine included a certain pressure in a handshake to which George responded, exchanging the password in syllables. The new contact had been very cautious, using the extra verification, 'How old is your mother?' and only after George's quiet reply of '966,' did he get to business.

'Jim McConnell, Caledonian Arch Chapter,' he clarified. 'A St Andrew's brother mentioned your name, said you were a good man, quick and shooting up the degrees like greased lightning. The thing is, George, we're damned short of men, lost a few good ones and you never know when someone's going to be sent to Timbuktu or wherever. We'll be looking for officer-bearers in October and it's not too soon to look around.' George's face must have shown his feelings because the man added hastily, 'I mean, for all we know you'll be on the boat in the spring… back home with the girl, all that… you and me both.'

George faced it. 'But if we're not?'

'Then you work up another degree and you'll be welcome in both Lodges, I can tell you.'

'Mark Master?' George, still glowing in his title of 'Master', contemplated yet another step up.

'Nothing to it. The Third Degree's the hardest, you know. All that spooky stuff, bit chilling.'

George was grateful that only looks were exchanged. It wasn't something he wanted to talk about it.

McConnell continued, 'No, the Mark Master ceremony is a doddle, even though I shouldn't say so. Repeats bits of the others, gives you a new pass-word, pass-grip, token, the usual sort of thing.'

'Aye and a free lecture, no doubt.'

'All part of it, man. And you'll need to choose a mark, of course. Got a pen and paper?'

George passed him the pen which was tied with a bit of string to the order book, and took a bit longer to find a scrap of paper, which was even scarcer. 'This is the sort of thing they're after.' McConnell outlined a little monogram composed of three initials, then scribbled over it. 'Not my real mark of course.'

'No, of course.'

'They'll put you up for it, next Lodge meeting.'

'Caledonian?'

'No, your usual… we don't meet as often and you'll find we're a cut above, when you do come to us…but you get your raise first. Glad that's settled. Good man.' George received a hearty slap across the shoulders to which there was no ritual response so he just smiled.

'Uniforms?' he queried, continuing with McConnell's requisition.

Wednesday 30.12.42
Moved ration store for the 5001 time. All the staff cheesed off at being worked so hard! Especially that _____ man Jackson!

Since Archie Pitt had been moved from stores to hospital duties, George had only seen him at Lodge meetings, and there was no chance of his company over Christmas as Mrs Pitt was still with him, still waiting to get off the island. No, there was only one likely pal for a New Year's Eve on the town so George went looking for Jock Wallace. There was no way George's New Year would start the way his Christmas had finished.

Five hundred Scotsmen felt the same way, or so it seemed to George and Jock when they reached the Gut. Valletta's welcome to servicemen had never been so stretched and Straight Street throbbed with singing, laughter, feet stamping and every musical instrument that could be mustered by the locals and the servicemen wailing into the night.

Tin whistles competed with some local form of bagpipe and the lilt of an accordion tipped George's heart sideways, with its reminder of his brother playing dance tunes on the keyboard and his father' disapproval. The likeness quickly vanished as George listened. This one lacked the reel rhythms of home, something Italian in the phrasing, a different note to the keys – David would have known whether the difference was in the player or the instrument. George shook off the nostalgia. He had not come out to muse wistfully on home; he had come out to seek oblivion.

'Come on, George!' Jock was already going in, heading straight through whirling bodies to the bar and ordering the beer, while George still hesitated on the threshold. 'George!' He stepped over, looking for Violet, looking for booze and looking for trouble.

'Cheers!'

George sank a couple of beers quickly, then started asking a few men he recognised whether they had seen that girl who used to come here. A few girls were pointed out to him as they shook their arms and skirts in some movements that passed for dancing, something which George avoided whenever possible, even in its more recognisable form. Then, one of the girls stopped near him, wiped the sweat from her brow, took a long swig of some fizzy drink and he recognised the friend Violet had been with, the first time George met her.

'You want to dance?' He had obviously been looking at her for too long.

'No, no... we met a long time ago.'

'Heard that one before too.' She gave an artificial giggle.

'No, honestly, I danced with your friend... and I was just wondering what she was doing now... Violet, that is?'

'What? You'll have to speak up. Can't hear a thing in this bloody racket.' There was now some enthusiastic accompaniment of the songs by men who made up the lyrics they couldn't remember. At least, George didn't remember 'in with some luck' in the original and he was not going to speculate on how the rhyming line would go. Emma, that was it, Emma.

'Emma,' he pronounced with triumph, catching her attention and repeating his enquiry.

'You're out of luck there,' Emma told him just as George winced at the predictable rhyming line clearly audible from the next table. Emma didn't seem worried. 'She was took home ill, coughing and all. Rumour is though,' she lowered her voice, 'she went to Bletchley Park but don't say I told you.'

'So she's gone.' Some sort of sanatorium, George assumed. He tested the depth of his disappointment and found it wanted another beer. He waved Emma off as she returned to the dance floor and he elbowed his way back to Jock and the bar.

'Spoof!' he was greeted. 'Are you better?' Jock had obviously been gossiping with the men who'd gathered round him, some R.A.M.C. drinking companions, some R.I.F., a submarine gang George recognised and some of their navy pals. The group was growing, despite the numbers splintering off to visit the hall opposite where the dance was in full swing.

'Does he look yellow?' George was subjected to inspection.

'What, like Malta beer?'

'No, like cat's piss.'

'Same thing.'

Another group of men was jostling for position and one turned towards George and sneered, 'Yellow, eh?'

His mate passed a curious glance at George's gang, asking, 'The greasy classes bothering you?'

'Being yellow bothers me. Chap could die in the blue relying on these monkeys. Hardly toilet-trained never mind technically.' He dismissed them, turning his back just as a submariner pushed past George to take him up on his comments. George made slightly slurred, vaguely calming comments on the lines of 'Forget it, Davey...can't help it, know what RAF stands for? Right Arrogant Fuckers...two months on Malta wears them out and they're off back to Mummy' and it might have been Jock who prodded the pilot in the back shouting, 'What's the difference between the Luftwaffe and the RAF? Only the vowels...' (with a posh accent and a quick punchline) '...Fokkers on one side...' or it might even have been the less subtle 'Having a difficult war, hen?' in broad Glaswegian.

Whoever threw the first punch lit a match across the entire room. Everyone tried to dispose of their beer as quickly as possible, the more determined downing beers in one, the others emptying them over their neighbours. Some with seats kicked them aside as they swung a hopeful fist; others picked them up speculatively and for the first time, outside the pictures, George saw stools smashed against walls and chair legs meeting heads.

The general tactic seemed to be to scream like a berserker, swing arms from side to side and make a fist whenever there was any chance of making contact with the enemy. Jock lowered his head and cheerfully butted a moustachioed neighbour, roaring like an Aberdeen Angus in the mating season. What could George do but join in?

The first crunch of human bone against his knuckle, hurt. You should see the other man George grinned to himself as he rubbed his right hand and waded in again, ducking a flying glass only to take a full punch in his left side.

A few minutes doubled up and then some chemical that really ought to be sold in bottles injected his body with sheer energy, focused entirely on the need to thump, and preferably avoid being thumped, but the latter no longer seemed important as George felt the softer response of muscle against his fist.

A bit of pushing and kicking added some variety, and, although organised teamwork was beyond them, there was the odd, 'To you, Spoof' as someone tripped an RAF man and George caught him – with a very satisfying crunch on the jaw. That was the one he would replay in his dreams. 'It's a goal,' he yelled, cavorting around a couple of fallen bodies, which he might accidentally have trodden on.

That one's for making up to Nettie and that's for Kesselring, Rommel, Himmler and that – he really put his back into it – *that's for Mr Hitler – and that's for every RAF snob – and that's for being English, you Sassenach...* so it went on.

Other men were lying down, falling over or just running out of steam long before George had run out of things to hit out at. As things came to a natural conclusion, slowing and leaving fewer and fewer men who had not stumbled off into the street, George was punching more air and fewer people, and suddenly his head hurt.

He could recognise people again, by name rather than by

'Hit/Don't hit,' and his body was just starting the dull throb that predicted spectacular bruises on their way.

Jock was stumbling towards him and the two instinctively felt it was time to leave, before there was any chance of the Military Police counting the costs and expecting some poor soldier to contribute to the clear-up fund.

Jock knocked against the door-frame. 'Ow.'

Satisfaction was a warm purr inside George's aching body. His grin was a little lop-sided – someone had caught the side of his mouth and he licked the iron taste of blood. 'Worth it.'

'I'll say.'

'We showed them.'

George shouted out across the remnants of Valletta's bombed buildings, 'Happy New Year.' A sheet of paper advertising cheap beds answered their prayers and 1942 was over.

Thursday 31.12.42

Went to St Andrews to get typewriter fixed, pleasant forenoon jaunt. Knocked off work dinner time. Cleared up – went for tea and left with Jock Wallace for Valletta. Half promised to visit the R.S.M. after midnight. Went to pictures first, then down S. St. (where we found some beer!) Then proceeded to Vernon's where there was the best fight I ever saw. In one hall there was a dance and in the other was just hundreds of drunken humanity. I didn't know there were so many Scotsmen on the island.

Anyway, it finished by the Navy and Army combined operations routing the aggressors – the Air Force – the _____ toffy-nosed blighters.

We wandered all over the place then looking for someplace to lay our heads – very luckily we found two beds in Straight. St. We both slept with our clothes on and greatcoat on top (prevention and cure of scabies! not because we were incapable!)

Up at 6 and caught 6.30 bus back to Naxxar and walked to Gargur. Spent a quiet forenoon. Left after dinner and cycled to Villa Blye. back at 7 o'clock. Went to the Officers' Mess for the evening at 8. Very pleasant. I won the dice championship and a prize of 10 cigs. I also flung a wicked dart and didn't half shake them.

Only Mac let the side down – the _____ fool finished by tipping his drinks in ashtrays or anything he could find! And he nearly got shot by a sentry on the way back.

Just a whisper as long as I remember – the Quarter Master Sergeant is carrying on a red hot romance with the R.I.F.s seamstress at every opportunity.

It had been such a long time since George had carried on a red hot romance; he kept writing letters and hoped that they would reach Nettie. He didn't wonder what would have happened if Violet had been there the night before.

Private George Taylor, aged 21, at the start of the war

George, aged 24, after three years of war on Malta

George with his red crss (medical personnel) arm-band, sitting on a rock
with Mtarfa and its famous clock-tower behind him

George and two different friends, one also RAMC. They must have taken
turns with the camera, ordinary young men taking snaps.
Maybe one was 'Lofty'.

George's Master Mason Certificate.

Chapter 23.

'The sacrifice of the Intellect' is the third and highest grade of obedience, particularly pleasing to God. the inferior must not only submit his will to that of the superior; he must also submit his intellect and judgement, must think the superior's thoughts and not his own… Such passive obedience is incompatible with genuine non-attachment.
Ends and Means

George could still not believe that he had exchanged the pass grip and password of a Master Mason with a total stranger. After his conversation with McConnell, he doodled variations of his initials on the rock, in the dust on a wall, on a scrap of paper whenever he was alone. He finally came up with a design he was happy with and he traced it in the sand.

The next Lodge meeting was on 22nd January and George making his mark was definitely on the agenda. No doubt, the Mark secretary would be able to expound on the rectitude of the angles, the importance of staying on the square and being straight with your Brothers but George just found the design aesthetically pleasing. He liked the straight lines and the interlinking of the three letters.

He added J M G underneath and drew a quick heart with an arrow around his collection of initials, then scrubbed it out, unwilling to leave it for the tide to wash away his hopes along with his cigarette stub.

Saturday 2.1.43
Spent the morning at work – quite a change really. Yesterday I received a letter from home so I sent off two cables and spent the rest of the day writing letters.

There is still talk that all schools, picture-houses and churches are to be closed down as infantile paralysis is now becoming serious.

Sunday 3.1.43
Usual forenoon's work. I went to lectures in the afternoon – and paid a visit to Bonnici.

Wonders will never cease – I actually saw – and ate two bananas – Heard today that there are now 270 cases of 'Poly' on the island.

Monday 4.1.43
Just a note – it is now 10 months since we had fresh meat – in fact all we have had fresh is a few tomatoes.

Wednesday 6.1.43
Another day nearer.

Thursday 7.1.43
Another day nearer what?

Friday 8.1.43
Have worked till bed-time every day this week – feeling tired and browned off.

Saturday 9.1.43

Well! All pictures, shops, churches, tombola, schools, etc. etc are out of bounds – all closed. The epidemic is now well under way.

Sleeping tail and toe or head or something. No congregating in groups. I prefer bombs to this! – Hardships! – You don't know what hardships are!!

One of our Corporals went in Hospital last <u>Monday</u> with it – he is 27 too!

About 500 tons of parcels have arrived on the island and they are opening up every one <u>and charging tax on them</u>!! It's a _____ disgrace!! Someday we will wreck this joint – already 'They' know that we've got to be relieved – or else!

And on top of this Roosevelt says this morning that the war will be over by 1944 – Do you think that cheers us up much! We won't live till then on this island at this rate.

Last but not least, we have had our first NAAFI issue in <u>months</u>:

1 tube toothpaste, 1 shaving. stick, 2 razor blades, 2 bars chocolate, 30 cigs and 1 cake soap which ought to keep us human for a fortnight.

Sunday 10.1.43

The paper today published one fact worthy of note – we have been existing on half rations for eight months.

On these I work a steady twelve hours a day, seven days a week if necessary. A convoy arrived last month which took a fortnight to load, and the army have unloaded it in 5½ days. It's funny just how much humans can stand – and yet in other cases – the slightest thing – and finish!

A sad thing happened though – one of our own subs torpedoed an Italian ship. Four men escaped through the torpedo hole and were picked up and brought to Malta.

800 British prisoners went down with the ship.

Monday 11.1.43

Staff Sergeant Mears received <u>15</u> parcels today and has now more goods than all the NAAFIs on the Island. I never saw such a mixture!

Extracts from daily paper: 7000 marriages of Sussex girls to Canadian soldiers results in 3000 babies – very cheering!! What ?!!

'A film 'Malta George Cross' is to be shown in London – depicts life on Malta during 2 ½ years blitz.' Remarks by G.S.T. – I don't think!

Still no pictures, no meetings, no schools, no churches – no nothing. What a _____ of a life.

Tuesday 21:1: 43

By the way – I was Warrant Substitute Sergeant last Wednesday – I'm expecting the Court Martial any minute.

Wednesday 22.1.43

Cheesed off. Just all the little things getting me annoyed. The final one just before lunch was – 'How long will it take you to wash 2,000 blankets.' Honestly, I am expected to supply anything from a peanut to a panda and know more answers than that. In fact I'm going to stop talking about it because it just makes me worse. It isn't good for my sunny disposition!

January 22nd brought George promotion, not the coveted R.A.M.C. commission – nor any prospect of it – but respect of a different kind. Word-perfect and mark perfect, he observed for the first time as the Lodge of St Andrew was raised to the Third Degree.

Last time, he had been outside the blanket (for they were still meeting in the crypt of the Cathedral), but then he had not been a Master Mason. Now he joined in automatically, knowing when to stand, when to speak, as the Lodge was reduced to the Second Degree, but with only Master

Masons present, for George to become the focus of attention once more.

While George waited yet again outside the Lodge, he knew from his little green book, which he had carefully indexed with strips of sticking plaster, the formulae that were duly expressed.

The Junior Warden would be speaking of his duties to observe the sun at High Twelve, to call the Brethren, to beware of and punish impostors; and the Worshipful Master of his duty to observe the setting sun, to pay the Master Mark Masons their wages and to close the Lodge.

George could have wished that the pay were not symbolic. His intentions to save hard for his marriage had suffered more irreversibly in Vernon's than had his knuckles.

Once the Inner Guard had given the proper knocks with the mallet, George was told, 'In the name of the Great Originator of The Universe, enter this Lodge of Master Mark Masons on the edge of the compasses, an instrument which demonstrates the moral advantages of discipline and education, by which means alone you can become a fit member of regularly organised society.'

George demonstrated his knowledge of the grips and passwords of the Third Degree, then made his mark carefully on a small card and presented this to the Registrar to be entered in the Lodge 'Book of Marks'. George had been too careful so there was a slight shake in the first line of the 'G'. He should have remembered that the bolder the freehand line, the better. No doubt the Right Worshipful Master could extemporise on that theme if he were allowed to; thank the Great Architect of the Universe that every word of the ritual was prescribed and any change to Lodge procedures absolutely forbidden or it would take all day. George took the card to the Master for approval and was told to present himself at the Senior Warden's wicket to receive his wages.

The token George had been given, another card with the

Mark Registrar's own mark on it, now had to be handed over. After that, George was instructed in the steps of the Mark degree and he made his Obligation, in which he promised to 'receive a Brother's mark when presented to ask a favour and to grant his request when just and lawful' so long as it was in George's power to do so 'without detriment' to himself or his family. Then the dramatic element of the ritual began.

George had once more withdrawn and been prepared as usual but this time he was also given a stone. He then took on the part of a mason of King Solomon, waiting his turn while the previous two masons had their stones, one square, one oblong, accepted by the re-named Junior Overseer.

George's stone was duly rejected but referred to the Master Overseer because of 'the beauty of its workmanship' and, truly, there was a beauty to the old stone polished and engraved by some real stone-worker who knew how many years ago, donated to the Lodge for this celebration of stone.

'Your work is rejected.' This far, the ritual struck George as only too much like a typical working day. The Brothers moved about the Lodge, shuffling their feet.

'What is the meaning of this confusion?'

'Right Worshipful Mark Master, it is the sixth hour of the sixth day of the week and the Brethren are impatient to receive their wages.'

'Every faithful labourer is worthy of his hire.'

The Brothers then moved in procession to the Senior Warden's 'wicket' where each Mark Master Mason put his hand in, using the correct approach for that degree, until George of course, who put his hand in as a Fellow Craftsman.

The offending hand was seized by the Senior Warden who exclaimed, 'An imposter! An imposter! Off with his head!'

George remained poker faced while the others mimed

indignation, more or less successfully. The deacons vouched for George being a good Craftsman and finally the crux of the ceremony was reached.

'What is the cause of this cessation of work?' asked the Master.

'For want of a Key Stone for the arch of the Sacred Vault of King Solomon's Temple,' was the Senior Warden's reply.

George then had to search for his rejected stone, present it once more – this time successfully – and receive the secret password and four signs of the Mark Master Mason. The last sign imitated the actions of the original Fellow Craftsman when he saw that Hasim Abif had used his stone, with his Mark on it, as the Key Stone, and he cried, 'Thanks be to God I have my wish.'

George had little time to wonder when he might feel the urge to clasp his hands together, roll his eyes and cry these words aloud. He felt it more likely that he would be shooting his arms in the air and lowering them in three clear stages in the Grand Hailing Signal of Distress – or using its verbal equivalent, 'Is there anyone who can help a poor widow's son?'

Still, as his Granny used to say, you never knew when something might come in handy. He accepted the mallet and chisel, the tools of the mark degree, and a 'jewel', a small brooch with a mallet on it, and it was done.

The Lodge was reduced to the First Degree, all brothers returned to the Lodge and they discussed the latest request for aid to the family of a distressed brother. It made distressing hearing as George heard the name of the Scotsman who had been a prisoner on the Italian warship sunk by a British submarine, the names not just of the man but of his wife and three children, still living in Stirling, a widow and her fatherless little ones. At least they would get some practical support from the Fraternity. In whom do we place our trust?

Wednesday 27.1.43

Still browned off. The intervening week has only been a matter of passing the time working eating and sleeping – pretty monotonous to say the least of it.

One ascorbic acid tablet is being dished out daily – at last!

In the past seven days Tripoli has fallen – which did cheer us up for about five minutes.

A Brigadier has arrived from M. E. to investigate the paralysis. He has also stated that all troops on this island are slightly mad. The Deputy Director of Medical Services is reputed to have said that he had ceased to be responsible for the health of the troops on the island and is pushing for the immediate relief of the island.

The 2ⁿᵈ Royal Inniskilling Fusiliers are certainly as mad as hatters – they're on another of their stunts at the minute. There won't be a fit man in the Unit by the end of the week. They came off convoy duty and were put straight on this stunt – all leave cancelled – so there will be the usual row.

This convoy coming in has apparently been pilfered to such an extent that it doesn't seem worth bringing it. Sergeant Majors, Sergeants, and right down the line are having Courts Martial by the score over it.

Well! That's all for today. Needless to say, I don't feel at all happy – I haven't even promotion to look forward to – the island is still static – a stagnant cesspit.

Sunday 31.1.43

Just another week past. Did Jury Duty on <u>Friday</u> – my first 'job'. Cigarettes appear to be back to 30 a week. All pictures etc. still closed. The NAAFI issue was as usual plus two handkerchiefs, of all things. No rumours or even hope of moving at present. Settling down for another summer here – and already have plans for next year – what a life! I think I have said this before but I repeat it – you get used to anything.

One thing there is to be thankful for – the weather. It's been a wonderful January. The difficulty is to get time to enjoy it. Yesterday I just forced myself out and spent the afternoon sunbathing. Today is even better – you would think a heat wave was on – and the glare of the sun hurts the eyes even now. I just can't think of suffering rain and snow after this. My winter dress is shirt and Battle Dress – and have worn my coat twice – groundsheet about six times.

Sunday 14.2.43

Just another week past and another week nearer. Tons of rumours floating about. Here are a couple of examples:
(1) A camp has been specially constructed at Reading and the Malta Garrison is going to be rested up there.
(2) American troops are relieving the island – and we're going to America to make a picture!!! There are dozens of these – but one thing I do know and that is that there are certainly big things in the air at the minute.

Well! The 'Poly' appears to be under control as schools, picture-houses, bars etc. re-open tomorrow – no children under 15 allowed though.

Food is considerably better – but we find that we can't eat now!!

It looks almost as if I'd have to live on bully and biscuits for the rest of my life!!

Today for instance I thought I'd try and have a decent day. Here is what I had. ONE <u>EGG</u> for breakfast with the issue breakfast of meatloaf (1oz). Eggs, by the way are almost museum pieces – I was lucky and got it for one and eight.

Lunch: <u>Steak</u> and <u>kidney pie</u> for which considerable scrounging was done. A small portion of rice pudding and then a small piece of Xmas pudding with white sauce (flour and water and whisky!)

<u>*Tea:*</u> *Meatloaf, cheese, jam tart, bread butter and jam and two pears.*

All I want to do now is go to a quiet corner and be sick.

I think there is a fair supply of food on the island now but they're not releasing it or we'd all be invalids.

We still get our daily tablet of Ascorbic Acid – 'Come and get your eggs and bacon' is the usual expression!

With regard to work – I've had a pretty rough week, got browned off early, and told too many people to go places, and where to put things. Still after being told one is aggressive and among other things that I resemble (1) a hedgehog (2) a mountain cat protecting its young – I've got to give them something to talk about.

I am sure that my salesmanship (if I ever had any) has suffered a severe setback as a direct result of my employment here. In fact I have been known to use the concise, pithy, forceful, direct expression consisting of two words beloved of QMs throughout the world, which are quite the antithesis of salesmanship.

Flask cookers are in full swing again. It's about the quickest way to make a place filthy I know.

All for this week and I may be home next week!!

Chapter 24.

At no period of the world's history has organised lying been practised so shamelessly or, thanks to modern technology, so efficiently or on so vast a scale as by the political and economic dictators of the present century.
Ends and Means

Sunday 21:2: 43
Well! That's my three years on this _____ island gone by. And I am wondering whether I will see another in here.

The food situation is now passable – we aren't starving anyway. The position as regards outside supplies is of course almost unchanged. Food can only be bought (on production of a pass) at three approved places in Valletta. This is a small improvement – typical of the present general trend of things.

A tunnelling Company actually arrived on the Island this week – they say that when at home they thought Malta was nothing – as they were at all the blitzed towns at home – now they are amazed and admit we have had a hundred times worse than anything at home. (And that's after we've been cleaning up for almost a year.)

There's another thing which is getting us mad at present – letters are being received which say that hundreds of men are on leave from Malta – why can't you get leave. The answer should be obvious – there are no men on <u>leave</u> from Malta. There are *only the men (very few and far between) who get home as unfit for further service.*

Had an egg for breakfast this morning — only 1/3 too! All for another week.

'Poly' has died a natural death in just over two months. The schools are open again — and the bars in bounds!

George's relief as the spectre of polio faded was as short-lived as his pleasure at getting two letters from Nettie. He had long ceased to consider the Censor when he wrote 'sweet nothings' in his letters to her but he had no option but to weigh every other word he wrote. How could this be 'correspondence' when there was so little he was allowed to say, when misunderstandings could not be cleared up, when she knew nothing and could say anything while he knew so much and could say none of *it?*

Saturday 27.2.43

I actually received two letters this week. One suggests I should like to see the CO to try and get home as I have a <u>strong case!</u> Do you mean to tell me that you think I can get home merely by asking the CO Look! If I could get home on any pretext whatsoever I would do so — I just can't. You remember me talking about Staff Sergeant. Johnson whose wife got in a spot of trouble — well! He applied for repatriation on compassionate grounds and got it? Yes? Like hell! He was put on a sub — taken to the Middle East and absorbed into the 8th Army.

I've got no grounds other than I've been away for three years.

There are several battalions on the island who were on their way home from India and Palestine when the war started who were dumped here. Most of them were time expired then — and none have been home inside eight years.

They are still here!

Then there are hundreds of genuine cases of applications on compassionate grounds which are turned down – cases of men whose homes have been blitzed – only the mother left with nobody to support her – men whose wives are still having babies – men whose businesses are collapsing. All turned down!

You can get home by aeroplane with two things – yes! 'Poly' and T.B. Although last week they sent a few patients with Dusty Miller in charge to the Mid-East on the 'Welshman' – she was torpedoed! – turned upside down. Miller's wife was notified he was 'missing'. However, he has turned up round about Tobruk.

I hear that any odd man who does get home from Malta is poked about for hours by Medical Officers – not allowed to inform his relatives he is home – pushed in hospital for three weeks and fattened up before being allowed out.

Tomorrow is by way of being a celebration. We have 6ozs of fresh meat for lunch! This is the first we've had for just over a year.

Well! It's been a very heavy week so far as work was concerned, varying from 12 to 16 hours a day. When I get back, if you ever try to tell me how difficult it is to run a house, I'll just suggest you try to feed and clothe 250 men spread over 20 different stations over half the island, equip these same stations with Ordnance and Medical Equipment, change and keep linen for 300 patients, issue fuel, soap, wicks, primuses, bicycles to these same stations – and then replace U.S. worn-out, lost, stolen – clothing and equipment – to ignore absolutely the red-tape, clerical and administrative side of the business. In our spare time we run MDS Gargur – the one and only underground MDS – complete with Operating Theatre. (1) It can possibly be seen that you can work 24 hours a day and just about keep things going. (2) All this is done by five men. In other words, I'm browned off as usual.

Just by the way – I noticed in one of your letters that you said *the food was rotten. Well! I can't. I mean I'm not <u>allowed</u> to.*

Here, you're not allowed to say such things but you can say, 'I'm enjoying myself immensely and the food is excellent.' Nor can you say, 'I'm browned off!' In fact the quickest way to be pulled in front of the CO is to <u>write</u> <u>the</u> <u>truth</u> <u>in</u> <u>a</u> <u>letter</u>. Our last Private, who told a little truth got 14 days for it. Well! That's about enough moaning for <u>this week</u>.

7.3.43

During the week 138 R.A.M.C. Other Ranks have arrived on the island and have been absorbed. We got 58 and a Staff Sergeant.

Otherwise not a great deal to report, just too much work. This appears to be the only efficient dept. in the unit – and unless we do a job it's hopeless.

Since last week things have got worse – I am now landed with (1) Unit Stores (2) MDS (3) Operating Theatre – in a disgusting state when I was forced to take it over as Lieutenant Dobbs signed for it (4) Disinfector (5) Have taken over Sergeants' Mess – also in a disgusting state.

Everybody's inefficiency seems to come our way for us to clean up. I know I'm browned off but after two years' work (which will probably cut years off my life) at this darned job, the fact that I still do a twelve hours stretch on <u>Sunday </u>is enough to brown anybody off. My ambition – and at least part solution to the problem – is to be able to turn work out effortlessly for 24 hours a day. This human frame limits me so much. There are hundreds of things I want to do and planned that I just never get to.

Writing is a thing that has long since dropped to the barest minimum. Everything comes in order of its importance – possibly unfortunately – work is first. And away down the list, almost so far as to be forgotten, comes health. I am not proud of it but merely state that I have had one bath in the past year.

Two more Sergeants at Imtarfa bumped this week. Our R.S.M. was threatened with bumping for inefficiency by the CO Rather nasty.

That's moaned another week away.

Sunday 14.3.43

Now! Let's see what happened this week. Received a letter containing photo of David – posted 17th Jan.

I am now Sergeants' Mess caterer – just add that to my previous list of responsibilities!!

On <u>Thursday</u> I attended a Field General Court Martial – R.I.F. – all polished up like a Xmas tree – was there from 9.30 until 5.40 when I was told my evidence wouldn't be required. Not a bite to eat or a drop to drink all that time. – Charge – cycles and butter and truck.

Yesterday I played football for the first time this year. Two results (1) Today I have decided that I am getting too old to play such games (2) I scored our only goal.

Further to my remarks re leave – R.A.M.C. ruling is now – men with <u>6 years' service and compassionate grounds</u> may be sent home accompanying patients – not much hope for me yet I'm afraid.

Mac went up to see Corporal White – he is completely in plaster and is third in priority for being flown home – his people at home have not yet been told. It's going to be a horrible shock.

Our Field Ambulance is definitely the only one of its kind in existence. We have just had added one complete company including Non-Commissioned Officers. We are now the heaviest, least mobile, most useless Field Ambulance in the world..

Everyone in billets – 20 stations – cooking on ranges – spring beds and mattresses for every man – one 30cwt Civvy truck as Store transport – an Officers' mess – a Sergeants' Mess (complete – separate buildings) Yearly – Use 10,000 gallons of paraffin, 5,000 lbs soap — 250 gallons Methylated Spirit, 500 gallons waste oil — And on and on and on. — There are few things you can name that I can't supply.

This is roughly what we hold:
Ordnance Equip:
Gen Equip — including complete range of linen for 300 patients
Curtains SF £600 alone.
Clothing: Enough to keep 300 men clothed
Survivors' Clothing
P.A.D. Equip.
Med Equip: (Including 1 complete Operating Theatre)
Red Cross Stores
Rations: Daily
Stewards' store for patients
Reserve 10 days — personnel
Reserve 10 days — 300 patients
I think I had better not write so much each week — or else I'll have to buy a new writing pad (which is still impossible by the way) before I get this home.
Played football today and scored the only goal — I was playing full back!
On Sunday afternoon went for a walk to Musta with Jack Reaves etc. and saw the church. Silly — isn't it! I was stationed there for a year and never was in the place.

If you said, 'Parish Church' to someone in Fife, he would imagine a squat building with a tower, maybe a stained glass window or two, and kneeling room for a hundred or so. He would never believe the scale of the Parish church in Mosta or 'Musta' as George called it. The famous dome could be seen for miles around and was supposed to be the third biggest in the world, after S. Sophia in Constantinople and S. Peter's in Rome, bigger by sixteen feet in diameter than St. Paul's in London.

George's only comparison was with St. Paul's and that after all was in London, where everything struck him as bigger and better, not in Mosta, a small village on a small island. The money for the Maltese architect had been scratched together in the nineteenth century by the villagers themselves, bringing eggs and vegetables amongst their donations until they could pay Grognet de Vasse for a design worthy of God. George had become so used to his surroundings that he had forgotten his first impressions of the island and its people. Now he remembered. Small wonder that they thanked their God for preserving – so far – this soaring act of worship carved in stone. With his finger, George traced his mark at the humble base of a pillar and paid his respects.

Monday 15.3.43
Usual 'orrible <u>Monday</u>!

Tuesday 16.3.43
Much as usual only the Sergeant Major elected to stay the night so we had a bit of a Mess 'do'.

Wednesday 17.3.43
'Pat's day.'

And what a day! Lord Gort inspected the Royal Inniskilling Fusiliers to start with and we were invited to their Mess in the evening. The only souvenir I have is a small piece of shamrock which I hope will eventually arrive home. Well! It was the longest session I have ever been on – from seven at night till three in the morning. Dance Band, Bagpipes etc, etc. – non-stop. A record was also set up as the RSM, QMS and myself drank 89 beers – and I've been trying to convince them ever since that I wasn't the one who drank only 29 – unfortunately they're two to one and they still insist I must have dodged one!

At three o'clock we walked – yes! – I said <u>walked</u>! the necessary ¾ mile to Gargur and so to bed.

On <u>Wednesday</u> afternoon previous to this effort I played two games of football – we won the first one 4-2 and lost the second 2-1 and then had a game of hockey.

Thursday 18.3.43

Is it to be wondered that I had a slight hangover – had as light a day as possible and went to bed at 8 as the R.I.F.s are giving us a return visit tomorrow.

I am still Mess caterer. Ours is the finest Sergeants' Mess I've ever been in.

Friday 19.3.43

A hectic day of preparation – with as much as possible done in the stores.

The Mess was really nice and then hostilities started at 7pm. I got rid of 12 dozen beer so fast I almost set my shoes on fire! The fun waxed fast and furious. One item was a song coupled up with a discarding of clothing – and the singer finished up naked in the middle of the floor, as happy as a sandboy.

The evening finished up quietly – no breakages!

Corporal White is still here – still in plaster – and he doesn't think that there's much chance of him getting off!!!

Sunday 18.4.43

I see I haven't put down a word for almost a month! It's funny how the time flies. As usual I've had too much work and have been considerably browned off. Received clothing and have equipped our new men. Sandfly curtains issued. Have requisitioned Gargur school.

Capt. Barber was on commando raid – now reported missing.

Gunnery practice going on every day. Received three letters including one with a photograph . Had my photograph taken *last <u>Tuesday</u>, was in bathing yesterday and this afternoon – quite comfortable – sun lovely and warm. Royal Engineers spent a night at our mess.*

I haven't done a stroke of work since yesterday at dinner time – If I don't get a rest I'll go mad. I <u>hope</u> (only hope though I'm afraid) that things keep a bit quieter so as I can keep myself clean and do a bit more writing.

You should see the gunnery practice – they can knock a sparrow off a wall! One Sergeant I spoke to has had 30 years' service – that's a long time!

Another week past – roll on tomorrow – every week's work brings me nearer getting home – I hope! Sa-ha!

Stone cutting by hand was a traditional Maltese craft. There was in fact a stone-cutting machine on the island, owned by the Strickland family, but it wasn't used so as not to antagonise the local workforce. On 28th August 1942 Lt Col Tanner Command Royal Engineers (North) discovered that the machine had been on the island for 12 years and put it to the work of building a new hospital, to replace one destroyed by bombs.

Chapter 25.

Traditional education is a training for life in a hierarchical, militaristic society, in which people are abjectly obedient to their superiors and inhuman to their inferiors. Each slave 'takes it out of' the slave below
Ends and Means

Saturday 1.5.43

Just as usual – all sorts of mad schemes – we are to make up equipment to take 450 patients – all personnel in tents. We have to post Englishmen to 161 – we get Maltese back. – The CO wants H1157s in duplicate for every man etc. etc.

The more I see of other messes, the more the following facts strike me –

(1) The average age of a senior NCO on this island is 40 – and average service 15-20 years.

(2) It is because of same experience that this island has pulled through.

(3) There is a colossal waste of manpower here at present – just imagine – I hear you are requiring officers at home still – and here are all these men who know the job from A to Z who can't even get promoted one step.

It's just the old, old, story I suppose – when you first arrive on Malta somebody's sure to say, 'Everything's different in Malta!'

And for the rest of your stay here you repeat that helplessly, realising all the time how true it is, and how futile it is to do anything about it. Just one among so many.

Very cheering news yesterday – I don't think!! Was informed officially that on completion of six years here they would <u>try</u> and get me home. If it wasn't so ridiculous I'd cry.

That's all today – still far from home and browned off. Oh! Joy! to be able to splash down on paper I'm browned off. If anybody ever censors this it's about goodnight for me.

By the way I told Uncle Bob and Aunt Nannie that I had had jaundice and some silly ass snipped it out!

5.5.43
Still browned off – too much work – no movement – just nothing.

I will just mention that we are now 15 Independent Brigade Group Field Ambulance R.A.M.C. and have now got static Medical Inspection Rooms and camp Reception Stations. An awful lot of plain mucking about!

Just been speaking to a QMS (Royal Engineers – 19 years' service) who flew to the Middle East on business. Says they don't know they're born – living in flats – never heard a gun or seen an enemy plane and promotion is colossal.

A remark was made in the mess tonight which just about sums it up. 'If Hitler only left the British Army alone they would kill each other for promotion.'

The whole trouble is of course that the men with the qualifications and service can't be promoted on the island and <u>can't</u> get off it. The most annoying thing of all though is to hear of someone you know to be a halfwit being an RSM or Lt in England or the Middle East.

To make matters worse the CO is a _____ If you just put in an application for anything, he puts it at the bottom of his tray and leaves it there – if you push, he just says, 'I can't recommend you,' and you're back where you started. The most I can say without being obscene is that he is a prig, a snob, a fool, an officer but no gentleman! I feel better after that! I'm back on the 'work hard and play hard' system with the result that I am now a fair exponent of the following:

Tennis, hockey, football, darts, solo, poker, poker dice, chess, draughts, cribbage, billiards, swimming, driving, boxing, cricket – in fact if this war lasts much longer I'll be a bit of an allround sportsman.

25.5.43

A few crazy new ideas since last time.

(1) Ten days leave in Tripoli. – <u>One</u> of <u>our</u> unit has gone – so if the war lasts ten years we'll each get ten days!!!

(2) 'Malta' – must never be written or mentioned in letters. No Maltese stamps etc. etc. We have two more units of our 'Gallant Allies' on the Island (1) Basutas (2) Mauritians. 'Senior' privates are leaving the island on trooping duties – this is another penalty of being a Senior NCO!! I would have been off the island by now had it not been for three silly tapes on my arm.

Malta is now definitely M.E.F. and promotions are on a roster basis.

This is worth recording though – I was up in a Beaufort torpedo-bomber on Sunday and didn't I have some fun. I was the rear-gunner and it's a good job I didn't see anything to shoot at or I would have shot half the plane away!

It's certainly more exciting than just to have a gun – (I've been on 3.7 positions and Bofors in action as I've probably reported before) – I know now why men stay in the air till it eventually gets them.

When we went up, we had 4 depth charges on and were looking for subs. Incidentally – no parachutes.

Sunday 6.5.43

This must be recorded while I remember it (half the things I forget you know!):

About 30 Senior NCOs and WOs put in for commissions (Special – age over 35) three months ago. – Yesterday they all arrived back 'Please submit on another form.'!! This is what is happening all the time – and the next step is to say all vacancies have been filled – yes! after M.E.F. Headquarters has sat on Malta's applications for three months!!!

Until the men are moved off the island, there is just no hope for me. I frankly admit they are better men than I – and also better than millions who are being promoted at home. There's just not enough room on this island and too many efficient men on it now.

However there is something coming off – this island is definitely offensive to a high degree – even old Eisenhower is on the island at the minute. All for now –

The 12th May saw AXIS surrender North Africa, allowing Allied commanders to increase the focus on Europe, including the plans for *Operation Husky*, the invasion of Sicily, which was to be launched from Malta. US troop convoys were heading across the Atlantic under the command of General Dwight D. Eisenhower, to join up with the Allied Navy under Admiral Sir Andrew Cunningham.

The wireless rang with morale-boosting speeches and praise for the troops who had defended Malta.

Eisenhower declared, 'Malta has passed successively through the stages of woeful unpreparedness, tenacious endurance, intensive preparation and the initiation of a fierce offensive. It is resolutely determined to maintain a rising crescendo of attack until the whole task is complete. For this inspiring example, the United Nations will forever be indebted to Field Marshall Lord Gort, the Fighting Services under his command and to every citizen of the heroic island.'

Grand Harbour filled with warships, submarines and landing ships of all kinds, such as the new US amphibian DUKWS, known inevitably as 'Ducks'. Naval stories were swopped as men waited for the 'off.' The one George liked the best was about the signalman on the minesweeper *Rye* who had a habit of 'correcting' signals before he sent them and who had been warned by his Lieutenant to send them exactly as received.

At some stage, the Commander had said, 'Make signal to Vice Admiral Malta. Sea trials completed.' At that point he was soaked through with spray and commented, 'Bloody awful weather,' before turning back to the Signalman and adding, 'Returning to harbour.'

The message received by the Vice Admiral read, 'Sea trials completed. Bloody awful weather. Returning to harbour.' For its role in towing the *Ohio* into harbour, *Rye* was one of the best known of the Malta Minesweeping Force, and it was also *Rye* which 'afraid for its chummy ship', rescued twelve survivors from the torpedoed minesweeper *Hythe*, and was greeted with a voice from the water, 'It's wee *Rye* – we knew you'd come.' *Rye*'s commanding officer, Lieutenant Pearson, was later awarded the Distinguished Service Cross for his gallantry and seamanship, while other members of the crew were awarded three Distinguished Service Medals and six mentions in Dispatches.

Once again, on June 20th, the Maltese lined the docks to watch the mine-sweepers herald the cruiser *Aurora*, on which King George VI paid the promised visit to praise his medal-winning island in person. The King's R.A.M.C. namesake was not at the dock, by choice, but the newspapers made the most of the visit.

The Telegraph and *the Times* (of England) eulogised, 'The King's visit seems to mark the recognition, by the Throne, of Malta as the symbol of the U.N.'s triumph and the coming liberation of Europe... Malta, lone speck, has been standing sentinel in the Mediterranean, flying the Union Jack and the red and white Maltese flag, fighting back, ever undaunted, 60 miles from AXIS territory, 1,000 miles from Gibraltar, and nearly as much again from Alexandria, for three and a half years. It was El Alamein that delivered Malta, but it was equally true that it was Malta that saved Egypt.'

Montgomery's prediction had come true and the General himself, wearing his famous beret, was also on Malta, in the new Headquarters at Valletta, preparing the 8th Army for their role in the invasion of Sicily.

Date of writing 27.6.43

In the interval Lieutenant Dean has left for England via the Cape. New Quarter Master has taken over. We have a 500 bedded R.S. and a 100 bedded RS and increased patients at other stations – fully equipped by 'Q'. Last Sunday four of us (Quarter Master Stores, myself and two sergeants) were standing talking on the road (goat track is nearer it – 8ft wide!) when who should pass but the King giving us a posh salute! It really amused me! I always said I wouldn't go to see him – he could come and see me and he did!

Today being Sunday we have all (Q staff) been recuperating – this being the first Sunday to be treated as a Sunday for a few weeks.

Staff Sergeant McPherson is off to M.E. this coming week – so that's another one away. (N.B. Address – c/o Dominion Bank, Canada)

News from home extremely poor. Nettie's address unknown. No answer to cable sent 16 days ago! Best correspondence at minute is with London – writing letters in answer at both ends.

Well! That's all the news in brief – very brief! Half the interesting things I forget when the time comes to write them down.

Still something brewing. Our Field Ambulance can now take

950 patients. Air and shipping movement is colossal – and there are empty camps (tented) all over the island.

Sa-ha.

There was indeed something brewing. Operation Husky hit Sicily on the 9th July, in stormy weather, with 2,590 US and British warships, and every form of small boat Malta could send. Many gliders were lost because of the weather but resistance from the Italian and German ground forces could not prevent the forward push from Syracuse into south-east Sicily and onwards.

17.7.43

It is now 17th July and since last writing I have been run over by a steam roller daily.

In the interval we have invaded Sicily. Ever since January, supplies of all descriptions have been piling up on the island – in dumps all over the island (in fields and quarries). Then about six weeks ago tents sprung up – also all over the island in mushroom fashion. Then the units began to arrive – 8th army – complete with equipment and transport. Two light Field Ambulances were included. They were only here a short time when 'the balloon went up'.

The administration for this do has been marvellous. Each soldier before leaving was given a booklet about Sicily – all information about the country being therein. Climate – sanitation diseases – cash to be used etc. etc. A branch here even prepared a <u>telephone directory</u> a week before they went over.

(I've had to change my ink for another brand)

Everything was merely a statement of fact!! As if it had already happened. Well! 15 Field Ambulance was supposed to pass <u>all</u> casualties through their hands. Hence our 500 bedded hospital.

So far it has only been the Quartermaster's nightmare as the total casualties since the invasion started has been 142 and the staff at S are all browned off as they have nothing to do.

QMS A. has just submitted his 5th application for a commission! In civvy street he was manager of insurance society and has done four years' army administration. All applications have been for administration and communications, and he still can't get there.

It has now been confirmed that the CO has *never* recommended <u>even one</u> man of this unit for promotion! I suppose you think that unbelievable – unfortunately it's true – and if you then think that there isn't one fit for promotion you must be crazy like the CO.

From a very bad start two years ago we are now the crack Medical Unit on the island, for the type of work on this island. 'Everything's different in Malta'.

The things which are turning my hair rapidly grey I seldom record. The daily madhouse existence.

I think I will record though that I don't intend to stay in the army. Promotion on a roster basis kills initiative and production of work. e.g. For three years I've worked hard without a break – result – three tapes. Now – I've had them a year and a half and know the job backwards – therefore I want to learn some more. But, unfortunately, it's no use me being able to take over a Quartermaster's duties as they'll post a QMS from M.E. to fill any vacancy. In a nutshell it means

(1) You get promoted if you are at the top of the roster irrespective of abilities.

(2) If the CO doesn't even recommend you – you have even less chance.

All tending to make you do as little as possible.

And when mummy's little boy becomes a lieutenant instead of being proud they ought to be ashamed – it's just another _____ fool that the NCOs on the unit have to carry. Particularly so in the R.A.M.C. where officers are doctors and know nothing at all of administration.

Well! I've had another good moan so I'll now proceed to recuperate.

P.S. Saw Staff Sergeant McPherson off on an invasion barge at 15.30 hrs 16/7/43 heading for Tripoli. The first parting I've had for some time – made me quite sad! Some of the lads I'd hate not to see again.

That's all.

Chapter 26.

When the destinies of whole nations are at stake, we do not hesitate to trust the direction of affairs to men of notoriously bad character; to men sodden with alcohol; to men so old and infirm that they can't do their work or even understand what it is about; to men without ability or even education. In practically every other sphere of activity we have accepted the principle that nobody may be admitted to hold responsible positions unless he can pass an examination, show a clean bill of health and produce satisfactory testimonials as to his moral character and even then the office is given, in most cases, only on the condition that its holder shall relinquish it as soon as he reaches the threshold of old age. By applying these rudimentary precautions to our politicians, we should be able to filter out of our public life a great deal of that self-satisfied stupidity, that authoritative senile incompetence, that downright dishonesty, which at present contaminates it.

Ends and Means

J *uly 43*
NO LETTER FROM NETTIE *since 27/5/43*
This must be recorded.

The 231 Brigade was the first on Sicily and have done excellently.

231 is ex-Malta garrison and all had a tough time manning airfields during the blitz. Have all been away from home 5-8 years. Consists of Devons, Dorsets and West Kents. We are all pleased they have done so well.

The R.I.F.s also left but have not yet gone into action – they're on the <u>next front</u>.

The troops on this island after three years defence are fighting mad. Still – most have moved now – exception – R.A.M.C..

Was talking to an American today – 23 – noticed two medals – asked what they were for.

(1) Tunisian campaign – he was in Cairo.

(2) Long Service and Good Conduct – <u>18 months</u> in the army.

And I laughed in front of him and he didn't mind in the least.

Mrs Pitt was finally to go home and George had twelve hours' notice, from when Archie told him the news, to make his decision. Should he send his diary?

He would not remain on Malta for ever and his diary would be increasingly dangerous if the Field Ambulance moved.

He should destroy it – why risk court martial over a hundred pages of rubbish? – but he could not. It had to go home, so that they would know, so that Nettie would know. Even if he himself never got home, she would know.

And so George gave the diary to Archie, his trusted Brother, to give to Jane who was to personally take it to 11, Cross St Kirkcaldy, where Nettie's sister Jean would keep it until Nettie was home on leave.

George handed over his diary, his closest friend, in a brown envelope, knowing that he could not replace the writing pad and that, from then on, whatever came must be contained within his own head.

Well! It is now 22/7/43 and I have the opportunity of sending this home – so off it goes.

I wonder if anybody will ever read this. It's just a lot of rubbish anyway. G.S.T

Mussolini was arrested and stripped of his power on 25th July and his replacement, Marshall Bodaglio, discussed with his new government ways to end the war, offering little resistance as the invasion of Sicily continued.

Despite the loss of some warships to the Luftwaffe, Allied progress was emphatic and on 11th September Admiral Cunningham had the honour of signalling the arrival of the Italian battlefleet in Malta, to offer surrender.

McConnell's suggestion that George should stand for office resulted in the appointment of G. S. Taylor as the new Junior Deacon for the Lodge of St Andrew, complete with trowel jewel. That same October also saw George raised to Royal Arch Mason with the Caledonian Royal Arch Chapter and a month later he was first Sojourner, the highest degree he was to ever reach in Freemasonry.

Malta's tally of VIP visitors was by no means over. In November 1943, Churchill stopped on Malta, on his way home from a conference. He complained about the domestic arrangements made for him by Lord Gort but made no public comment on Malta's contribution to the war.

President Roosevelt made no such omission when he too called on Malta in December, returning from the same conference. 'In the name of the people of the United States of America, I salute the island of Malta, its people and defenders, who in the cause of freedom and justice and decency throughout the world have rendered valorous service far and above the call of duty.

Under repeated fire from the skies, Malta stood alone but unafraid in the centre of the sea, one tiny bright flame in the darkness, a beacon of hope for the clearer days which have come.

Malta's bright story of fortitude and courage will be read

by posterity with wonder and with gratitude through all the ages. What was done on this island maintains the highest traditions of gallant men and women who from the beginning of time have lived and died to preserve civilisation for all mankind.'

The Times of Malta contained a full report of the speech with exuberant commentary from its editor, still the redoubtable Mabel Strickland. *The Times* had not missed a single edition during the war and was to keep this proud record.

George read as much between the lines as in the papers and, although he faced another Christmas on Malta, he knew he would be on the move some time soon.

He could still write letters, on the thin blue paper of the regulation air letter, with its fragile hopes of reaching home. He still believed that home was there for the reaching.

His letter of 3rd December 1943 was to be labelled by Nettie as 'my favourite letter sent from overseas'.

7265587 G S Taylor
HQ 15 Idep. Bgde. Gp. Fd. Amb.
R.A.M.C. – C.M.F.

My Dearest Adorable Darling,

I have an idea that if half these letters get home you will still think me crazy. However, I am writing this specially for Xmas as I will be unable to send a cable or present – just due as usual to the exigencies of the service – and hope that this letter will arrive in lieu at just the right time. I wish you as happy a Xmas as possible in the circumstances and wish you all you wish yourself in the New Year.

Some day soon I hope to make up to you for the lack of birthday and Xmas presents – I did once send you some lace you know but to my knowledge it has never arrived. Nor has any parcel arrived from you – not even the one you told me you sent about a year ago. What was it? You quite excited my curiosity by the little hints you did drop about it.

My first present to you will be a wedding ring. You are the only girl in my life and always will be – you alone – and failing that your memory will live with me forever. Your eyes still haunt me – in glimpses of fleeting expressions of yours.

Do you still have those funny curls stuck on top of your forehead? Do you still blush furiously? Would you still rush to me if I keep on looking at you? Do you still say you don't want to dance just to please me? Do you refuse to smoke and drink? (I suppose that isn't done on a P.T. course)

I'm afraid I'm just as bad as ever. I should have been born 200 years ago because everything that's been done since then I consider 'not done' or 'not right' or intemperate. My motto should be 'Let temperance chasten in all things.' Next week I'll probably be a philosopher – or a madman – or a monkey!

Something I want to ask – do I keep repeating the same things over and over in my letters? I suppose (hope! even!) that you have quite a few of my letters tied up in (blue? – or pink?) ribbon and so you can easily tell me what to stop saying as I've said it already too many times.

Except of course the phrase 'I love you' which I have special orders to repeat 'three times daily after meals in a wineglassful of water'!!

Certain other items too I keep on repeating – but that is because you have not yet given me a satisfactory answer. So, buck up! Darling! And, instead of going on leave, write me hundreds of letters because the more you write, the happier I am, the harder I work and therefore the sooner the war will be over.

Give my regards to all at Kirkcaldy and Colton of Wemyss and when the toasts go round at New Year, don't forget 'Absent Friends'.

And that – my own sweet Darling – is all for now.

Yours as ever
All my love
George

AFTERWORD

All men desire peace but very few desire those things which make for peace... In the modern world 'the things that make for peace' are disarmament, unilateral if necessary; renunciation of exclusive empires, abandonment of the policy of economic nationalism; determination in all circumstances to use the methods of non-violence; systematic training in such methods. How many of the so-called peace-lovers of the world love these indispensable conditions of peace? Few indeed. The business of private individuals is to persuade their fellows that the things that make for peace are not merely useful as means to certain political ends, but are also valuable as methods for training individuals in the supreme art of non-attachment.
Ends and Means

'Can you imagine he went through all that?' Nettie asked me when I had read the diary, sitting in a comfy chair while she watched my face. 'We didn't know... about the censorship or anything... when I sent him the blank writing paper, I was just so cross he hadn't written... I didn't know, none of us back home did. Even when they showed the Pathe News with all the pictures of the bombing and the excitement over the George Cross, we didn't know what it was like.'

When I asked Nettie whether George was sent home after all that, she told me he was sent to Anzio – from blitz and starvation to bloodbath. He was among the troops landed on the beaches and he was there at that monastery, Monte Cassino. She said the name with awe but it meant nothing to me. Is our generation – or rather those of us who do not live in war zones – lucky or ignorant to have buried so completely the horrors our fathers knew?

I found out a little more. At Monte Cassino, George worked in a field ambulance in the mud, among rotting corpses and constant shelling, conditions more usually associated with the First World War. He dealt with maimed and sick soldiers, who had to remain at the front, due to lack of a communication line to any hospital.

Then, after five years, after Malta and Anzio, he walked back to Nettie along a station platform. His only contact with her had been through censored letters and a diary smuggled back home.

He said, 'Hello.'

'Can you believe it?' Nettie asked me. 'All that time and all he could say was 'hello'! But that was your father for you. All he wanted was a car, children and a wife – in that order!'

They married as soon as they could, on December 18th, 1944 – not the splendid church ceremony she had dreamed of, but a quiet civil ceremony in a hotel, with wartime frugality. She wore a blue two-piece and he wore khaki, a sergeant's stripes on his arm. She always hated chrysanthemums, 'flowers for the dead', because those were the only flowers available for a December wedding bouquet. She was still an officer in the army but George didn't hesitate as he wrote 'housewife' in the space for her occupation and 'soldier' in his.

If he noticed the tightening of her small mouth as she drew up the battle lines, he quickly forgot it in his plans for the honeymoon he had dreamed of during the long moonlit lights in Malta. No woman had ever been loved like this. He would shower her with presents, not too expensive of course. He would surprise her with a treasure hunt for presents ending at the final slip of paper reminding her 'I love you silly', and then he would show her exactly what that meant. She kept the little slips of paper from that treasure hunt, along with her favourite letters, tied up with blue ribbon.

Perhaps it was weeks later or even months, when one turned to the other and said, 'Five years is a long time,' meaning the war years, and the answer to the unspoken question was, 'A chapter closed. We'll leave it at that, shall we.'

George had not survived the war in order to re-live it. On that, they were always of one, strong mind, although George could not even stay in the same room as any television story of love affairs between Yankee soldiers and British girls. He never parted with his diary, which lived in secret on a high shelf, wrapped in paper, out of reach of the children, but there were no companion volumes to his account of the Malta years.

Unsettled by war, he was to stay in the army his entire career, working his way slowly up the ranks to become a Major. It seems unlikely that the man I knew ever used a particular pressure of the hand to gain either favours or help and, although reluctant to talk of 'men's business', Nettie did say that George had become disgusted at the corruption within Freemasonry in the U.K. and only attended Lodge meetings when posted abroad, to Germany or Hong Kong.

As a soldier, he was not allowed to join a trade union, and he had good reason to doubt how much care the army would provide for his widow and children if anything happened to him; he had no doubt that his Brothers would provide that care.

There were occasional visits to George over the years of two or three men from the old days. Archie Pitt remained a friend for life and, when he called, Nettie would whisk the children out of the way so that George and Archie could talk 'men's talk' over a game of chess.

There is certainly no evidence that George's career was aided in any way by his Masonic status; his must have been one of the slowest progressions to the rank of Major on record, particularly for someone with his war history (and, yes, the medals that went with it). One reason for this was his refusal, immediately after the war, to accept a commission that required him to be parted immediately from Nettie.

In fact, their regiments seemed to take perverse delight in separating the newly-weds, until Nettie could resign and follow George, as she did, all over the world for thirty-two years. There were still times when George was posted alone somewhere for a few months and, once again, he would write to her all that he found difficult to say, face to face.

My own Darling,

I'm sure I received two of the nicest letters ever written today. I think it must be because my wife wrote them whom I cherish so much. Many many times in Malta I used to sit outside in the cool of the night, in the moonlight, just anxiously wondering – but then you never came any nearer as you do now, it makes such a difference….

George considered it demeaning to switch on a kettle if there was a woman in the house to do it for him but he always kept the army habit of polishing his own shoes, belts, buttons and, on ceremonial occasions, his medals and sword. He smelled of leather and metal polish, Old Spice and cigarettes, his 'blues' smoother against a little girl's cheek than his everyday khaki. He and Nettie would have forty-two years together and four children; he would disappoint her frequently and she would strike sparks off the ironing board, the pressure-cooker and us children, without even deepening the blue of his eyes. He was a very rational idealist.

Nettie's wedding ring wore thin so she asked a jeweller

to protect the eighteen-carat original with two thin bands of nine-carat. When I slip the triple-band off my finger, where I usually wear it beneath my grandmother's diamond engagement ring, I can still read the initials engraved inside, 1944 G.S.T. and J.M.G., George and Nettie, my mother and father.

George and Nettie's Wedding, 18ᵗʰ December 1944

Major George Taylor wearing his blues at his eldest daughter Anne's wedding 9ᵗʰ May 1970. The ribbons above his left pocket represent all the many medals he won during his career in the RAMC

Between 1966 and 1969, George was the only regular army officer tasked with setting up a Field Dressing Station staffed with volunteers. He was supported by one regular army sergeant-major to help him. This was the reference given by his superior officer, a doctor and a T.A. Colonel.

1969
Testimonial for Major George Taylor

223 Durham Field Dressing Station
RAMC (Volunteers)
Bishop Auckland, County Durham

This officer is a very competent administrator. He very ably set up the organisation of a Field Dressing Station and due to his efforts the transition to a Field Ambulance is progressing smoothly.

He tends to look on all problems as serious, partly because of his nature, and partly because he realizes all the possible ramifications, due to his wide experience of army matters, which also results in him giving a well-reasoned solution.

His relations with his brother officers and men are very good. He is prepared to undertake any task that presents itself. Of temperate habits and equitable nature, he is seldom visibly flustered and I have never known him to show evidence of anger.

Historical Note

This story is as factually accurate as my research and sources could make it. It is not a memoir; it is a reconstruction based on a live report from Malta during the 2nd World War, written by an ordinary, sensitive young Scotsman in his diary. It is not my story; it is George's story.

The diary extracts included are used verbatim, with small changes to clarify acronyms, and some changes to names where these are not key historical figures. The diary itself was written between 1940 and 1943, is 30,000 words long, and was kept hidden in a cupboard for the rest of George's life, too dangerous to be made public and too precious to destroy.

I have tried to create a context for the diary, but I could have written chapters on so many aspects of wartime Malta that I had to be selective. So much shocked me when I first read the diary: football and killing, juxtaposed; cigarettes as rations; X-rays used as lightly as band-aids, with no protection for the radiographer and no thought to the patient's health (X-rays on pregnant women are mentioned). George blamed the cancer that killed him at seventy on his work with X-rays, but he never wanted to accept that cigarettes – also an aspect of army life - might have been the cause.

I invented a name and a background for Violet, but I know that there was indeed a 'Violet' for George. To bring the story to life, I also created the dialogue in the hospital from all the diaries I read of men in different military forces. Each of the characters is rooted firmly in real people. George's mental breakdown can be inferred from the gaps and hints in the diary, the change of job, and the fact that so many in his situation did 'go crazy'. This was, of course, considered to be a matter for shame, and to be concealed at all costs: being 'bomb crazy' was a hazard of the job and there was no sympathy for what we now call

PTSD. I think those meetings with brothers in war, later in life, were a way of sharing the burden, without necessarily talking about it.

I also gave a nickname, Lofty, to George's friend, whose death he records as having taken place at 10.35pm on 10.7.40. There is no military death recorded on the 10th July 1940, but George is so precise that I suspect the official records are wrong, not George. The most likely person to be George's unnamed friend is a young private from the Dorsetshire Regiment, as they were billeted with the RAMC. George Edward Le Prevost died at twenty-four years old, on 12th July (according to the record).

I also attributed actions by anonymous soldiers in George's diary, to Lofty, to bring some personality to this man who was special to my father. George rarely expressed emotion, so this diary entry would be an extreme outpouring of grief in a more open man. Whether Le Prevost was 'Lofty' or not, he was somebody's friend – and son. The Dorsets defended the coast, repaired bomb damage, mended roads and runways, manned anti-aircraft guns and prepared for an invasion that happily never came. Thirty-three were killed while all faced hardship, hunger, danger and deprivation.

I cannot reveal my sources for all the details of George's induction and progress as a Mason because I have taken a terrible, binding oath of secrecy, so you will just have to trust me. My research into wartime freemasonry did challenge my own prejudices against the Brotherhood and I tried to show this secret society as it would have appeared to George, not according to my own opinions.

My father and I had thousands of discussions about the universe and everything, and he never lost his temper once, however much he disagreed with my politics and philosophy. He sharpened my brain, and, after thirty years without him, I still miss him. He always said that *Ends and Means* was THE book of philosophy to read and so all the quotations as chapter headings are from *Ends and Means*. I love the ironic counterpoint they give to George's story and I can imagine him nodding in agreement as he reads them – then getting back to work.

A soldier's daughter like me knows how such a gentle man can be a soldier all his life, and how aware he can be of the paradox. Being a soldier was his way of stepping up, of protecting all he held dear, however much he hid that in cynical humour. Remembrance Day for our family was personal and, for me, it will always be a time to re-read George's diary, in remembrance. I think he would be pleased to know that this witness statement has been read so many times, via this book. He would smile and say, 'I was there.'

Acknowledgements

The 2nd edition of this book owes much to input from Colonel Walter Bonnici (retired) who has created a wonderful site dedicated to RAMC history on Malta *maltaramc.com* Here, men serving in the RAMC are shown the respect they deserve. They don't even get a mention in some WW2 Malta books purporting to be 'comprehensive'! Walter helped to identify photographs and events. More than that, he brought his knowledge of and love for both Malta and the RAMC to his comments. His father was a Maltese gunner during the war and I like to think of him chatting to a young Scottish soldier. Who knows – maybe the 'Bonnici' George refers to was one of Walter's relatives?

And with special love and thanks to George's brother, Dave, for all the many background details and for the fun we had together, despite the tears, while I was writing this book.

Thanks also to Babs, Kris and Jane for their invaluable input.

Excerpts from *Ends and Means* by Aldous Huxley. Copyright © 1937, 1964 Aldous Huxley. Reprinted by permission of George Borchardt, Inc., for the Estate of Aldous Huxley.

Other quotations are from:
My dreams are getting better introduced by Marion Hutton in the film 'In Society', lyrics by Les Brown as recorded by Doris Day with the Les Brown orchestra
When is a man a mason? by Joseph Fort Newton
The Mother Lodge by Brother Rudyard Kipling
The Annihilation of Freemasonry, article by Sven G. Lunden
Ecclesiastes is quoted from the King James version of the

Holy Bible (also known as the Volume of Sacred Law)

Photo Credits
Cover image: Combat Aircraft © Keith Tarrier
Masonic Headstone: © Walter Bonnici

Other images: George Taylor, © Jean Gill
Maps © Michael Tamelander

Selected Sources
Fortress Malta by James Holland
Siege: Malta by Ernle Bradford
Malta by Sir Harry Luke (Lieutenant-Governor of Malta 1930-38)
Air Battle for Malta by James Douglas Hamilton
Mabel Strickland by Joan Alexander
The Kapillan of Malta by Nicholas Monserrat
Army Medical Services, a guide published in 1969 with a foreword by N.G.G. Talbot, Director-General Army Medical Services
The perfect ceremonies of craft masonry published 1938 by A Lewis
The constitution and Laws of the Grand Lodge of Antient Free and Accepted Masons of Scotland
The Standard Ritual of Scottish Freemasonry published by CC and AT Gardner 1927
Villa Blye Pawla Malta G.C. by Brother Douglas Shields
The Malta Story (film)

And among many useful internet sources:
Jack Williams' memories of mine-sweeping at Malta – now part of www.bbc.co.uk/ww2peopleswar/
Eyewitness in Malta: 1940-1942. The diary of Reverend Reginald Nicholls, Chancellor of St Paul's Anglican Cathedral maltafamilyhistory.com

4.5 Years: memoir of a WW2 POW
By David Taylor

If you liked *Faithful Through Hard Times,* you might enjoy
the war memoir of George's brother, Dave, who tells his
story of 4.5 years as a POW in France and Germany, a
story which complements *Faithful Through Hard Times.*

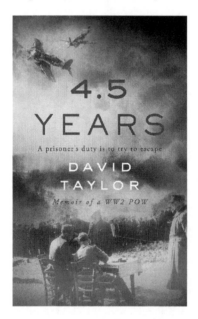

The true story of a young Scottish soldier stranded in France
during WW2 and sent to a Prisoner-of-War camp.

The story of 4.5 years in a world where one egg is an illegal
treasure, where knives are hidden and get used, where Jewish
prisoners are glimpsed and, inexplicably, disappear.

This book is a tribute to the human spirit.

'A fascinating Prisoner of War-Internee story. Dave's
personality, technical skills, common sense and Scottish
entrepreneurial attitude shine through.' *Don Marshall, Military
History Enthusiast*

About the Author

I'm a Welsh writer and photographer living in the south of France with two scruffy dogs, a beehive named 'Endeavour', a Nikon D750 and a man. I taught English in Wales for many years and so am as much Welsh as I am any nationality, given my nomadic childhood. My claim to fame is that I was the first woman to be a secondary headteacher in Carmarthenshire. I'm mother or stepmother to five children so life has been pretty hectic.

I've published all kinds of books, both with traditional publishers and self-published. You'll find everything under my name from prize-winning poetry and novels, military history, translated books on dog training, to a cookery book on goat cheese. My work with top dog-trainer Michel Hasbrouck has taken me deep into the world of dogs with problems, and inspired one of my novels. With Scottish parents, an English birthplace and French residence, I can usually support the winning team on most sporting occasions.

www.jeangill.com

For news, offers and a FREE ebook of 'One Sixth of a Gill', please visit www.jeangill.com and sign up for my newsletter. This collection of shorts was a finalist in the Wishing Shelf and SpASpa Awards

A book with 'Wow' factor - Geoff Nelder, *Aria*
A fantastic array of wonderful prose, from bee-keeping to Top Tips on Dogs! A FINALIST and highly recommended - The Wishing Shelf Awards

Five-minute reads. Meet people you will never forget: the night photographer, the gynaecologist's wife, the rescue dog. Dip into whatever suits your mood, from comedy to murders; from fantastic stories to blog posts, by way of love poetry.

Fully illustrated by the author; Jean Gill's original photographs are as thought-provoking as her writing. An out of body experience for adventurous readers. Or, of course, you can 'Live Safe'.

Not for you
the blind alley on a dark night,
wolf-lope pacing you step for step
as shadows flare on the walls.

Printed in Great Britain
by Amazon

32694120R00178